Crisis and the Everyday in Postsocialist Moscow

OLGA SHEVCHENKO

Crisis and the Everyday in Postsocialist Moscow

INDIANA UNIVERSITY PRESS
Bloomington and Indianapolis

This book is a publication of

Indiana University Press
601 North Morton Street
Bloomington, IN 47404-3797 USA

http://iupress.indiana.edu

Telephone orders   800-842-6796
Fax orders   812-855-7931
Orders by e-mail   iuporder@indiana.edu

Library of Congress Cataloging-in-Publication Data

Shevchenko, Olga, date
  Crisis and the everyday in postsocialist Moscow / Olga Shevchenko.
    p. cm.
  Includes bibliographical references and index.
  ISBN 978-0-253-35248-4 (cloth : alk. paper) — ISBN 978-0-253-22028-8 (pbk. : alk. paper) 1. Moscow (Russia)—Social conditions. 2. Moscow (Russia)—Economic conditions. 3. Post-communism—Russia (Federation)—Moscow. I. Title.
  HN530.2.M67S54 2009
  306.0947'3109049—dc22

                                                                                      2008023840

1 2 3 4 5 14 13 12 11 10 09

To my parents

Contents

Acknowledgments

Expressions of gratitude, as Simmel reminds us, always leave an aftertaste of inadequacy. No matter how much one appreciates a favor, there is always one thing that remains impossible to reciprocate: the good will and spontaneity that went into the initial act of kindness. Since I embarked on this project in 1998, I have been fortunate to receive such spontaneous acts of kindness from a wide range of people. All I can do here is mention by name a small number of them, truly only the tip of the iceberg.

Looking back at the early stages of my fieldwork, I am well aware that its spirit and direction were profoundly shaped by the sociological intuition of Renée C. Fox. My debt to her since has only grown. The many long conversations we had over coffee in Philadelphia, Moscow, St. Petersburg, and Williamstown helped me in more than just thinking about my data; these were lessons in work ethics, responsibility, and sociological imagination. The powerful theoretical mind and firsthand knowledge of both socialism and postsocialism made Ewa Morawska an invaluable mentor and colleague. Many of the ideas that shaped this book were first tried on Ewa and her husband, German sociologist Willfried Spohn, and their enthusiasm, along with their occasional skepticism, kept me going.

In the writing and revising of this book, I was fortunate to benefit from the keen intellect and wide-ranging expertise of many friends and colleagues. From the early stages of fieldwork and onward, conversations with Oksana Sarkisova, Alexander Semyonov, Maria Stoilkova, and Alexei Yurchak gave me multiple opportunities to reformulate vague intuitions into research questions, and often helped me see old realities in a new light. At different points in time, Melissa Caldwell, Sheila Fitzpatrick, Laura Levitt, Katia Makarova, Maya Nadkarni, Serguei Oushakine, Kim Lane Scheppele, Yakov Schukin, Olga Sezneva, and members of the University of Chicago Russian Studies workshop read chapter drafts, discussed key themes, and offered most insightful advice and comments. Kai Erikson and Michele Rivkin-Fish read the full manuscript, and I thank them for their intellectual generosity and constructive suggestions. Victoria Frede took several days of her Christmas vacation to read an early draft of this book and to provide what remains to me a model of an intelligent and sympathetic critique at a strategic juncture. I am grateful to her, as well as to the other members of our postdoctoral *kruzhok* at the Harriman Institute (Hilary Appel, Rebecca Neary, Ethan Pollock, and Katrina Schwartz) for their crucial comments and suggestions. Throughout my work on this project, my Russian friends Yulia Goidenko, Maria Klenskaia, Nastia Leonova, and Oksana and Sergei Sarkisov were unfailing adventure companions, sounding boards, kindred spirits. I thank them for that, and for having been my eyes in Russia when I could not be there. I owe the same debt to the Russian sociologists Boris Dubin and Oleg Yanitsky. Each in their own way, these people have both inspired and challenged my analysis, warning me against easy explanations. The research and writing of this book have also been facilitated (and at times, temporarily interrupted) by my friends Greg and Clark Collins, Theo Davis, Richard and Jude Fox, Julia Kalmanson, Joanna Kempner, Solene Lardoux, Tina Lupton and Heiko Henkel, Sophia Malamud, Sarah and Morgan McGuire, Normin Mobassera, Sonya Ovrutsky, Lily Panoussi, Kashia Pieprzak, Rebecca Seamans, and Eleanor Sharpe. I thank them for their company and good humor, and for making America feel like my second home.

Three institutions provided supportive networks of colleagues and generous institutional resources without which this book would not be possible. I am grateful to Charles Bosk, Diana Crane, Jerry Jacobs, and Susan Watkins at my alma mater, the University of Pennsylvania, and to Catharine Nepomnyashchy and Jared Ingersoll at Columbia University where I enjoyed the luxury of uninterrupted work on the manuscript during my residence at the Harriman Institute as a postdoctoral fellow. Finally, I received ample support from my home base, Williams College. I am grateful to two successive Deans of the Faculty, Thomas Kohut and William Wagner, as well as John Gerry, for never failing to exceed my expectations of intellectual and administrative support available at Williams. I am also indebted to my colleagues, most notably Michael F. Brown and Robert Jackall, for their intellectual engagement with the project, and for the many wise suggestions on matters of craft and substance. Donna Chenail did all in her power to bring my manuscript from jumbled prose to a more organized whole, and helped coordinate many of the logistical details involved in preparing a manuscript for publication. Many Williams students contributed more than they realize to the shaping of this book. I want to thank them, and to express special gratitude to Robin Kim and Jonathan Earle for their close readings of the text, and their editorial and bibliographical assistance.

The list of my benefactors would not be complete unless I mention the enormous help I have received in the course of my fieldwork from a team of six Russian transcribers who went through hundreds of meters of audio tape, transferring the interviews I had collected into the word processor. The computer wizardry of my brother, Pavel Shevchenko, made many tasks far less laborious than they would have been otherwise. And certainly nothing can exceed my gratitude to the subjects of my study, the Muscovite men and women who let me repeatedly enter their lives and their homes, question them about their struggles and victories, share their fears and joys, and hopefully bring at least a reflection of their personas to the pages of this text.

Ethnographic fieldwork for this book was funded by the National Science Foundation (grant no. 9901924), by the Otto and Gertrude Pollak Summer research fellowship from the Sociology department at the University of Pennsylvania, and by Williams College. While writing, I was supported by the Global Supplementary Grant from the Open Society Institute, and by the postdoctoral fellowship from the Harriman Institute at Columbia University. I would like to thank these institutions for their generous support, and to point out that they are in no way responsible for the content of my findings.

At Indiana University Press, Rebecca Tolen, Candace McNulty, June Silay, and Laura MacLeod provided invaluable editorial and logistical assistance. I also thank Tom Broughton-Willett who did the index.

I thank my husband, Christopher Marcisz, for treating this project as if it were his own, for the critical engagement, companionship, and patience, and for many delicious dinners. I am grateful to Shirley Kosciol for her company, her timely assistance, and for her learning to like tea. And to Mila Marcisz—thank you for reminding all of us what it really means to take joy in discovery.

None of the projects I have ever endeavored would have been possible—or meaningful—without my parents, Inna Izrailevna and Anatolii Konstantinovich Shevchenko. This work is dedicated to them.

Some of the book's arguments have been previously published in article form in *Communist and Post-Communist Studies* ("Bread and Circuses: Shifting Frames and Changing References in the Ordinary Muscovites' Political Talk," 34:1, 2001), *Journal of Consumer Culture* ("'In Case of Fire Emergency': Consumption, Security, and the Meaning of Durables in a Transforming Society," 2:2, 2002), *Europe-Asia Studies* ("Between the Holes: Emerging Identities and Hybrid Patterns of Consumption in Post-socialist Russia," 54:6, September 2002), and *Social Identities* ("'Wiggle Your Wits!': Social Restructuring and the Transformation of Entertainment Genres in Russia," 13:5, 2007).

Photographs are by the author unless otherwise indicated.

Crisis and the Everyday in Postsocialist Moscow

1   Introduction: Living on a Volcano

In the mornings, Lina's bedroom serves as a playroom for her granddaughter. In the evenings, it becomes a living room. This is where she and her husband receive guests, socialize, watch TV. Sitting in this modestly furnished room with a view onto a quiet Moscow yard, its hostess, a fifty-five-year-old retired chemical engineer and the matriarch of a family of four, was treating me to homemade pumpkin jam with tea. Our conversation wandered back and forth between culinary recipes and political developments. Before long, we hit the topic of *Avgustovskii krizis*—the financial breakdown that had occurred four months earlier, in August 1998, and had, in a matter of days, led to a rapid escalation of prices. "The scariest part," she remembered,

> was a few days after August 17, when the dollar exchange rate jumped up and immediately all the food vanished from the stores. Absolutely all of it. That is, you come into a store and you see nothing but boxes of oatmeal and of the most expensive cigarettes. Me, personally, I was just terrified. Because there's family, kids . . . How am I going to feed them? How are we supposed to live? What if it stays this way forever? Little by little, products appeared, but at much greater prices, that was the next shock. But at least I knew: all right, there is stuff out there, even if I can only afford minuscule amounts. And after a while, we got used to the way it became. Because, what are you going to do? . . .

In December, a few months after the ruble collapsed, the consequences of this event for everyday life in Moscow were still acute. For a sociologist with an interest in the experiential dimension of social change, this dramatic event presented an opportunity to explore how individuals' methods of coping evolve under the influence of sudden political and economic disruptions. It was not long, however, before I realized that I had been interpreting the situation all too narrowly. A few days after my conversation with Lina I met with Konstantin, an engineer in his early fifties who lived on the opposite side of town with his wife and school-aged daughter in a small-sized *khrushchevka* apartment.[1] Konstantin's life during the 1990s was full of twists and disappointments. After a lifetime career in an aviation research institute, he was forced by economic need to turn first to retail, then to small-scale commerce, and finally to contract construction work. At the very end of the 1990s he returned to his old post at the institute, which, in the course of the decade, managed to piece together enough commercial contracts for its staff to get by. The conversation with Lina was still fresh in my mind, and so I asked him how he and his family were affected by the recent crisis. But instead of sharing his experience of recent events, Konstantin looked at me with feigned incomprehension and said, "Which crisis do you mean? We are in crisis all the time."

Konstantin's response illustrates the inadequacies of viewing crisis and everyday life as polar opposites. The notion of crisis typically evokes connotations of a sudden rupture, of a breakdown in the natural order of things, of all that everyday life is not. It is an event out of the ordinary, a powerful force that inevitably destroys the habitual patterns of existence. With its roots in the Greek *krinein*, "to decide," crisis was traditionally used to indicate the decisive stage in the development of an illness, after which the patient either recovers or dies.[2] Although the medical associations have given way to a far broader contemporary usage, the term retains its connotations of emergency and impermanence to this day.

Such a discrete vision of crisis is blind to the possibility apparent in Konstantin's response: that a crisis may be perceived not as an isolated occurrence, but as a routine and unchanging condition. In such circumstances, the crisis evolves from a singular and alien happening into the very stuff of everyday life, the immediate context of decisions and actions, and, after a certain point, the only reality with which individuals have the social and cultural tools to deal. Crisis may become the default expectation that organizes people's priorities and desires, as well as the benchmark against which they measure their successes or failures. How are we to approach crises such as these, and what are the tools with which one can assess their workings?

The closing pages of Kai Erikson's classic study of the Buffalo Creek flood propose a framework for thinking about routinized emergencies in terms of what he calls chronic disasters, ones that "gather ... force slowly and insidiously, creeping around one's defenses rather than smashing through them" (1976, 255). While many of my Russian interlocutors would take issue with this definition of a chronic disaster (there was nothing slow or creeping about the avalanche of social, political, and economic transformations they had witnessed over the past decades), the value of Erikson's distinction is undeniable. It points to a far closer connection between disasters and everyday life than was previously recognized, and it pushes one to investigate the links between the two.

This study builds on Erikson's insight into chronic disasters (or, as I call them here, *total* crises) as diffuse conditions without boundaries and expiration dates, which blend with everyday reality and transform it in a myriad of complex ways. But Erikson's distinction should be pushed further. For all the conceptual value of classifying chronic disasters as a separate category, their effects have so far been considered identical to those of acute crises. Here is the (by no means finite) list of symptoms outlined by Erikson: "A numbness of spirit, a susceptibility to anxiety and rage and depression, a sense of helplessness, an inability to concentrate, a loss of various motor skills, a heightened apprehension about the physical and social environment, a preoccupation with death, a retreat into dependency, and a general loss of ego functions" (1976, 255–256). These traumatic symptoms are sufficient for one to conclude that a disaster has taken place, but does this also mean that any chronic crisis inevitably generates these, and only these, symptoms? Even a cursory observation of the streets and squares of Moscow in the late 1990s would suggest otherwise. One could observe in Muscovites' behavior plenty of apprehension about the physical and social environment, but also a pronounced, almost obsessive preoccupation with the beautification of their personal living quarters. There was a sense of helplessness but very little retreat into dependency; if anything, postsocialist Muscovites took a certain amount of pride in their learned self-sufficiency and independence. In short, the scope of reactions to what was unanimously recognized as the "crisis decade" was far wider than the traumatic symptoms enumerated by Erikson.

Given this observation, one may question the applicability of crisis imagery in this particular case. But one should also question the a priori assumptions about the necessary and inevitable outcomes of any chronic crisis. The theoretical value of setting chronic crises apart as a separate category is in the recognition that a routinized long-term condition has a different dynamic than an acute event. It seems logical to propose that it may have different effects as well, and that it should be subjected to a different pattern of inquiry.

Indeed, from the works of Fernand Braudel to the tradition of disaster research in sociology, instances of social crisis have been conceptualized as singular and unique, while everyday life is imagined as the realm of routine and repetition.[3] Even where the crises in question are considered chronic, crisis is opposed in this binary vision to the "normal" flow of everyday life.[4] This assumption is buttressed by the metaphors used to describe the workings of crisis. When one speaks of the "impact" or "imprint" that crises leave on a community, a conceptual separation between the two is taken for granted: the "crisis" is always an alien force, while the "community" is the recipient of its destructive impact. This imagery encourages the researcher to frame her agenda as a balance sheet, concentrating mainly on the damage the crisis inflicts upon the community's morale, solidarity, and patterns of trust. Such logic is justified in application to disaster research and short-term crises, where the primary goal is to assess the losses and to formulate a program of recovery. But in situations where the crisis is embedded in everyday life and represents for its constituents the most familiar and habitual operating environment, the conceptual separation between its manifestations and "normal" existence becomes more problematic. This dictates a different set of questions than the ones asked in situations of acute disasters. Without doubt, a state of routinized emergency has a bearing on the community's patterns of association, social trust, and solidarity. But it is also true that a chronic crisis may become the very essence of a community's identity, a mode of living and a way of self-imagining without which the community is inconceivable. In order to assess these patterns in their complexity, then, one has to explore them for their own sake and not merely in terms of their deviation from some past standard. In fact, the very notion of the past standard can be dangerous, because as the crisis unfolds, particularly if it spans generations, it begins to form its own standards. This means that at a certain point, the "damaged identity" becomes merely an "identity," "survival" becomes "life," and the crisis itself, originally conceptualized as a temporary breakdown in the social and economic *field,* becomes indistinguishable from the people's *habitus.* The traditional question of the immediate effects of crisis (i.e., what crisis does to people) has, then, to give way to an exploration of the durable forms of social organization in its midst (i.e., what people do in crisis). Such a question calls for a systematic investigation of the art of living, as Konstantin put it, "in crisis all the time."[5]

Studying Everyday Life

Everyday life is an immediately appealing and yet elusive object of sociological inquiry. Its appeal is both political and epistemological. In terms of epistemology, it is grounded in the intuitive, taken-for-granted character of everyday perspectives—the quality identified by Garfinkel (1967) as their indexicality, their ability to skip over controversial or questionable evidence and definitions, and thus to preserve the coherence and continuity so crucial for the maintenance of the social order. In other words, the realm of the everyday embraces the sphere of unquestioned practical knowledge, and as such it comes closest to the shared foundations of action and relation-formation that make society possible.[6] An inquiry into everyday life holds the promise of revealing the unspecified assumptions that underlie the patterns of routine interactions and that account for much of the resilience and variability of daily existence.

The political allure of the everyday in sociology stems from its role in the critique of capitalism. In sociological literature, everyday life is constructed as a last vestige of poetry and spontaneity lost during the capitalist era, as opposed to the rationalization and alienation of most modern-day activities. This perspective on everyday life was explicitly formulated by Henri Lefebvre and the Situationist movement[7] and later developed in the works of Michel de Certeau (1984), who, drawing on Bakhtin and the tradition of the Annales School, emphasized the spontaneous, subversive, and anti-authoritarian character of daily practices. By championing the value of routine experiences, students of everyday life deliberately expand the scope of sociological inquiry in order to include and legitimize the perspectives of the powerless, who rarely leave behind anything other than the marks of day-to-day existence. The sociology of everyday life shares this inclusionary vision with cultural studies, analyses of resistance, and the *Alltagsgeschichte* tradition in history, all of which seek to redress the redundant emphasis in the social sciences on the outstanding at the expense of the trivial, the recognizable at the expense of the anonymous, and the heroic at the expense of the self-effacing.[8] Reclaiming the analysis of everyday life as a legitimate method of inquiry into social reality, these approaches effectively affirm the democratic ideal of a total history without excluded categories and silences of omission.

And yet, despite the considerable attractions of this inclusive vision, as a conceptual category, everyday life presents certain difficulties. Some of these are direct extensions of its democratic pathos, since in its openness to the experiences of the "ordinary people," everyday life comes close to turning into a class category: once it is equated with the life of the powerless, there is little space left for considering the possibility that it could figure equally prominently in the experiences of elites (and indeed, studies of everyday life rarely engage the routine details of the wealthy few). Operationalizing everyday life raises other problems as well. At its most ambitious, the concept could be interpreted so widely as to subsume the totality of experience of a social stratum. In more modest interpretations, everyday life designates a fixed range of chores but fails to address the principle of their selection, as well as their structural connections with the wider sociopolitical context, without which it remains close to impossible to comprehend their significance.[9]

In order to redress the conceptual fuzziness of everyday life without losing its heuristic potential, this study defines it as all activity based on everyday knowledge, on notions widely shared and largely accepted without question in the contemporary Russian setting. The spontaneity of this activity, or its promise of resistance matter far less than its taken-for-granted character. This definition of everyday life encompasses, as I quickly discovered, ideas and practices relating to spheres as varied as consumption, political sentiments, moral order, and safety. In other words, I address everyday life as the stock of practical knowledge and activity that can be, and is, widely considered self-explanatory and comprehensible, not only to one's friends and colleagues, but to generalized hypothetical others. Through such a definition, I aim to get at ideas and practices representing what Sewell (1992) calls *deep cultural schemas* that cut across social categories and provide for the possibility of interaction and collective identification among individuals, even if this identification is informed by assumed, rather than actual, agreement regarding the fundamentals. This interpretation owes more to Garfinkel (1967) and Berger and Luckmann (1967) than to the substantially more romantic vision of de Certeau (1984) and Lefebvre (1991), although it shares the latter's interest in the mutability and creativity of everyday strategies. The project of exploring everyday life thus amounts to, first, figuring out what the activities are that constitute this sphere in the people's eyes; second, understanding the meaning of these activities in a larger social context; and third (and this is where the mutability of everyday life comes in), grasping the role they play both in the reproduction of habitual cultural patterns and in their selective reinterpretation in response to novel social conditions.

An important consequence of this pragmatic definition of everyday life is that its actual content could not be defined a priori, but could only be delineated in the course of the fieldwork. Ethnographic observation alone could identify what my informants designated as the areas of commonsense understanding, the problems and ways of mastering them that required no further clarification, and the expectations that were most likely to be violated by my inappropriate requests to specify and explain things that "reasonable people can understand as is." In this sphere of inquiry, interviewing techniques turned out to be questionable allies, since they often undermined the expectations of presumed understanding. While in certain ways such violations were helpful, since the surprise and bafflement of the interlocutor were the best confirmations of the fact that the conversation was treading into the waters of everyday life that "reasonable people understand as is," I often chose to resort to implicit markers (trajectory of the narrative, selections of examples, comparisons and metaphors) instead of repeatedly asking people to explain themselves.[10]

This, of course, does not mean that initial stages of fieldwork amounted to drifting in an open sea of information with no conceptual map to steer by. The set of guiding themes I have used to organize the interviews emphasize the connections between the large-scale social transformations and their experiential dimension and cover many of the "usual suspects" in the everyday sphere, such as leisure, consumption, gender, and family relations. But I was far more interested in using them to identify the relevance of these topics than to ensure that all of them were covered in equal detail. Thus, I discovered that, because of the household-centered logic of postsocialist daily life, my contacts preferred to talk about the household as a single unit, blurring over gender inequalities, which they considered marginal to the task of collective navigation of the crisis. While the awareness of gender inequality turned out to be less than I had anticipated (although its very suppression, as I will argue elsewhere in this book, put enormous pressure on the family unit), the awareness of other issues exceeded my initial expectations. For one, the degree of politicization of routine daily developments was striking. This was not because politics as a topic was considered particularly interesting (if anything, an important part of practical knowledge was the realization that politics was a "dirty business" not worth talking about), but because the most trivial and diverse phenomena, from postal mistakes to currency fluctuations, were linked directly and routinely to failures of the state. In an inversion of the socialist logic through which the state and its main agent, the Party, attempted to permeate all spheres of daily life and to claim credit for all achievements, however minute, postsocialist actors ascribed to the state (now imagined by turns as overwhelmingly present and as hauntingly absent) full responsibility for the troubles they were encountering on a day-to-day basis. To a greater extent than I imagined it would be, a study of everyday life thus turned out to be a study of everyday life's place in the larger framework of political relevance.

This study's interest in the shared structures of everyday knowledge enables it to explore how common communicational and cognitive frameworks evolve, fuel symbolic practices, and animate action. But it also dictates that, for the purposes of this investigation, the shared is more important than the particular, and that group-specific perspectives do not have the same value for advancing this quest as do those that are practiced across the board. Insofar as one aims to capture the inner logic of the practices and opinions that contemporaries will expect to make sense to everyone, rather than identifying the features that vary widely across generational, gender, and class divides, the search for practical knowledge turns a researcher, to use Zerubavel's (1996) terminology, into a *lumper,* rather than a *splitter.*

The decision to concentrate on commonalities rather than differences between the representatives of various social groups was not an easy one to make, considering the undeniable fact that, practically and psychologically speaking, the postsocialist transformation affected different strands of the population very differently. Several considerations made this methodological sacrifice more tolerable. First of all, a number of recent studies have explored group-specific responses to postsocialism in the 1990s, and the number of works in this category is growing,[11] while a systematic exploration of the logic governing the shared sentiments and practices remains rare. Second, the specificity of the first postsocialist decade was precisely that the broad, imagined community of *narod* (the people) continued, despite discernible inequalities, to hold a far greater sway than more narrowly conceived group-forming interests and identities.[12] Identifying the shared meanings that made such collective identity possible in the late 1990s appears no less important than distinguishing the actual cleavages within it.

Yet, rather than ignoring group-specific experiences, I pursue them with a different aim. In addressing diverse reactions to postsocialism, I outline the gamut of ways in which people experienced particular phenomena in order to identify the themes that unite them. In other words, the variations here are important as evidence of underlying patterns, yet it is the shared patterns that made dialogue between differently positioned individuals possible; and it is these patterns, in their various manifestations, that this book pursues in depth.

Everyday Life in a Postsocialist Metropolis: Paradoxes of the Changing Times

At the end of the turbulent decade of the 1990s, Moscow was both a unique and a propitious locale for investigating the workings of a perpetual crisis. Substantially more affluent than other Russian regions and offering greater opportunities for advancement, the Russian capital was not marked by the uniform socioeconomic depression characterizing the many collapsing smaller cities and towns across Russia, or, for that matter, the sites of classical sociological studies of communities in crisis.[13] Yet Muscovites framed the awareness of this privileged position vis-à-vis other cities and regions in catastrophic terms, like the ones used in a 1996 monograph whose author chose the title, "If Russia is doomed to perish, then . . . Muscovites will be the last ones to die!" (Simakov 1995, 92).[14] Much like the rest of the Russian population, Muscovites, suffering from low income and fears of unemployment, reported each year of the decade to be more difficult than the one that preceded it.[15] The city was affected by the same macro-social developments as the rest of the country, from repeated currency devaluations to political upheavals. It was the site of two violent clashes: in 1991, a coup by Communist hard-liners, and in 1993, a power struggle between President Yeltsin and the parliament. Moscow was undergoing simultaneous restructuring of the political, legal, and economic system, which meant for many of its inhabitants not only a loss of income and security, but also a fundamental ambiguity concerning the most basic issues of legitimacy, authority, and accountability. The city's relative prosperity did not shield Muscovites from instability, but it did offer them a variety of options for navigating it: through their consumption and employment strategies, through organization of family life and leisure, and through a variety of other ways of reestablishing a measure of control over their immediate environment. It was in the everyday topography of this navigation that the crisis and the daily routine merged into one.

This book draws upon conversations and interactions with Muscovites from various walks of life, and of various ages and political persuasions. Its core are the 103 in-depth interviews that I have conducted recurrently with a sample of thirty-three Muscovites over the span of two years, from 1998 through 2000.[16] In my research agenda as a participant observer, and in the published materials I collected and analyzed, I followed up on the themes that emerged in the course of these interviews, looking for tangible everyday forms in which social change could be observed, and exploring the ways in which the experience of a societal crisis was embodied in a variety of diverse daily practices, from shopping for furniture and watching the news to seeking medical attention and solving crossword puzzles.

While it was hard to doubt the scope and impact of the changes experienced by people over the span of the first postsocialist decade, I quickly learned that change for them was almost never a good thing. Even those whose personal encounters with the reforms of the 1990s had been lucrative—those whose personal and family circumstances improved, who could make their first trips abroad and who encountered other previously unthinkable opportunities—did not consider such markers to be their main achievements. Rather, they praised themselves for being successful in the preservation of their families' peace and well-being, a preservation which could, of course, bring unforeseen and pleasant advances, but which was valuable primarily for its own sake. Improvement was a by-product; stability was what counted most.

And yet stability almost never came to mind without a direct link to crisis. The expression in the title of this chapter, "living on a volcano," is one I often heard in the course of the interviews. The metaphor of a volcano turned into one's home turf, a volcano rendered habitable, conveys the notion of fragile, laboriously cultivated, and yet ephemeral stability better than any comparison I could purposefully invent. It also highlights the kernel of personal and social transformation that is inevitably rooted in it. Living on a volcano implies not merely building stronger homes or better shelters; it also connotes the unceasing labor of remaining attuned to what could be the ominous rumblings of coming calamity, so that one's instincts are trained to pick out signals indistinguishable to an outsider. For a community, this amounts to a revised hierarchy of skills and talents, a distinctive and unique conception of what it means to be a practically competent individual, a different notion of order, safety, caution, and responsibility. It also means that, while the volcanic nature of one's home ground is never quite forgotten, it is also accepted as inevitable and accommodated through a multiplicity of small adjustments, so that the threat is normalized and domesticated at the same time as it is resented.

The exploration of life in the midst of social change, therefore, had to zero in precisely on what did not change in the midst of a perpetual crisis, and on the formation of modes of self-organization that made preservation of stability possible. Two interrelated trends emerged as central to the attainment of stability in late-1990s Russia: first, the symbolic weight of domesticity and of the household, accompanied by the declining relevance of wider networks of belonging, such as professional communities; and second, the high premium on achieving and displaying one's autonomy—almost autarky—from the disorderly postsocialist milieu. In the midst of the first postsocialist decade, the family was construed both as a symbolic and practical refuge from the confusion of political and economic restructuring, and as the safety buffer absorbing the shocks and failures emanating from the outside world.

Both of these drives, together with the images and expressions associated with them—fortified doors to private apartments, investments in home furnishings, abandonment of savings banks in favor of mutual lending among relatives, and the like—could be considered merely leftovers from the prior times of socialist atomization.[17] But there are reasons to resist such an easy connection. First, the drive for autonomy fostered not atomization, but its opposite: a conscious cultivation of largely informal and particularistic connections and loyalties.[18] Second, while many skills vital to staying afloat in the economy of the 1990s could indeed be traced back to the old days of distributive socialism, by the end of the 1990s they developed a value of their own, and their singular importance was regarded (and vocally asserted) as a recent and significant discovery of the postsocialist era. To draw on a useful distinction articulated by DiMaggio (1991), yesterday's cultural *resources* were being reinterpreted as today's cultural *capital.* In other words, skills previously deemed merely helpful to some began to be seen as imperative for any competent member of postsocialist society in general.

A notable implication of this reorganization of the cultural universe is that mental and practical autonomy became an important quality both to cultivate and to demonstrate, since it lay at the very foundations of the competent navigation of a perpetual crisis. The new lines of distinction revived and rehabilitated many Soviet-era habits, such as stockpiling, networking, or reading between the lines, but they also took the logic of autonomy further, applying it to the emerging private structures and public institutions, and thus defining the lines along which these were forming. A skeptical sensibility essential to the preservation of moral autonomy found its reflection in the new genre of revisionist historical literature and in consumer defense publications, in public attitudes toward politics and mass media, in the spatial organization of the city and the public's conception of its own place in the political process. Paradoxically, while crisis and destitution were understandably resented, they also provided a backdrop against which to demonstrate the cultural capital of postsocialist autonomy. In a context where other forms of collective self-imagining were only beginning to evolve, this was particularly valuable. In a sense, crisis turned into a symbolic resource, creating a situation in which people could most easily achieve trust through affirmation of universalized distrust, and the shortest path to building solidarity was an assertion that "nowadays" solidarity was impossible.

The focus of this book, then, is on the traditional sociological question of societal self-organization, but also on the less traditional (although, due to the impressive expansion of the new cultural sociology, increasingly important) question of cultural categories and their role in times of change. On the one hand, cultural and cognitive classifications are notoriously conservative; indeed, their function is to preserve cultural and social continuity. On the other hand, they are themselves products and facilitators of change, since individuals inevitably assess emerging situations and distinguish new opportunities through the prism of culturally available vocabularies. It is precisely this combination of rigidity and transformative potential that makes cultural categories so interesting from a sociological standpoint. The category of crisis, with its unrivaled popularity among Muscovites during the 1990s, both in discourse and in practice, thus provides an ethnographically rich opportunity to explore how cultural categories and cognitive classifications both shape and impede social change.

By linking discourses of crisis with their articulations in practice, we need not assume that one flows unproblematically into the other; on the contrary, as I show in later chapters, notions of crisis came to life in a wide array of mutually contradictory practices. But in order to understand the linkages between them, one has to view *both* practices and discourses as essentially two branches of the same tree: both are profoundly semiotic in nature, in that they obtain their meaning through relating themselves to the other elements in the cultural system. To speak of "nowadays" as "the time when solidarity was impossible" meant, in the context of the Russian 1990s, to draw on a different set of practical knowledge and cultural assumptions than if the same argument were advanced in the context of the contemporary United States.[19] It implied passing a judgment on the moral and economic toll of the reforms, and emphasizing one's personal difference from the "drab background" (*seryi fon*) of the postsocialist existence. But the same message was embedded in things other than discourse: in the immediate distrust of strangers that sharply contrasted with in-group solidarities, in the elaborate questioning aimed at discovering forgeries when shopping, and in the physical objects that became integral parts of Moscow's urban environment: security guard checkpoints,[20] iron doors, and makeshift car garages. It is in the linkages between these discourses and practices, the "suturing" of these "diverse semiotic modalities," as Sewell (2005, 339–340) puts it, that the common cultural logic of action is to be discovered.

Integrating discourses and practices into a single analytic framework has yet another advantage. It permits scrutinizing one in the light of the other, and consequently taking note of the method through which images and ideas translate into actions, and actions and experiences fuel rhetoric. Particularly with chronic, ongoing crises, this opens up the possibility of tracing not only the reported "effects of the crisis," but also the strategies through which individuals navigate the crisis and inevitably transform and reproduce it in the course of their engagement.

This means that crisis has to do with security and control as much as with instability and powerlessness, and the book documents the resourcefulness and imagination with which Muscovites selectively drew on their old skills and dispositions and applied them to the new and unfamiliar reality, unwittingly turning them into threads in the weaving of a new social fabric. And yet this is a story not so much of resistance as of absorption and normalization, a story of how a perpetual crisis can turn into a symbolic resource and grow to become the individuals' second nature, a source not only of daily aggravations but, paradoxically, also of a sense of identity, dignity, and status. Finally, this is a story of social change, albeit of a different kind than I had imagined at the outset of this research. When one thinks of social change, one tends to conceive of it on a grand scale—in the case of postsocialist Russia, in terms of the transformation of property relations, the formation of new elites, and the restructuring of industries and entire economic sectors. While it is hard to doubt the reality and significance of these developments, this study primarily targets a different, more elusive breed of metamorphosis—the piecemeal patchwork of social change that occurs through myriad private actions. Each may be aimed at nothing more than the preservation of stability, yet, taken collectively, these acts contribute to the formation of new institutions and infrastructures, and in effect transform society from within. That this transformation should be carried out in the explicitly conservative interests of self-protection from perpetual crisis is just another testimony to the power of the unintended consequences of human action.

Scope of the Book

This book follows two main lines of inquiry. The first (covered in chapters 2 through 4) concerns the interplay of interests, needs, and narrative traditions standing behind the emergence of crisis as the dominant framework of interpretation (or, in W. I. Thomas's words, the definition of the [postsocialist] situation) in the 1990s.[21] I explore the contributions that various groups of actors, from intelligentsia to public politicians, made to the evolution of this framework in the course of the late 1980s to early 1990s, and trace how, in the course of this evolution, crisis imagery obtained overtones of finality and timelessness, and the crisis itself was reimagined from a temporary developmental challenge into an all-embracing and ahistorical condition. Crucial to this metamorphosis was the transformation of routine daily consciousness, which by the late 1990s began to regard a skillful navigation of total crisis more generally as a central measure of individuals' practical competence.[22] While many forms of self-identification along professional, economic, or cultural lines lost their legitimacy in the face of shifting social boundaries and rapid societal restructuring, the stance of a hardened crisis subject, capable of maintaining composure in the face of adverse circumstances, could offer postsocialist Russians the sought-after sense of personal solvency. This symbolic importance of the crisis framework for articulating one's practical competence contributed to the steadiness with which it was evoked across a range of seemingly disparate instances.

The second line of the book's interest (covered in chapters 5, 6, and 7) deals with the consequences that crisis as a framework of interpretation had for the postsocialist milieu. It explores the organization of life in the midst of a perpetual crisis and addresses the bearing that the specific features attributed to this crisis—its permanence and its all-embracing, total character—had on the ways people developed for navigating it. The diffuse, ubiquitous threats expected to emanate from everywhere were countered with equally universal and versatile self-protection arrangements. Moreover, the crisis framework was so central to connoting practical competence that the individual's responses functioned as ways of self-presentation as much as they were coping strategies, for they performatively indicated that the subject was in control. In other words, the crisis framework became so essential to people's self-conception that it was put into practice whenever they felt a need to mark themselves as adept postsocialist subjects; the cultivation of autonomy was not merely instrumental but also symbolic, and this created a power field in which a variety of statements and behaviors could be reproduced simply because they served as testimonials to the individual's practical aptitude.

Thinking of crisis as a framework of interpretation and self-presentation, and not just as an objective and indisputable fact, allows us to recognize an additional dimension to the frequent distresses of postsocialist life by addressing the gravitational force that they created around themselves. In this gravitational field, phenomena of great diversity functioned as mutually replaceable. Old socialist traditions, both narrative and pragmatic, were selectively revamped and infused with new life, and new social forms emerged as by-products of Muscovites' efforts to preserve stability.

My two analytical foci are complementary in that they both concern themselves with everyday experience, albeit in distinct ways.[23] The interest in crisis as an interpretive frame addresses experiences in the aggregate, as phenomena "construed by those who lived through them, as having meanings that need to be recovered" (Sewell 1980, 11), and seeks to comprehend the logic by which these meanings were ascribed. Later, the book turns to experience in the singular—experience as the know-how, as the wisdom that Muscovites felt they developed in the course of the 1990s. While most agreed that their multiple postsocialist experiences were predominantly traumatic, the cumulative wisdom they drew out of them was nonetheless highly valued. The value of this accumulated experience was inevitably tied to the crisis that engendered it, and in a sense depended on it.

The book's chapters deploy these analytical foci as follows. The second chapter surveys the public discourse of the 1990s in Russia, in particular the lasting appeal of crisis imagery, which stemmed partly from socialist-era narrative traditions and partly from the embedded interests of various groups in the public arena. The chapter argues that as the decade progressed, the crisis imagery, which was initially used as pretext to begin discussion, obtained overtones of permanence and gravity. It went from being the question to becoming part of the answer. Parties from all over the political spectrum contributed to this loss of *telos,* and while the historical trajectories on which they plotted the crisis differed—from the linear progressivist model of the liberals to the eschatological vision of the neotraditionalists —the mere routinization of the term played a role in blurring the public's memories and impressions of the period.

The next two chapters analyze, on the basis of the interviews, the contexts in which the images of a total crisis circulated in everyday conversations. Chapter 3 describes a common theme of the public discourse in late-1990s Russia: the theme of drastic deterioration. The chapter concentrates on a number of important historical moments, as well as personal experiences perceived as symptomatic of the downward spiral of postsocialism. It addresses the gaps and inconsistencies, as well as the internal logic, of the deterioration discourse, and discusses some of the reasons for its powerful appeal even among those who by narrowly economic criteria could be considered "winners of the transition."

The fourth chapter addresses the frequent companion of the deterioration framework—the framework of permanence. While people typically imagined the first postsocialist decade in terms of decay, this decay was portrayed as everlasting and ahistorical. The chapter locates the theme of the permanence and eternal return of crisis in the larger field of postsocialist temporality and conceptions of history, exploring the reflections of these altered perceptions of time in everyday practices. Furthermore, it suggests that the seemingly contradictory themes of decay and permanence supported and conditioned each other, creating the image of a world in which crisis was perpetual and continuous, and in which all adverse developments emanated from the same core condition. The chapter outlines the interpretive constraints that this vision exerted over individual's assessment of the situation, but also the ways in which, by the end of the 1990s, it became a crucial resource for building rapport, shaping ideas of safety and autonomy, creating solidarities, and asserting one's practical competence in everyday interactions.

The fifth chapter treats crisis not only as a narrative but as a broad behavioral orientation. The chapter is centrally concerned with the phenomenon of domesticity and the centrality of the household, both of which were constructed as types of symbolic and practical refuge from the postsocialist crisis. It takes up the theme of domestic consumption and, in particular, the discourses and practices surrounding purchases of large domestic equipment, as ways of assessing the role played by the total crisis framework in the organization of daily life.

Chapter 6 looks beyond domestic consumption to examine everyday rituals, health beliefs, and informal exchange as sites where pragmatic responses to the uncertainty intrinsic to the postsocialist condition were converted into signs of personal distinction. This chapter explores the drive toward autonomy, toward maximally insulating one's daily life from all interactions with the state, which in practice generated informal parallel structures and arrangements that replicated the mistrusted public institutions. It argues that the cultivation of autonomy was the overriding coping mechanism allowing postsocialist actors not only to accommodate and resist change in their everyday lives, but also to perform their criticism of the postsocialist order in practice and to project an image of themselves as able and competent postsocialist subjects.

The seventh chapter deals with the unintended consequences of crisis and the drive toward autonomy, both for the social actors and for the larger social structures and institutions of a society slowly and painfully coping with the process of developing a capitalist economy. It suggests that, although crisis terminology was instrumental in helping people function in an unstable environment, its repeated use contributed to an inflation of the concept. Taking successful attainment of autonomy as a measure of practical competence in the postsocialist context, my subjects invested much effort into demonstrating their emotional and practical independence from what they perceived as a consistently threatening and disorderly reality, inadvertently reproducing the civic withdrawal, generalized mistrust, and power-avoidance that plagued the period of late socialism. However, while this unquestioning acceptance of crisis as the ultimate postsocialist reality may have inhibited forms of active civic involvement, it also provided the individuals with an incentive for creating defensive institutions and a basis for developing collective solidarities, even if this occurred through affirmations of generalized mistrust. The book concludes by considering the implications of this paradoxical situation for Russia today, as well as for sociological approaches to long-term social crises more generally.

2 How the Crisis of Socialism Became a Postsocialist Crisis

As is the case with the worlds we all inhabit, the first postsocialist decade was shaped by developments of many decades, indeed centuries, that preceded it. But the turning point that many Russians recognized as particularly critical to the shaping of their present situation occurred in the mid-1980s. Mikhail Gorbachev's initiatives, launched in May 1985, just two months after his election to the post of the General Secretary of the CPSU, began as a call for increased economic efficiency of enterprises (the so-called *khozrashchet* and *gospriemka*). This quickly broadened to include a campaign for a more thorough reform and renewal of the socialist system, with increased transparency of public life and openness about societal ills (the so-called *glasnost*).[1] These initiatives, however, were partial and somewhat inconsistent, and existed in the context of intensifying shortages of food and consumer products, increasing interethnic tensions in various regions of the Soviet Union, and deepening conflicts within the Communist Party of the USSR. Toward the end of the 1980s the partial reforms of Gorbachev's team proved incapable of ameliorating the situation, and Gorbachev lost the lead in public opinion to a team of democratic reformers with a far more radical political and economic agenda.[2] While the socialist project received a heavy blow in 1989 in the wake of the fall of the Berlin Wall and the "velvet revolutions" in Eastern Europe, its decisive end on Russian territory occurred in 1991 after Boris Yeltsin, recently elected president of the Russian Federation, issued a ban on all activity of the CPSU in Russia. Declared immediately after the August coup d'état in which Communist Party hard-liners attempted to oust Gorbachev, the ban effectually delegitimized Gorbachev, who was left little choice but to resign from his post as the General Secretary of the now-suspended CPSU. His removal from power was sealed by the dissolution of the USSR in December 1991.

The country's economic situation in 1991 was dismal. Gorbachev's government had already taken measures against inflation and food shortages in the late 1980s. In 1990, ration cards were introduced for the basic foodstuffs, and the year 1991 brought the infamous "Pavlov's reform," which withdrew high-denomination banknotes from circulation virtually overnight, wiping away millions of people's savings.[3] Economic upheavals continued under Yeltsin with the policy of "shock therapy" and the abolition of price controls in 1992, causing rapid inflation and escalation of prices (prices rose by 350% within a month and by 2,600% within a year [White 2000]). A privatization campaign, investment scandals, and pyramid schemes in the mid-1990s were followed by several relatively calm years. During this time the variety of goods and services available to Russian consumers increased dramatically, and an entrepreneurial infrastructure developed just enough to justify a discussion of the slow emergence of a middle class in Russia. This category, however, was small even by optimistic estimates,[4] and its formation coexisted with increasingly grave payment arrears in the "budget sector of the economy." Budget deficits remained a problem, and in 1998 a sharp devaluation of the ruble, partly triggered by the Asian financial crisis and partly resulting from state fiscal policy, precipitated a nationwide financial default. This in turn spurred a cycle of price hikes and inflationary expectations, which had a substantial impact on both middle-class Russians and their worse-off counterparts.

Much like economic developments, political events throughout the decade were diverse and often unpredictable: the attempted coup of 1991 and the breakdown of the Soviet Union; the fall of the iron curtain, which made foreign travel possible; the lifting of ideological controls and the end of the CPSU; the parliamentary crisis of 1993, which resulted in Yeltsin's controversial suppression of the parliament and subsequent alteration of the Constitution to strengthen presidential power and autonomy; the electoral shock of the 1993 parliamentary elections, when the eccentric nationalist LDPR party, led by Vladimir Zhirinovsky, received nearly 23 percent of the vote; Yeltsin's reelection by a slim margin in 1996; his incessant reappointments of favorites and occasional dismissal of prime ministers (within the two years of my fieldwork, four governments came and went); the two Chechen campaigns, the second one prompted by a mysterious apartment bombing in Moscow in October 1999; and finally, Yeltsin's sudden voluntary release of power in favor of then–prime minister Vladimir Putin as the country prepared to celebrate the new year on December 31, 1999. All these developments were gradually shaping the postsocialist order in irreversible and dramatic ways. But a recounting of events, by themselves, cannot tell us much about their significance for Russian citizens. In order to comprehend how they were perceived by the public, one has to examine the rhetoric that evolved in the course of the 1990s in reference to the ongoing transformations.

Two Contradictory Messages

In any culture, standard responses to greetings reflect to a much greater extent the culture's rhetorical conventions than the actual circumstances of the particular speaker. No competent listener would take a "Fine, thanks" reply to be indicative of anything but the speaker's command of the Anglo-American rules of small talk. Similarly, no one would expect an in-depth explication of the speaker's circumstances (should it take place) to conform to the benign spirit of this formulaic response. Yet, interest in these conventions on the part of the social scientists is well warranted,[5] for they reflect some of the basic principles that structure both the ways people live their lives and the terms in which they comprehend them.

Repeated conversations with Muscovites over the span of 1998–2000 gave me plenty of opportunities to explore the patterned responses to the initial wellness inquiry in all their variances. Two types of responses seemed most standard: the ones centered around the idea of stability ("All goes as usual," "Nothing is new, same old stuff"), and the ones emphasizing sharp deterioration ("It's much worse than it used to be," "After the default, of course life has gotten worse"). As with the "Fine, thanks" reply, subsequent elaborations of the speakers' circumstances did not necessarily follow from initial tonality of the response. That is not to say that the initial claim of stability or deterioration received no support in the further discussion. Rather, the discourses opened in such a divergent manner seemed to unfold toward each other, in the sense that opening lines notwithstanding, they mixed the themes of stability and deterioration, alternating between images of an increasingly aggravating social and political situation, and those of a static, unchangeable routine. Here are, for example, two fragments of the same interview, voiced within a twenty-minute interval of one another:

> *Fragment 1*
> You know, nothing global has happened lately. The government has changed,[6] but that wasn't anything that I would feel as a change. Nothing has changed in our lives, it's just going as it is, little by little . . .
> *Fragment 2*
> It's all changing right now. I can't even figure out how to save money. Even with dollars . . . well, I hope they aren't going to restrict [their circulation] right now, but still, there is no stability. . . . In our life, you just can't relax: today you have one situation, and tomorrow it's completely different. (Lena, female, 37)[7]

As with many others, Lena's interview started from an affirmation of stability ("Nothing is new, all is normal"), a statement that received support in the course of the conversation, but that was also countered by comments exemplified by Fragment 2. Neither the message of stability nor the one of perpetual change was constructed as dominant. Rather, much like Konstantin, Lena was drawing here on the idea that her life was unfolding "in crisis all the time," which made the themes of stability and deterioration equally applicable and even mutually replaceable.

Both the framework of deterioration and the one of permanence drew support from the very same evidence of economic and psychological privations experienced in the course of the 1990s, yet the permanence perspective cast the past years as an undifferentiated period devoid of internal heterogeneity and development, while the deterioration framework emphasized the dynamic aspect of the decade. This duality could be traced on the level of terms frequently used in discussions of the decade, both in the media and in everyday conversations. Some terms, such as *boloto* (mire, swamp) bear an overtone of the permanence framework, while *katastroika* (a merger of *perestroika* and *katastrofa* [catastrophe], authored by the former dissident Alexander Zinoviev), or *razval* (collapse) support the more dramatic vision of deterioration.

Let us make a brief detour into the historical and sociological underpinnings of the two discourses outlined above. What allowed affirmations of constant instability and of unbreakable persistence to peacefully coexist in the discourse of the same individuals? What were the rhetorical traditions and public sphere discussions that people could draw upon in framing their experience as one of a perpetual crisis? And why were these rhetorical traditions so susceptible to the crisis imagery to begin with?

These questions call for an investigation of rhetorical forms available to the public, in the spirit of Hilgartner and Bosk's discussion of the "rise and fall of social problems" (1988). Hilgartner and Bosk point out that the definitions of social problems, and the types of issues labeled as such, are never uncontestable. These and similar labels ("crisis" being one of them) always represent a product of choice among many alternative interpretations, and as a result they inevitably simplify and distort the totality of complex sociocultural, political, and economic developments they refer to. In order to understand how particular labels evolve to become widely acceptable definitions of given phenomena, one needs to look at the public arenas in which the definitions were forged and at the communities that were involved in negotiating framing categories.

This is the task I set forth in this chapter. The data for the examination of how "crisis" became such a durable and widespread way of looking at the post-socialist reality (or, in Sewell's [1992] words, a widely available cultural schema) comes from several sources. In 2001 I conducted interviews with thirteen Russian public intellectuals, journalists, and political analysts.[8] I supplemented these with a close reading of the debates that took place on the pages of Russian periodicals—thick monthly journals (*Oktiabr, Nash Sovremennik, Znamia*) and thin weeklies (*Ogonek, Argumenty i Fakty*)—as well as political pamphlets and sociological publications in the course of the late 1980s and 1990s. In addition, I drew on the resources of the electronic database *Integrum*, which allows text search through thousands of Russian-language publications. The sources available through *Integrum* were further supplemented by select publications identified by the interviewed experts as having been centrally involved in the public polemic of the late 1980s–1990s (e.g., *Vek XX i Mir*). My aim here is not only to identify the primary "carrier groups" of the crisis rhetoric, but also to trace the subtle shifts that occurred to the meaning of the term "crisis" as it grew in popularity. This chapter discusses the significance of the term for the public's perception of postsocialist change, both in terms of the interpretations that it empowered and the selective blindnesses inevitably associated with it. Finally, it addresses the ways in which the shifting meaning of "crisis" fed into the two seemingly contradictory interpretations of the decade which I discussed above.

Defining the 1990s

In June 2001 a book presentation took place in a reception hall of the Moscow Interbank Currency Exchange, an ultra-modern office building situated on one of the quiet side lanes off Bolshaia Nikitskaia Street in Moscow. The reception was well attended and featured easily recognizable figures as speakers, such as former prime minister and author of the Russian economic reform Yegor Gaidar, former minister of the economy Evgenii Yasin, and the controversial power-broker and image-maker Gleb Pavlovskii. The book under discussion was co-written by the political scientist and vice-director of the Enterprise Development Foundation Irina Starodubrovskaia, and Vladimir Mau, a former member of Gaidar's economic team. Titled *Great Revolutions: From Cromwell to Putin,* it argued for a thorough revision of conventional interpretations of the decade of the 1990s in Russia, to portray it not as the period of postsocialist disorder and infrastructural collapse but as a decade of a great revolution, no greater or smaller than those known by other industrial nations such as France and Great Britain.

The merits of the authors' arguments are a subject for another discussion. But what made this event most interesting for the purposes of this study was the amount of high-profile attention it received, and the timing of its occurrence. At the turn of the century, when the closing of the decade and the election of a new president in the spring of 2000 appeared to complete a self-contained and finished period, the impulse to forge a definition for what had happened on the territory of the former USSR after 1989 was becoming acute. Starodubrovskaia and Mau's book was just one of many manifestations of an interpretive struggle taking place to that end. Other examples appeared in the special issue of a popular bimonthly essay magazine, *Neprikosnovennyi Zapas* (Private Stock), dedicated to the tenth anniversary of the 1991 coup; in the Carnegie Endowment–sponsored journal *Pro et Contra*, which dedicated its spring 1999 issue to the theme "Transformations in Russia: Outcomes of the Decade";[9] and in multiple retrospective television series, such as *Ten Years That Shook Us,* filmed in 2002 and aired on the TVS channel.

This vibrancy of public discussion and activity of various parties aimed at forging an appropriate "label" for the decade stood in sharp contrast to the lack of discussion as the events of the decade were still unfolding. The few official designations for the period—"time of transition" (*perekhodnyi period*) and "changes" (*peremeny*)—did not take root in popular discourse. In far greater abundance one could encounter pejorative names for designating the post-1985 period.[10] In her perceptive study of late-perestroika-era discourse, Nancy Ries (1984, 44, 46) enumerated several, such as "complete disintegration," and "collapse." They coexisted with others: brothel (*bardak*), no-limit zone (*bespredel*), and of course, crisis (*krizis*) come to mind. But one would be hard pressed to come up with a widely accepted but relatively neutral term. It was this worldview, which was described in the early 1990s by Russian critics as "clinical alarmism" (Rubtsov 1992, 16), that allowed the term *catastrophe* (*katastrofa*) to emerge as "run-of-the-mill for describing both the entirety and the components, however minor, of public life" (Guseinov 1996).

How did it happen that this catastrophic rhetoric developed in Russia into a virtually uncontested interpretive framework for much of the 1990s? Assessments produced in Western Europe and the United States demonstrated no firm consensus on the success and long-term implications of post-Soviet reforms throughout the 1990s. There was, and there still is, a gamut of opinions, from neoliberal celebratory panegyrics to harshly critical accounts, with many more-moderate positions in between. In contrast, in the Russian political rhetoric, both in everyday talk and in the media, crisis terminology visibly prevailed,[11] even leading to certain stylistic excesses, such as a poetry collection published in 1999 by a well-known poet, Andrei Voznesensky, under the title *Zhutkii Crisis Super Star* (Awful Crisis Superstar).[12] It was not until the very end of the decade that works like Starodubrovskaia and Mau's began to question the authority of the crisis framework and propose alternative terms of analysis. To understand why the catastrophic sensibility turned out to be so appealing, and why "crisis" represented such an unproblematic rhetorical choice within it, we need to take a look at the recent history of the term.

Perestroika Rhetoric: Crisis of Socialism

Other scholars have pointed out continuities between the Russian folkloric tradition of litanies and laments and the ritualized complaints of more recent times.[13] The story of the recent uses of crisis in the public sphere, however, starts not from a historical analogy but from an instance of cultural discontinuity.

Terms like "crisis" were not uncommon in late Soviet political and economic discourse. However, in the years prior to 1985–1986, they referred primarily to the state of things in the "capitalist camp" and were almost always accompanied by the label "bourgeois." While many speakers actually meant it, it is also crucial to remember that this terminology was the only guise in which any kind of research and discussion of the Western intellectual, political, and economic trends could be conducted. Thus, it would be hard to take these terms as instances of genuine criticism. Books with such titles as *Crisis of Contemporary Bourgeois Political Economy, Mass Literature and the Crisis of Western Bourgeois Culture,* or *Crisis of the Contemporary Currency System of Capitalism and Bourgeois Political Economy* provided many with a legitimate pretext to explore non-Marxist approaches in the social sciences, engage important themes in non-Soviet literature, and study economic and political realities of Western democracies. Maintenance of a critical stance was essential for receiving access to bibliographical sources published abroad, and all research drawing on foreign sources, especially in the social sciences and humanities, had to be framed in the language of unmasking crises of capitalism. For example, Igor Kon, one of the few psychologists in the Soviet Union who was well-read in Freudian theory of psychoanalysis and who lectured publicly on it in the 1960s, used the language of "crisis of capitalism" repeatedly.[14] Kon's very access to Western publications was strategically presented in his petitions to censorship committees as crucial for the task of "criticism of bourgeois methodology," for "it is impossible to adequately carry out ideological struggle without knowledge of the enemy."[15]

The metaphor of crisis was, in other words, the only legitimate introduction to any discussion of certain ideologically sensitive matters. Examining the ways in which crisis terminology was first applied in a more or less consistent way to domestic realities in the mid- to late 80s, one distinguishes a similar pattern. The notion of a "crisis of socialism" was initiated from within the system by Mikhail Gorbachev and his reformist team (Lewin 1988). It was taken up and developed further in order to legitimize the economic and political reform which was, to use a phrase from one of the most resonant publications of the time, *Inogo ne dano* (*There Is No Other Way*) "a precondition of the viability of our society. There is no other way" (Afanasiev 1988).

As Soviet writers had done in their critique of "bourgeois ideology," these new commentators used crisis imagery instrumentally. They acknowledged particular social problems as a prerequisite for reforms, and it was the nature and direction of such reforms that commanded the authors' true interest. An example here could be the exchange that took place between the publicist Viacheslav Karpov and mathematician/journalist Igor Shafarevich in 1989–1990 after the publication of Shafarevich's much-discussed essay *Russophobia* (1989). In this text, earlier available only in samizdat form, Shafarevich maintained that the USSR's contemporary social problems were due to the anti-Russian elites, who unreflexively applied Western solutions to the uniquely Russian national context. In his response, Karpov justly pointed out that Shafarevich's arguments sounded chauvinistic. At the same time, he fully embraced Shafarevich's assessment of the "crisis state of our society," saying that "the interest in labor is diminishing, we are witnessing expansion of violent crime, fertility is declining," and "real-life social illnesses [are] growing on a truly threatening scale" (Karpov 1990, 151–152). The term "crisis" referred here to the state of Soviet society and was, in a sense, a rhetorical figure allowing the authors to advance to the discussion of their immediate agenda, the trajectory of a proposed reform. In other words, both authors agreed on the existence of a crisis in order to move beyond it. It was the possible resolution of this crisis that evoked real debate (in Karpov's case such resolution involved pluralistic democracy, while Shafarevich leaned toward Russian national consolidation).

Two things point to the close affinity between this usage of crisis terminology and that of the preceding period. First was the sense of the rhetorical necessity of acknowledging the crisis before one could move to more substantive debates. Second, these later writers essentially understood the crisis in a Marxist fashion, as an expression of lasting and unavoidable systemic contradictions. Despite sharing the same origin, these two aspects were actually in a state of tension. It did not take long after the beginning of perestroika for it to become apparent that the nature of the socialist system was far from a clear matter, and that in order to formulate strategies of reform, the public discussion needed to reach some modicum of consensus on what precisely the socialist system was and what were the origins of its crisis. The acknowledgement of the crisis, therefore, could not remain merely a rhetorical matter, but had to take its place at the very center of the public polemic regarding the deficiencies of late socialism.

The public discussions of 1985–1990 structured themselves around the need to conceptually clarify the nature of late socialist economy and society and to critically assess its susceptibility to reform. The boom of "thick journals" and analytical newspapers that occurred during these years can serve as an indicator of this issue's significance in the eyes of late Soviet subjects. Over the period from 1985 to 1990, the circulation rate of all publications involved in this public polemic grew manifold. The popular weekly newspaper *Argumenty i Fakty* increased its circulation from 3,000,000 to 32,900,000, the thin monthly *Ogonek* from 1,480,000 to 4,600,000, and the thick monthly literary-critical journal *Novyi Mir*, known for its publications of formerly suppressed materials from Solzhenitsyn's *Gulag Archipelago* to Pasternak's *Doctor Zhivago*, from 422,000 to 2,620,000.

While the interpretation of the Soviet system as "command-administrative" or "planned economy" prevailed, other interpretations emerged as well. Mikhail Voslenskii's analysis of Soviet political leadership, or *nomenklatura*, came out in Russian in 1991.[16] Voslenskii's terminology was adopted by, among others, Viacheslav Kostikov in his 1991 article "The Splendor and Misery of the *Nomenklatura*," as well as by many authors for *Vek XX i Mir*. Lev Timofeev (1990) argued that the shadow economy, rather than the "planned economy," was the backbone of the socialist order.[17] Each commentator proposed different solutions to a differently theorized systemic crisis. Ideological positions on the issues varied widely (as did the prescriptions for action), from the pro-socialist and reformist visions voiced in an edited volume titled *On the Brink of a Crisis* (Zhuravlev 1990) to the anticommunist and far more extreme suggestions put forth by Solzhenitsyn in his pamphlet *Rebuilding Russia: Reflections and Tentative Proposals* (1990). Yet, divergent as they were, these discussions shared one crucial precept. This was the conviction that the crisis they were dealing with was surmountable, and that the historical situation in which the discussion was taking place was an open one. The abundance of policy proposals, actual recommendations, and prognostic debates that occurred in the press during these years signaled the participatory position of the parties involved with the discussion and their intellectual investment in the project of deliberating the future of the reforms.

Post-1991: Crisis of Reforms

The advent of the 1990s brought with it an avalanche of political and economic upheavals, from the failed coup of 1991 and the breakdown of the USSR to the repeated devaluation of currency through monetary reforms, inflation, and liberalization of prices. Amid these developments, the images of crisis did not disappear from public discourse. However, the participatory attitude of the former years had all but vanished. Increasingly, newspaper and magazine publications communicated a sense that the course of events and political decisions was set in advance. More importantly, the very meaning of the "crisis" started to change. When the socialist project disintegrated in 1991, the crisis of the socialist system was reinterpreted as the crisis of reforms themselves.

This change of framing is significant, because it signaled a shift of historical perspective. Crisis, as Reinhard Koselleck points out, is "a concept that always posited a temporal dimension which, parsed in modern terms, actually implied a theory of time" (2002, 237). Yet, while the early-perestroika-era conception of time was rather straightforwardly linear,[18] the trajectory implied in the later accounts was far more ambiguous and diverse. The events under criticism, at least for the first several years, remained substantially the same: growing inflation, social unrest, diminishing industrial output, and increase in crime. However, their larger meaning shifted. No longer did they indicate a need for public discussion of policies and measures for their amelioration; rather, they were seen as an unchangeable circumstance, a given, which was not so much the starting point as the end point of a discussion. Some authors explicitly noted this transformation of meaning. "Year 1991 will enter history as the year during which the socioeconomic crisis of the Soviet society turned into a national catastrophe," said Gennadii Osipov (1992) in an article tellingly titled "Myths of the Passing Era." But for the most part, the supplanting of a temporary crisis of socialism by an ahistorical catastrophic condition occurred implicitly. The terminology of denunciation remained, while its legitimate purpose was lost. In the absence of the modernist project of endowing socialism with a human face, the historical significance of the ongoing changes remained unclear.

This loss of clear historical perspective was closely connected to the ideological vacuum which, many argue, accompanied the collapse of communism. While the former socialist countries of Eastern Europe could frame the time after 1989 as the period of national liberation from oppression, such an option was closed to Russia, in which the seventy-odd years of Communist rule were not imposed from abroad, but rather fueled by an internal political dynamic. In the immediate aftermath of 1991, this led, among other things, to peculiar political exorcisms described by Michael Urban (1994), in which Russian politicians of different ideological persuasions competed in projecting onto one another the culpability for the discredited past. Indeed, in the absence of an external oppressor, the responsibility for past mistakes had to be ascribed to someone within the country—or else the communist project had to be exonerated altogether. Neither of the two (much-utilized) options offered an opportunity to generate a working consensus regarding even the most basic principles of the transformation. In this respect, the East European countries had a wider spectrum of ideological opportunities available to them, since they could employ rhetoric of national liberation and nationalism more broadly. Since socialism could in their case be externalized as a Soviet (or, in the case of the former Union republics, Russian) import, this rhetoric worked in Eastern Europe alongside, and not against, the push for democratization and for a "return to Europe" (Derluguian 2003).

If some semblance of an ideologically coherent framework existed in Russia at the time, it would have to be the neoliberal view associated with the privatization crusader Anatolii Chubais and his team.[19] This vision, however, was limited narrowly to the sphere of economics, where it was so dominant that dissenters, such as the leftist sociologist and author Boris Kagarlitsky, found it bordering on orthodoxy.[20] This doctrine also had two fundamental problems. First, it was implemented in a top-down fashion and without the benefit of public discussion, which was bound to make it illegitimate in the eyes of much of the population. Second, and just as importantly, it was narrowly technical; it failed to translate into a larger strategic vision of the transformation that could give meaning and coherence to a protracted process of social, economic, and political change.

The pragmatic disregard of the neoliberal economists for participatory politics and strategic discussions did not come from nowhere. In fact, outright dismissal of all-embracing ideological strategies was characteristic for the entire Yeltsin government during the early 1990s. Moreover, this distrust of ideology was among Yeltsin's most attractive features for many of his anticommunist supporters. What seemed to go unnoticed was that by refusing to generate some version of a "Yeltsin doctrine" in dialogue with major social groups and organizations, Yeltsin's government was leaving its subjects without a way to meaningfully relate to the ongoing changes and to the very real sacrifices that these changes entailed. As a result, it became easy to see the events of the early 1990s as either suspended in a historical vacuum, or meaningful only as an endpoint (but certainly not a starting point) of the historical process.[21]

I had several conversations with political actors who participated in the making of Yeltsin's policies. These discussions made apparent how strikingly little effort was given in the course of the 1990s to legitimizing the reforms in the eyes of the Russian population, and to inscribing them into a larger meaningful framework in a manner that public politics would require. The general assumption, according to Georgii Satarov, a long-time member of the team and one of the authors of Yeltsin's 1996 program, was that "the needs of the citizens were purely practical. Such things as the meaning of life were just not part of it. The task was merely to satisfy their physical demands, and that was it."[22] Similarly, according to Andranik Migranian, a member of the presidential council for most of the 1990s,

> Yeltsin never developed any strategic vision. Mostly, he limited himself to a number of catchwords: the market, freedom of the press . . . but very inconsistently. Somehow, there were always more urgent things (*kak-to ne do togo bylo*). At some point there was a struggle with the parliament. Then, after 1993, fear of Zhirinovsky, and in 1994–1995 he had to defend himself against Communists. After the victory all his illnesses started, the fights around property and so on. So he never had it as one of his aims to articulate some kind of vision.[23]

The ideologically barren landscape of the 1990s, therefore, had few viable alternatives to offer to the crisis rhetoric it inherited from the perestroika period. Moreover, even if this interpretive frame was not readily available, it had to be invented to give voice to the difficulty post-Soviet individuals faced as they tried to rationalize, in at least minimally meaningful historical terms, the sacrifices they had to make. However, this was already a different crisis, one that did not fit into a clear teleological schema of reforming socialism, but that instead operated in a historical void of postsocialist politics.

A number of social groups, or as Hilgartner and Bosk (1988) would have it, "communities of operatives," implicated themselves in the reproduction of this resigned and atemporal crisis rhetoric. All of them did so in response to the tectonic shifts in the social structure, which were first felt as early as 1991, and which transformed (albeit in different ways) the prior position of these groups in the social arena. The most profound challenges affected the social layer that was professionally involved in the articulation and dissemination of meanings: the intelligentsia. I will discuss this group's role before addressing the contributions made by its specific subgroups: the social scientists, media professionals, and political actors.

Intelligentsia's Crisis

Defining the Russian intelligentsia is notoriously difficult, not only because any definition of an intellectual is, by necessity, a self-definition.[24] A product of two centuries of autocracy, the Russian intelligentsia always understood itself in terms beyond merely objective occupational characteristics which exist in any industrialized country: a stratum "with specialist qualifications, including engineers and technicians as well as employees in executive, political, artistic, scientific, and administrative roles, and self-employed professionals" (Zaslavskaia and Arutiunian 1994, 150). Rather, it viewed itself as a moral and ethical community endowed with a particular social mission. Without straying too far from the topic to explore the social and historical sources of this missionary drive,[25] suffice it to say that the intelligentsia's identity rested on two self-professed callings: offering education and enlightenment to the masses, and providing a moral and spiritual opposition to the authorities. As some authors point out,[26] the intelligentsia's two callings, or to use a more prosaic sociological language, social functions, were in a state of (typically misrecognized) tension. In its conventional Soviet-era version, enlightenment of the masses frequently amounted to dissemination of canonical forms of culture, which were sanctioned from above and whose further sacralization could hardly be interpreted as a form of dissent. However, this contradiction did not undermine the late Soviet intelligentsia's sense of significance and missionary purpose. It was not until the early 1990s that the two callings of the intelligentsia began to crumble, together with the regime that made them possible, and the intelligentsia, to use the formulation of Boris Dubin, "lost [its] social place" (2001, 329).

Along with members of many other occupational categories, the bulk of post-Soviet intelligentsia members experienced rapid downward mobility, while the prestige and economic position of managerial and business professions improved. In the intelligentsia's case, this loss of economic and social standing was accompanied by a fundamental uncertainty about the group's social and cultural mission in the rapidly opening environment where canonical conventions were in flux, while the notion of "authorities" became both more diffuse and more readily open to questioning by anyone.

The intelligentsia's articulations of its frustration over the loss of its social mission did not remain muffled. For a number of years, discussions of the Russian intelligentsia's fate and its expected implications for Russian society in general abounded in the media.[27] These debates were especially intense on the pages of thick journals—traditional venues for the intelligentsia's discussions since the 1840s. Two aspects are noteworthy in light of this chapter's interest in crisis as a frame for interpreting reality. First, although the debates were led by and concerned with the intelligentsia, they construed the problem as one of universal importance. As Natalia Ivanova put it on the pages of the thick monthly journal *Znamia*, the decline of thick journals, which started as early as 1991,[28] signified not only the agony of the intelligentsia as a social group, but "the agony of society," for "without the brain, without the head, a body cannot exist, while it can exist without an arm and a leg, even if on crutches; and the death of a brain leads to immediate lethal outcome for the entire body . . ." Probably unaware of the social-Darwinist implications of the above argument, Ivanova expressed hope that "at the long last, finally, society?—the state?—will come to think better of it," although the article stopped short of proposing any specific solutions to the problem (1993b, 173).

This inconclusiveness of Ivanova's discussion brings forth the second important aspect of post-Soviet debates about the fate of the intelligentsia, which was precisely the absence of a clear positive referent that could be juxtaposed to the crisis of the intelligentsia in order to provide a model for policy purposes. This does not mean that the referent was entirely absent, but rather that it was elusive and unfixed. To return to Ivanova's article: at one point she unfavorably compared the postsocialist-era disregard for the intelligentsia in Russia to the situation in Poland; at a second point, to the financial independence of intellectuals in Europe and the United States; and at a third point, to the high esteem and social importance that the intelligentsia commanded during the time of late socialism. This foregrounded the deficiency of the postsocialist Russian situation at the expense of a more systematic analysis not only of differences but of parallels between the experiences of other national intelligentsias and that of Russia in its new sociopolitical reality. Furthermore, because she examined no alternative national models in their full complexity, investigating both strengths and weaknesses and their potential for Russia, the normative model implicit in the article's critique turned out to be truly *u-topian*,[29] revealing that the ultimate standard for the intelligentsia's social role had no historical or geographical referent and existed only in the writer's imagination.

The same logic was characteristic for everyday discussions of the postsocialist crisis that I witnessed several years later in my respondents' kitchens. There, too, it was more important for the speakers to assert that the situation they were discussing was fundamentally deviant than to systematically explore what it deviated *from* (and by extension, what it might have been similar *to*). As a result, events under discussion developed an aura of exceptionality, incomparability, and uniqueness, much like the "tragedy of the Russian intelligentsia," setting Russia aside from the rest of the world in a move that was nothing short of self-orientalizing. However, while the early publications on the fate of the Russian intelligentsia viewed the ongoing changes in eschatological terms,[30] by the end of the 1990s the proclamations of an imminent collapse had sounded so often that they acquired a ritualistic, repetitive ring.

Ideological Factions and Unlikely Alliances

The broad label of "intelligentsia," as outlined above, covers many ideologically and socially divergent groups, each of which had its own stake in the reproduction of crisis as an interpretive frame for understanding postsocialist reality. Thinking of the intelligentsia as a whole stratum is not entirely unhelpful, since the susceptibility of its members to the crisis rhetoric can be linked to the actual crisis of the intelligentsia itself, as a collective entity and a category of self-perception. However, at this point I would like to move from this totalizing label (which, indeed, became increasingly irrelevant in the course of the 1990s) and briefly examine the embedded positions of the specific interest groups comprising it: scholars, mass media professionals, and political actors. As this discussion will make clear, a crisis of the category of intelligentsia did not necessarily mean a crisis for all of its members. However, even those who personally profited from the ongoing transformations had their own structural reasons to continue the reproduction of crisis rhetoric.

Academia

The situation in the field of the humanities and social sciences became highly complex after perestroika.[31] On the one hand, the share of these fields in the state budget shrank significantly in comparison with the Soviet period. This put them at the mercy of grant-giving agencies, leaving their practitioners dependent on piecemeal income from teaching and lecturing as a supplement to the deplorably underfunded research. An indicator of the toll that the inadequate state funding exerted on post-Soviet academia is the shrinking acquisition rate in research libraries, many of which (about 50 percent of regional research libraries) were reported unable to afford to purchase any foreign literature. This could only exacerbate the divide between the Russian academic community and the rest of the world.[32] On the other hand, freedom of academic contacts with the West made joint research projects possible. Cutting-edge foreign-language publications became available in translation without the rigid ideological controls of the prior era,[33] and the institution of censorship vanished from academic research.

Despite this mixed record, many scholarly commentators found the undifferentiated crisis rhetoric convincing when addressing both the state of academic knowledge and the larger social condition that engendered it. This may be explained by a combination of institutional and ideological factors.

Institutionally, the inadequacies of research financing led many Russian scholars toward a disproportionate dependence on international grantmaking agencies, such as the Ford Foundation, the John D. and Catherine T. MacArthur Foundation, IREX, and so on. In their turn, these agencies were understandably concerned with the potentially explosive effects of reforms to a greater extent than, for example, with pure social theory or literary studies. As a result, the general consensus formed among academics in the course of the 1990s that grantmaking organizations were biased in favor of particular themes, such as corruption, violation of human rights, environmental threats.[34] One's chances of being granted research funding, consequently, were considered to be directly proportionate to one's ability to word a grant proposal in terms of severe social problems. To put it more paradoxically, affirmation of a systemic crisis became a prerequisite to personal academic success. The reliance on, and perpetuation of, crisis terminology could thus be considered a tactical response of Russian academics to the existing socioeconomic situation. In a private conversation, a young historian colleague put it in the following way: crisis was "a category of practice." "When you say that all is well—that the transition is complete, and it is possible to convert your intellectual product into its green crunchy equivalent[35]—it becomes unclear why they have to help us," he continued. "Given this, I'm all for [crises] and for assistance in breaking through in the Western academic market."

But considerations of funding were not the sole factor in making the crisis rhetoric appealing for the members of the academic community. Prior histories of ideological commitment played into the highly critical response that many scholars had toward the decade of Yeltsin's reforms. This in itself, of course, was not particularly surprising; far more interesting was that former ideological rivals found themselves, in the course of the 1990s, drawn to the same crisis terminology, although through different logic and for different reasons.

In ideological terms, the fall of socialism represented a threat to a number of ideological projects important to particular factions of the Soviet academic community. In the case of the countless ideological workers, whose careers were built on the refutation of bourgeois theories and the propaganda of "scientific communism," the fall of socialism signified the loss of a guiding perspective with which they had associated both their public and their private identities.[36] Their frustration thus had both an ideological and a practical dimension: they lost their niches in the teaching curriculums of post-Soviet universities, and they felt a threat to their funding and publication opportunities in the restructured research and publishing industries. Social scientists loyal to the ideology of Russian nationalism (a train of thought with a following not only among some scholars but also among high-ranking members of the Soviet *nomenkla-tura*[37]) fared somewhat better, in that they did not consider their ideological project so thoroughly compromised by the fall of the USSR.[38] However, they had their own reasons to frame the era of the 1990s in crisis terms, since the Westernizing pathos of the early postsocialist transformations amplified their sense of humiliation over the ending of the Cold War. In the meantime, the ideological project of the formerly liberal and pro-Western scholars was not faring much better. The highly idealistic expectations of the latter faced the harsh reality of the early post-Soviet *realpolitik,* in which democracy and the free market brought not only personal freedoms (such as they were), but also rampant inequality, unemployment, and the triumph of mass culture. For these critically inclined academics, discontent and opposition to the Soviet regime (the traditional self-identification of the intelligentsia) logically led to a simi-larly vociferous opposition to Yeltsin's policies, since these had failed to produce the type of liberal democracy they had anticipated. As a result of this ideo-logical somersault, the harshest criticisms of the first postsocialist decade that came from liberal sociologists started to sound quite similar to those voiced by their former ideological adversaries.[39] In both cases, developments of the 1990s were all too often dismissed as manifestations of crisis, corruption, and dis-order, at the cost of a more subtle group analysis of the multidirectional effects of the reforms.

Mass Media

Gorbachev-initiated change began in the 1980s with the call for a more open discussion of the problems of socialism. The early programs of pere-stroika, such as *Vzgliad* (Gaze) or *Prozhektor Perestroiki* (Perestroika's Projec-tor) saw their mandate as fulfilling the public demand for a frank discussion of formerly avoided issues, which were phrased in the terms of a "crisis of so-cialism." With the breakdown of the USSR and the end of media censorship, many of the old problems remained. They were exacerbated by new instances of ethnic violence, economic deprivation associated with the rapid devaluation of the ruble, and political tensions that eventually erupted, in 1993, in a vio-lent clash between Yeltsin and the parliament over the future direction of the reforms. Seen in these terms, one could argue that the mass media's gravitation toward crisis rhetoric (which the media themselves labeled *chernukha,* or "the dark stuff") merely reflected the consensus that had already existed in society regarding the darker aspects of the ongoing changes. To some extent this was the case; however, the media's own transformation, proceeding hand-in-hand with the transformation of post-Soviet society, doubtlessly contributed to the readiness of TV and newspaper commentators to dress their accounts of the news in various shades of black.

On the level of a more general critique, many stylistic and format constraints experienced by media professionals after the advent of the market in Russia resembled those noted by media commentators elsewhere (Bourdieu 1998;

McChesney 1999; Grindstaff 2002). An element of sensationalism, a disproportionate representation of shocking and at times gruesome material, and a tendency toward simplification and, indeed, flattening of represented perspectives are endemic to commercial media around the globe. Market-driven logic, which came to replace the ideological controls of the Russian media in 1991, brought with it these new and unfamiliar standards of visual and narrative presentation. Furthermore, this tendency was exacerbated by two uniquely local developments.

First, the initial easing of censorship during the late 1980s understandably released a wave of previously suppressed information regarding the past. Revelations about the scope of Stalinist repressions, as well as previously undisclosed information about the social ills of late Soviet society, made crisis imagery sound more than appropriate. But even this initial "elective affinity" with crisis rhetoric might not have been as lasting had there not been a second factor at play. This had to do with the simultaneous political and economic struggle over property redistribution which defined the 1990s, and in which the media were centrally implicated.

Struggles over redistribution of state property affected the media in two ways. On the one hand, the media's mandate was to provide critical coverage of the newly formed empires of the first post-Soviet oligarchs. On the other, as former state property themselves, the media institutions were being bought, sold, and restructured at the same time as they were supposed to work objectively documenting the same processes happening elsewhere. It would not take exceptional foresight to predict that, in the context of such a conflict of interest, media outlets could become easy tools in the informational struggle between different economic and political camps.

The role that the Russian media played in the struggles waged by the oligarchs is a matter of great complexity.[40] In the interest of the task at hand, it will suffice to say that already by the mid-1990s, the media landscape was heavily shaped by the political struggles of various interest groups who often used the TV channels and newspapers they controlled to voice their agendas, or to get at their opponents. Considering the contentious character of the political process of the 1990s, combined with the weakness of the judicial system, this meant that the informational space became a site where scandalous and compromising information, with varying degrees of accuracy, was routinely posted (or, to use a formulation of the late 1990s, "poured off" [*slivalas'*]) with virtually no consequence for the individuals involved in the corresponding stories. For example, a two-hundred-word front page article in a 1999 newspaper could nonchalantly evoke scandals concerning billions of dollars illegally smuggled out of the country, or make allegations about the criminal activity of highest Kremlin officials, but offer no follow-up journalistic investigation into similar themes raised in prior issues. Given the dearth of such systematic follow-up, whether journalistic or juridical, politically motivated and fabricated allegations blended with justifiable information in a way that made them indistinguishable. With all the diversity of compromising information available everywhere, the only stable fact that carried over from one publication to the next was the fundamental gloominess of all things public.

I do not claim that the effect of post-Soviet media was to single-handedly generate a "mean world syndrome" in the manner described by Gerbner in his lifelong work on the power of the media.[41] With respect to the crisis imagery of the 1990s, mass media actors represented but one group in a complex field of public rhetoric shaped by the interplay of interests, cognitive possibilities, and rhetorical traditions. However, as many of my interviews testified, the mass media provided an array of examples, reasoning patterns, and terms of reference highly compatible with the crisis framework. The fact that in the Russian case these were the products of political struggles, and not simply considerations of market profit, only made them more compelling in the highly politicized climate of the first postsocialist decade.

Political Actors

Unlike the members of the downwardly mobile technical intelligentsia, mass media actors reproduced crisis rhetoric not because it was true to their own life experiences after perestroika, but rather because this rhetoric was instrumental in their own professional projects. This would also be the case with political figures, although their aims were understandably different from those of journalists.

Political parties and movements of the early 1990s drew heavily on crisis imagery as a mandate for political action. Practically all program documents of that period started from the affirmation of a deep systemic crisis, which was attributed either to the heavy burden of the Soviet past or to the mishandling of the reforms by President Yeltsin. Unsurprisingly, in this case the divide depended on the parties' prior participation in the reforms. The documents put forth by political parties or actors involved with the reform process heavily emphasized the weight of the Soviet legacies and their resistance to change. Meanwhile, those who had been marginal to the policymaking of the perestroika and post-perestroika years were quick to reinterpret the travails of the early 1990s as evidence of flaws in the reforms themselves. For example, the program statement published by a short-lived pro-Yeltsin Russian Democratic Reform Movement (*Rossiiskoe Dvizhenie Demokraticheskikh Reform*) in 1992 blamed the crisis on incompetent political predecessors: "Today's crisis of Russian society is the consequence of the fact that for decades, the country has been governed by people incapable of comprehending the course of the social development of the country and of world civilizations, to learn the lessons of history"(Koval' 1993, 172). A year earlier the nationalist movement the Russian All-People's Union (*Rossiiskii Obshchenarodnyi Soiuz*) blamed not the legacies of the Soviet past but the "perestroika launched in 1985" for "fail[ing] to prevent our society from slipping into a crisis, but instead deepen[ing] and intensify[ing]" this slippage (336).

The rhetoric of crisis persisted throughout the decade, but the arguments tracing the sources of the crisis to pre-perestroika years waned as time went on. By the mid-1990s, "crisis" meant squarely the failure of the reforms. This, however, did not imply agreement on definitions. For some politicians, primarily of a neoliberal pro-Western persuasion (such as Yegor Gaidar or Anatolii Chubais), it referred to the necessary costs of Russia's economic reforms. Others— national-patriotic proponents of the "third way" (Alexei Podberezkin, Vladimir Zhirinovsky)—interpreted the term as a civilizational crisis, Russia's loss of its unique worldly mission. Yeltsin's "party of power" gravitated to the former position. In the context of one all-embracing social crisis, specific periods of the 1990s were characterized in crisis terms as well, from the constitutional crisis of 1993, to the crisis of voters' confidence in 1994, to the identity crisis put on the public agenda by President Yeltsin in 1996.[42]

An important caveat here would be that the rhetoric of crisis was frequently used by politicians instrumentally, and was therefore hard to tie into a consistent ideology. In other words, it often emerged either as a by-product of criticism on the part of the oppositional political parties (as the Communist leader Gennadii Zyuganov put it in his 1996 political program, "Why today's power is unable to devise a way out of the crisis"),[43] or as rationalizations put forth by the political group in power to justify the downward social and economic dynamic as inevitable and objective (as in Gaidar's or Yeltsin's rationalizations of inflation, which Yeltsin, in his pre-election materials called "the terrifying staircase of the economic crisis").[44] In the latter case, crisis obtained the form of something external and overbearing, something that had the power to explain any malfunctions and failures, and to legitimize things inconceivable in the posited ideal of a "normal civil society."

Crisis as a Tool of Interest Struggle

Varied as the uses of crisis rhetoric were among different groups, there was also a common logic that applied across the board. This logic had to do with the legacy of Soviet political and economic culture. Politically, decisions under socialism were never formulated as benefiting particular social strata. Rather, they were cloaked in the language of universalism and social consensus, on the assumption that all progressive political developments were to benefit society—indeed, "all progressive humanity"—as a whole. In the post-Soviet years, public discussions remained faithful to the ideal of consensus, as opposed to bargaining or compromise, and the rhetoric of all-embracing crisis was instrumental to that end. Among the intelligentsia and political actors alike, it helped legitimize specific collective grievances by making them appear universal and applicable across the societal spectrum. In other words, the notion of crisis was congruent with the idea that the political program promoted by a given group was not a stake in a struggle of interests, but a proposal advanced for the benefit of everyone in the country. The notion of a massive, all-embracing crisis was thus a useful ally in morally legitimizing one's agendas and rallying support. Overtones of this motivation are discernible in Ivanova's article about the fate of the intelligentsia, in which the author argued at length that the decline of the intelligentsia signified "the agony" of the entire society, and thus a threat to the entire nation's future. Coming from a different ideological standpoint, the Communist leader Gennadii Zyuganov used the same approach in his 1996 political program, in which he generated a similarly all-inclusive list of grievances so as to demonstrate that the proposed solutions would benefit everyone.[45]

In addition to providing morally legitimate grounds for articulating group interests, crisis imagery also had an economic application, equally rooted in the economic realities of state socialism. Under the distributive logic of Soviet economy, demonstrating an economic need was an important precondition for getting state funding. The more severe the reported situation, the more likely it was to receive assistance (Verdery 1996). It is easy to see how the narrowing of federal support for industries and regions in the course of the 1990s could only intensify the pressure to compete for scarce resources among administrative actors (local and regional politicians, representatives of industrial enterprises, etc.). The notion of a crisis, be it of a particular industry, region, or social group, thus served as a useful tool for navigating the unclear economic terrain of the postsocialist decade in that it allowed economic and political actors to obtain subsidies, subventions, and other types of "special consideration" on the part of central authorities.[46]

Several themes thus appear central to the evolution of the crisis rhetoric in postsocialist public arenas. First, like many rhetorical tropes, "crisis" had its antecedents in the rhetorical politics of a prior (in our case, pre-perestroika) era, and in many ways its uses were conditioned by this prior history. However, the crisis rhetoric slowly lost its telos as the decade of the 1990s marched on. Initially taken up as a shortcut toward the discussion of sensitive political issues, it quickly became a subject of discussion in its own right. The events that initially marked the crisis of socialism began to be interpreted as evidence that the reforms were in crisis, while crisis itself obtained a character of inevitability and permanence. An ever-expanding range of phenomena began to receive explanation in crisis terms. One factor behind the proliferation of crises of various kinds was that this rhetoric resonated with the crisis of the Soviet intelligentsia as a social-stratificational category, the loss by its members of economic well-being and missionary purpose. However, since this rhetoric provided a tool for mounting criticism of political opponents and for responding to these criticisms, for obtaining scarce resources and for legitimizing one's demands as just and universally valid, other interests and group solidarities were at work as well.

Emphasizing the strategic importance of crisis imagery for many collective actors on the postsocialist scene is not the same as questioning the severity of the grievances many suffered during the protracted postsocialist transformation. However, as we acknowledge these, we also have to be aware that crisis rhetoric became an easy answer to developments much more diverse and multi-dimensional than the "crisis" label would make them seem. Magnifying and universalizing dramatic decline in all spheres, this rhetoric made it impossible to separate the more urgent problems from the less severe ones, to distinguish the areas of positive dynamics and to resolve the isolated issues all lumped together by the assumptions of one total crisis.[47] All this contributed to the paradox that the crisis was seen as both omnipresent and comfortably familiar, a calamity and, at the same time, an easily recognizable backdrop of everyday life. The facility with which this label was deployed signified that the ruble's inflation was accompanied by a certain rhetorical hyperinflation of key sociopolitical terms. And much as with monetary logic, a wide circulation of various "crises" through diverse communities of stakeholders detracted from the significance of every particular instance, to the point that societal crisis became so much a part of everyday rhetoric as to fade, ironically, into the background, diminished by the very forces that perpetuated it. Debates on the pages of print media represented in this respect only the tip of the iceberg, and I shall now turn to the voices of ordinary Muscovites in order to explore the ways in which the crisis rhetoric permeated the sphere of everyday conversations in the late 1990s.

3   A State of Emergency: The Lived Experience of Postsocialist Decline

As one might expect, the face of crisis in everyday life differed markedly from its description on the pages of the printed media. Of course, some points of similarity remained. To start with the most significant, the label of "crisis" was used widely to describe a variety of diverse phenomena whether of a macro-social (the economic crisis, the educational crisis, etc.) or a micro-social (payment arrears, incompetent or abusive teachers) nature. It formed the frequently taken-for-granted rhetorical context in which discussions of specific experiences and memories took place. In fact, the appeal of crisis imagery was such that even an individual's successes were narrated through its prism, as something exceptional and unrepresentative of the state of affairs in the country as a whole.

Like the public debates described in the previous chapter, private memories also located the first signs of crisis in the era of perestroika. Significantly, this is also the period in which earlier ethnographies of political talk in Russia located the particularly dramatic instances of catastrophic imagery. Observing narrative conventions and speech genres in Moscow in 1989–1990, Nancy Ries remarked:

> The phrase "complete disintegration" and similar phrases such as "complete breakdown" or "collapse" . . . resounded through many of the Moscow conversations in which I participated. *Polnaia razrukha*[1] was an abbreviated reference to everything that was supposedly disintegrating in Russian society at the time: it was a discursive signpost that embraced the escalation of crime, the disappearance of goods from the stores, the ecological catastrophes, the fall of production, the ethnic violence in the Caucasus, the "degradation" of the arts, the flood of pornography, and other signs of immorality which some people saw everywhere. (1997, 46)

Similarly, Buckley (1993) recorded the proliferation of variously defined "crises" both in media and in popular narratives during a somewhat longer period than the one Ries described (1985–1991). Both Ries and Buckley underscored the specificity of the phenomenon they observed and assigned it to a rather narrow historical period (in the case of Ries [1997, 165], to the "central, liminal phase of perestroika,"[2] whereas Buckley [1993, 13] spoke of the "Gorbachev era and a little beyond"). But ten years later catastrophic narratives persisted, and this stability of the crisis metaphor begs a closer look.

If notions of crisis and deterioration made more than a little sense to the

Russian people in their own lives in the late 1980s–early 1990s, it was for many of the same reasons that made them resonate in the public sphere. For one, the easing of censorship associated with the beginning of perestroika was embraced as a long-awaited opportunity to raise legitimate criticisms regarding a wide gamut of issues. The volume of articles and letters to the editor scrutinizing the drawbacks and oversights of late socialist and, subsequently, democratic governance mushroomed,[3] as did critical voices regarding enterprise management, bureaucratic excesses, and shortages of consumer goods. Individuals who were used to the state taboo on criticism and dissent experienced freedom of speech primarily as freedom to voice negative information. Dmitrii Kirillovich, a fifty-four-year-old doctor whom I interviewed in his home in one of Moscow's most remote suburbs, put it succinctly when he said,

> What Gorbachev really did, it's that he gave us freedom.
> AUTHOR: What do you mean, freedom?
> DK: I can go out to Red Square and say that Gorbachev is a fool, rather than, as it was before, that Reagan is a fool. You know this joke—that an American says [to Brezhnev, boasting about freedom of expression], "I can come out to Times Square, and loudly say that Reagan is a fool." And Brezhnev says, "Well, I can also come out to Red Square and say that Reagan is a fool." And now I can come out and say anything, and not be afraid that it will reflect on me.
> AUTHOR: How would it have reflected before?
> DK: Very directly. I could not talk politics at work. All discussions were taking place on the kitchen level, and always with fear of consequences, at work or from the Party, or in some other fashion. Now, clearly, we have freedom.

We know from the preceding chapter that the freedom to voice concern with the negative aspects of the Russian society was fully picked up and developed by the media, which heavily emphasized the problematic aspects of the transformation but had significantly less interest or skill in developing a pluralistic dialogue aimed at exploring the opportunities for further development.[4] A similar tendency marked developments in the fine arts, especially in film-making during the late 1980s, where the dark genre of *chernukha* catered to the audiences' "appetite for further revelations as to the decayed state of Russian society" (Faraday 2000, 178). This association between civic freedoms and denunciatory rhetoric—in Dmitrii Kirillovich's terms, the freedom to say that Gorbachev (and later Yeltsin) is a fool—made the metaphor of the crisis not only conventional but also the socially approved way of viewing things, since it gave this framework overtones of civic concern.

The paucity of alternative interpretive frames that was characteristic of the media and political discourses of the time affected everyday political talk as well. This particular predicament was described by Serguei Oushakine as *post-Soviet aphasia*—"*regression* to symbolic forms of the previous historical period that has been caused by . . . the society's *disintegrated* ability to find proper verbal signifiers for the signifieds of the new socio-political regime." Oushakine argued that post-Soviet Russia had yet to witness the emergence of a distinctive post-Soviet cultural and discursive style. In the meantime, post-Soviet subjects found themselves confined to the symbolic repertoire of Soviet times, and therefore unable "either to put into words normative ideals and desired goals of the post-communist period or to express the changes that have already happened in Russia" (Oushakine 2000a, 994, 997; italics in original). The attraction of crisis imagery in this context was particularly strong because it resonated with the logic of aphasia, in which postsocialist gains had no name (and thus no value). Furthermore, it allowed post-Soviet citizens to voice not only their discontent with the felt effects of the transformation, but also their frustration regarding the deficiencies of terminology through which one could process these effects.

But similar as the everyday narratives were to the media and political rhetoric of the time, they displayed no recollection of the optimistic telos of the early perestroika-era discussions, which started out by viewing crisis as a surmountable obstacle on the way to a more humane socialist society (in Gorbachev's famous formulation, "socialism with a human face"). Instead, at least in the reverse perspective that I could observe firsthand in the late 1990s, already the first signs of changes were remembered as indicative of the decade to follow, in which sacrifices and losses were not legitimized by any larger ideals or visions of the future. As a result, the era of perestroika (1985–1991), which is viewed by historians and sociologists as a period analytically separate from the post-socialist decade (Dunlop 1993; Walker 1993; D'Agostino 1998), was treated in the folk historical knowledge as essentially indistinguishable from it.

Perestroika as a Watershed

Karina is a soft-spoken sixty-three-year-old woman who lives in a solid five-story apartment building located in a leafy suburb in northwest Moscow. Although she described herself professionally as an architect, today's table of ranks would most likely classify her as an interior designer, with one important qualification: the interior plans Karina created at the Planning Institute of Residence, where she worked all of her life, were implemented not in the residential apartments of wealthy clients, but in public offices and apartment buildings across the country. Karina's first recollections of postsocialist change are characteristic of the responses I received from others in the sense that she located the first signs of change in the late 1980s, when a number of reforms were implemented by Gorbachev in an effort to change the socialist system. For her, as for many others, the earliest signs of change in the system seemed to come from the workplace, which became a site of experimentation with various new labor practices as early as 1985–1986. Reflecting upon her first experience of postsocialist change, Karina concentrated on the toll that the new practices took on the relationships between colleagues:

> Somehow, it all started changing . . . I remember the last years I was working in the institute, it was around '88—I left earlier than official retirement age—it was when *khozrashchet*[5] began. And I remember, it was completely striking for us then.

AUTHOR: What was it like, khozrashchet?

KARINA: Before, what was work like? The planning institute, everyone receives a certain salary, according to their qualification and position in the hierarchy. And with khozrashchet, the situation was that the money had to be earned. Before, a committee would establish how much money we needed and pass everything to us. And here, we have to earn everything ourselves . . . And what do you think? The relations within our department . . . We used to have a completely amazing department, we dealt with interior decor and were the elite of the institute, . . . relations changed immediately, because each person had to find some way to earn. Everyone started looking for contracts. And it was amazing how it changed everything. Architects—they are supposedly intelligent, cultured people, and suddenly they started to behave in a completely different fashion. Conflicts began, lies began, relations were spoiled. It was so unpleasant and so unusual and unexpected that I decided to leave as soon as possible.

Karina's first encounter with the market left her disappointed and unsure that she would be able to successfully integrate into the new system of roles and relations. Her subsequent involvement with the new system was more productive: at the time of my fieldwork, she and her husband were employed in a commercial distance-learning institution, earning much-needed money for daily necessities, and most notably for the expensive British food supplements that her husband's diet required. But these developments did little to ameliorate Karina's overall attitude to the changes of the past fifteen years. She attributed her successes to a fortunate stroke of luck, all the while retaining her skepticism regarding market-based economic relations.

In a different vein, the same belief was voiced by those who remembered welcoming the perestroika-era ideas and practices as a refreshing change from the old and ineffective way of doing things. For example, Gennadii, a forty-three-year-old former engineer who provided for his family by working as an office equipment repairman, remembered the advent of changes at his factory:

When *gospriemka*[6] came along to our factory, it was somehow prestigious [to be involved with it]; first—the salary [was higher], second, it was something new, so there was competition to be transferred to this sector, and I managed to get through, it was all very interesting. But as time went on, it completely discredited itself, because it had to coexist with the plan . . . But what is interesting, these were these very early 1990s [sic], if you remember, that's when all this cooperative movement started, and the so-called perestroika.[7] And our team in gospriemka, it was so strong that everyone who left, they never returned to the factory, they left to start their own firms. And I know these guys who were the first to leave, this gospriemka gave them the opportunity to show their initiative, and this aspect became very useful later on, in commerce. But me personally, somehow it didn't work this way with me, and I stayed at the factory. . . So we divided into two camps, those who went into commerce and those who didn't. And of course, we were still acquaintances, still friends, but this tension, you could feel it already then.

Different as they were, the recollections of Karina and Gennadii were united by the theme of the inevitable transformation of personal relations that came hand in hand with the new social and economic realities. This transformation was so radical that to some it felt like emigration. Remembering his return from the obligatory army service in 1987, Nikolai, a thirty-one-year-old freight operator, put explicitly what many others evoked indirectly:

> I returned [from the Army] in 1987. Those were certainly some interesting times. We were drafted in one country, and two years later, came back to a completely different one . . . All these economic changes had started, this one was leaving for business, other ones stayed. People were trying to earn capital somehow, and for a while it was all like fishing in muddy waters. Some people were still serving sentences for speculation and currency operations, whereas others were already conducting these operations in the open. They might be arrested, but they might also be left alone. In the "old" Soviet Union things like that would never be allowed. But the old structure was falling apart in front of our very own eyes.

The experience of observing the dissolution of structures formerly considered indestructible and absolute had a triple impact. First, as the excerpts from Gennadii's and Karina's interviews confirm, this structural reorganization, or *perestroika*,[8] triggered massive social shifts, in the course of which old socialities and communities broke down and new ones were forming. Second, it created among the disoriented Soviet subjects a fundamental ambivalence regarding the legitimacy and legality of the newly emerging social order, since the new order was taking shape on the basis of such formerly forbidden practices as commercial activity and currency exchange. Lastly, given the massive extent to which the late Soviet state regimented the lives of its subjects, the experience of perestroika also meant that the newly emerging opportunities could easily be interpreted not in terms of the advance of freedoms, but in terms of the retreat of the state. Considering that the growth of the state in the Soviet Union was associated, in good Hegelian tradition, with the unfolding of progress (Gross 1985), it was not surprising that post-Soviet subjects often interpreted the disappearance of state structures as a sign of impending trouble.

"Before" and "After" the Great Divide: The Many Faces of Postsocialist Decline

The period of perestroika indicated a sharp rupture in people's perceptions of their lives and of the nation's history more broadly. In their eyes, a gulf had opened between the first postsocialist decade and the rest of their lives, which they had spent in the disappearing socialist universe. This gulf had any number of dimensions—the breakdown of working collectives, shifting notions of professional identity, a loss of the sense of embeddedness in a nationwide professional network, the increasing importance of, and at the same time pressures on, the kinship network, lack of faith in the workings of administrative infrastructure, and deepening skepticism regarding the controllability and responsibility of power. All these developments marked the advent of the era of postsocialism that was so widely referred to as the time of crisis.

Individual recollections of the time were split into the "before" and "after" periods, with "before" serving as the ultimate antithesis of "today." "Before" stood for the era of stability, predictable (although modest) incomes, relative social equality, and personal and social security. "After" was the time of rampant crime, social polarization, and insecurity, both in terms of personal situations and of the larger political and economic realities. Karina, whose discussion of the first perestroika-era shocks was cited above, singled out the issues of trust and accountability as an important dimension in which postsocialist developments represented a sharp contrast to her Soviet-era experiences:

> There is this uncontrollable process, the prices keep growing, people get poorer and poorer, and there is no one to turn to for protection. I remember, in Brezhnev's time, whenever you had a complaint, you could write a letter to the local Party organization and things got done right away. Even in the late 1980s, I remember our roof was leaking and we couldn't get the local powers to do anything about it, so we wrote a letter to Yeltsin—he was then the head of the Moscow administration—and that was all it took. The roof was repaired right away. And now, in this anarchy, if you are trying to find some channel for your complaint, you won't find anything; there is nowhere to go with your problems. So it's our luck that we live in a decent neighborhood, in a decent building, because if something went wrong, we'd get no help at all . . .

Leaking roofs and rapidly deteriorating housing stock were common metaphorical representations of the postsocialist crisis of accountability. Writing in 1997, Jussi Simpura and Galina Eremitcheva noted that for many St. Petersburg dwellers, images of dirt and urban disrepair served as symbolic ways of expressing their larger anxieties regarding the declining social order. Karina's usage was consistent with this observation. She too viewed material disorder as indicative of a larger societal breakdown. Tellingly, the fact that her own building was rather well maintained did not prompt Karina to relinquish her criticism of the infrastructural deficiencies, and when during a subsequent conversation it turned out that the building just underwent a thorough renovation, she made no effort to interpret that event as indicative of any large-scale improvements in the social order. For Karina, the fundamental problems of social order remained, this time metaphorically represented by an unresolved murder case she had recently heard about.

Crime—another oft-cited dimension of postsocialist disorder—was an important topic indeed, in that it too bridged the issues of large-scale infrastructural failures and individual moral decline. For many, the increased instances of crime signaled not only the state's inability to assert social control, but also a fundamental demoralization of their fellow citizens. As Georgii, a forty-three-year-old self-employed car mechanic, put it,

> Yes, indeed, the Party dictatorship is no more, and I appreciate that. But look at today's life and see for yourself: rampant crime, mafia everywhere, general aggressiveness, empty promises [from politicians], homelessness. All these things. And I also

don't appreciate the young generation, which is growing up to be cruel. It's enough to look around at how the youth, the children don't want to give their seats to the elderly in transport, how they are all ready to push people over, a man or a woman, anyone . . .

For Georgii, crime was thus one instance of a general state of social anomie. A thirty-seven-year-old nurse, Maria, used other metaphors to stand for the postsocialist crisis of morale and sociability:

The very first issue on everyone's mind is all this politics. You come to work, let's say, and it starts with politics and it comes down to money. Life is gloomy, joyless . . . You know, before, they used to have meetings, Pioneer and Komsomol meetings, and even these *subbotniki,*[9] all in all, it was still interesting. There was more sociability [*obshchenie bylo*]. And now, in school, they finish classes—and go straight home. I finish my shift—I go straight home. There used to be some committees in every enterprise, they would organize activities . . . You see, it used to be interesting, people used to socialize. And now every person has his own life. After work, I rush home as soon as I can, and indeed, what else is there for me to do . . .

Nelly Romanovna, a fifty-seven-year old retired math teacher, had an equally bleak view of the moral decline she considered emblematic of postsocialist society. For her, the decline originated, first and foremost, in the corrupting influences of capitalist sensibilities, although she excluded herself and her generation from the tendency she was describing:

There has never been such a global break in Russia before . . . There has never been such a gap between people. Before, one person would have an apartment, and another a room, perhaps . . . [but] people, simple people were much closer to one another. Our generation still has this sense, but we're losing it, and it will eventually completely vanish. If I needed money right now, I could call any of my friends. And I can bet that, in an hour, I would have collected at least ten to twenty million. Because as I calculate, a million[10]—that's an average monthly salary. And my friends, they would never consider asking me for any interest, whereas the young generation—they have more, they earn more, and they already know these words that, even if a disaster has happened, they would ask you for interest. This, to me, is nonsense; I cannot even imagine this . . .

Later on during the same interview, Nelly Romanovna made a further qualification, admitting that her thirty-year-old daughter and her social circle were also to be excluded from the trend she described. However, like Karina, she continued to maintain that the tendency was universal, preferring to frame the unconfirming cases as exceptions rather than to part with the imagery of a society-wide moral crisis altogether. It was almost as if the reality of the "global break" Nelly Romanovna was discussing was so undeniable to her that it did not require evidential support.

The specter of the lost collectivity of socialism (a collectivity that was often perceived as fundamentally egalitarian in nature, as the above quote testifies) did not mean that today's individuals were deprived of their old friends and acquaintances. On the contrary, as the following chapters will make clear, it was through informal connections and kinship networks that most individuals obtained new employment and information throughout the 1990s. However, the aspect of stability and continuity of the old-time collectives seemed irrevocably lost. And although this stability of close-knit networks often had its negative aspects, frequently portrayed in the films of the period,[11] the very permanence (even if illusory) of these ties inspired a sense of nostalgia:

> I stopped by recently [at the planning institute where she worked for over twenty years]. There are about a dozen small companies there. You open each door—and there is something unfamiliar going on. They've rented out the space . . . Some floors are renovated so well, not the way it used to be before. But our department . . . We had such a large room, practically a hall, it's all locked up, and everything is piled up in disarray inside. Our old things . . . Someone's tea mug, all these memories . . . Some schedules are still posted on the wall: Department Twenty, ten subdivisions—the distinctions were so incomprehensible . . . It all looks so strange now . . . Like a cemetery, a total cemetery. Our room is a cemetery, and in many other departments the situation is the same. One or two people stayed, and the rest are elsewhere . . . Some were told to retire ahead of time . . . And one department, they used to develop driers, they somehow tapped into the world market and now are supplying these driers to, I believe, Argentina. They feed themselves. So, each and every one is out there on their own now. (Alena, female, 48)

The image of a cemetery speaks volumes about the unbreachable distance Alena perceived between her socialist-era existence and her current life. In this context, material relics (in Alena's case, a cup and the schedules of some forgotten project she discovered still posted on the wall) played the role of an emotional mnemonic recalling the investments and loyalties associated with the long-gone era when, in contrast to "now," people were not "out there on their own."

Alena's nostalgic gaze could hardly be relied on for accurate information regarding human relationships under socialism, and comments from others testify to that. The same sociability that was fondly described by Alena or Maria as "companionship" was remembered by some others as a "socialist terrarium" (*sotsialisticheskii gadiushnik*), and viewed as part and parcel of such socialist-era problems as incompetence and inefficiency. This disagreement, however, only highlights what both evaluations took for granted: the fact that there had been a sea change in how work was organized and experienced, and that the turning point of this transformation occurred at the moment of perestroika:

> [Had things remained unchanged], I would still be working at the factory where I worked till 1989 as a programmer, calculating salaries . . . The accountant would be coming to me regularly with tea, bringing me tasks. I would tackle them, and she would be saying, "You know, I had the funniest dream last night," and tell me all about it . . . And then my month's worth of work would have to be dumped, because they would gather together and decide that they would rather go back to abacuses . . . (Zhenia, female, 34)

The problem with sociability, according to Zhenia, who at the time of our meeting held a well-paid accounting job in an oil company, lay not in the dissipation of the close-knit Soviet-era work collectives. Rather, it had to do with the rapidly widening income gap that was tearing apart old friendships and solidarities. An avid camper, she remarked with regret that some of her long-standing camping companions could no longer afford the lifestyle that their group led, while others became so rich that they preferred luxury resorts to the less glamorous camping:

> For you and me, this may seem an ordinary thing—splitting a bill, buying tickets. But for some of them [the downwardly mobile] this is a real dilemma. They can't spend on par with everyone, and they are too proud to be taking advantage of others. And this is very sad, because you are losing friends you've known from college times, people with whom you share a great deal. . . .

The ruptures in the social fabric Zhenia identified were painfully familiar to many others. Almost everyone had a story of friends whose upward or downward social mobility effectively ejected them from their social circle. In other words, the sense of a gap between people's current realities and their lives under socialism could have different origins, but it was something known to all. The transformation of personal relations, changes at the workplace, and an increasing emphasis on competition and effectiveness (to the detriment, as many would argue, of loyalty and interpersonal ties) made the departure from socialism feel objective and irrevocable. But as telling as all these sites of change were by themselves, none would warrant the label of "crisis" when taken individually. Rather, the crisis resided in the web of connections that individuals saw between all the isolated instances of postsocialist decline.

The Long End of the Rope

According to the periodic bimonthly opinion polls conducted in the course of the 1990s by the Russian Center for Public Opinion Research (VTsIOM),[12] the percentage of the Russian population that endorsed the statement "our miserable situation has become intolerable" fluctuated between 28.7 percent and 34.5 percent in 2000. In 1997, the same numbers hovered around 36 percent; in 1993, around 33 percent.[13] But more significant than the relative stability in the number of those ready to claim that they had reached the end of their rope was the scope of response options the poll question offered. The two alternatives to the desperate response above were (1) Everything is not that bad, and it is possible to live, and (2) Life is hard, but one can still carry on. Even the most positive response option was framed by the survey authors apologetically and in terms of a downward trend, quite in line with the already normalized assumption of universal decline.

The same assumption of crisis as the ultimate postsocialist reality was shared by the population to an extent that made explicit statements to that end unnecessary. Consider the following string of themes that were discussed in uninterrupted succession by one of my Russian interlocutors: the incident of the confrontation between Yeltsin and the parliament in October 1993, the war in Chechnya, poverty, scarcity of pensions, unreliability of medicine, virtual disappearance of stipends in education, financial pressures forcing students to combine education and work, corruption in business, the putsch of 1991, the unpredictability of the future, the brevity of yearly vacations, the collapse of northern Siberian cities. Seemingly unrelated, the themes (and the discrepant phenomena they referred to) were tied together by the speaker's underlying conviction that there was one single source from which all of them emanated. In the late 1980s–early 1990s, the same developments—the dangers of state disintegration, moral decline, the degradation of the municipal housing stock, bureaucratic inefficiency, and the inevitability of an environmental catastrophe—were rehearsed and recycled as evidence that the country was about to descend into "chaos and anarchy" (Ries 1997, 47). Now, a decade later, Muscovites relished the same evidence, although the formerly apocalyptic overtones were slowly being replaced by resignation. The circumstances remained unacceptable, and yet the only conceivable response was to learn to live with them, since they were there to stay.

But despite the relative familiarity of the situation, it remained imperative that one's discontent be registered explicitly, even if at the expense of logic or consistency. It was not uncommon for the same narrator to switch from dramatic descriptions of destitute street beggars to expressions of distrust and contempt for the same beggars, who were believed to "fake their poverty," while in reality "earn[ing] more than you and I do." While obviously incoherent if taken as a description of the speaker's attitude to the poor, such logical leaps seemed perfectly understandable when taken as veiled statements about the sorry condition of the society at large. From this standpoint, the referent of both statements was the social crisis, which in the first case was demonstrated by referring to an image of financial deprivation and in the second one by evoking a narrative of moral decline. It was in the same spirit that frequent comments about corruption and the extortion of bribes among the medical profession existed side by side with striking images of doctors' and teachers' deprivation and self-sacrifice.

A similar play with reference points and examples took place in my conversation with Natalia Konstantinovna, a fifty-three-year-old manager in a chemical research laboratory:

> I don't look down on business, in fact I have a huge respect for it . . . Myself, I used to dream with this colleague of mine, when our institute falls apart, we'll open a drugstore. Of course, we imagined it the way it would be in a normal country, where you can apply your knowledge productively. That was in 1989 or 1990, and shortly afterward this colleague left for the States, and that was that. But if he'd stayed, it wouldn't have changed anything. We wouldn't have opened this drugstore; Kobzon[14] opened it instead. Because, you understand, this is one of the most profitable spheres, and it was all divided up beforehand. . . . You see, the worst thing is, we all

lost our future. What is it going to be like? We are not so young anymore, but in 1985, when I was forty-something, we all knew what was in store for us. That's what this state was. We knew what our pension would be, although we were still relatively young . . . I knew exactly what my retirement would look like . . . There was a kind of stability. For instance, I have completely lost any opportunity to vacation [*otdykhat'*].[15] Now it's an impossible luxury—to go somewhere, just normally, for a month, or for the whole summer. We always did that before. All we have left to us is to just sit at our country dacha.

AUTHOR: So as far as going places, you haven't been able to do that for a while? . . .

NK: Twice. I went with my husband—accompanied him to conferences. We went to Germany and to Spain last year. But that wasn't without assistance. They paid for the tickets, and we paid for the rest of it. So, formally speaking, we traveled out [*vyezzhali*] twice in the past two years. Recently our daughter went abroad for vacations [*vyezzhala*]. So it's possible if you put all you can into it. But that is not *otdykh*—it's an intense, emotionally positive break, but you don't rest. My opinion is—a week is not *otdykh,* and two weeks is not *otdykh* either.

Natalia Konstantinovna's account is interesting in a number of ways. As her narrative proceeds, one becomes aware that the references she uses in order to evaluate her postsocialist circumstances are unstable. In the recollection of her business plans, Natalia Konstantinovna comes across as a person who was initially oriented toward some model of a contemporary market society. The term "normal" she uses in this instance is quite vague, but in conjunction with the frequent references to the United States that are scattered throughout the interview, it invites the listener to conclude that Natalia Konstantinovna's disappointment is based on Russia's failure to become, as was widely expected in the early 1990s, a "modern capitalist country." Yet, if that were the case, the second part of our exchange would hardly be possible, since the narrative takes a nostalgic turn, downgrading the benefits of newly acquired transnational mobility in favor of the lifestyle—relaxed, although clearly not conducive to economic growth—associated with Soviet-era social policies. This shift in the point of reference is reflected not only on the level of content, but also in style. Drifting into nostalgic mode, Natalia Konstantinovna also chooses a rather peculiar term for referring to the activity of going abroad. Instead of using the words *go* (*ezdit',* or *s'ezdit'*) or *travel* (*puteshestvovat'*), she repeatedly speaks of *traveling out* (*vyezzhat'*), recreating the characteristically "iron curtain" image of the world separated into Russia and "the abroad" (*zagranitsa*).[16] This stylistic detail suggests that, using Sewell's (1992) language, the change of reference involves a reactivation of the cultural schema associated with the period in question. The instrumental character of this reactivation merits special notice—Natalia Konstantinovna resorts to it only in the context of her discussion of vacation styles. Her earlier memories of perestroika-era hopes are expressed in a different vocabulary—that of enterprise and business opportunity.[17]

This excerpt illustrates the selectivity with which the crisis rhetoric used evidence. It would be naïve to assume that Natalia Konstantinovna was unaware of the counter-examples to her statements. Her comments contain multiple references to successful small- and medium-size businesses that sprang up in the country over the course of the 1990s (one of which employed her twenty-four-year-old daughter, furnishing her with income greater than that of her parents combined). In fact, Natalia Konstantinovna's own career trajectory illustrates the complexity and multidimensionality of the changes in the structure of opportunities marking that decade. From her position as a research chemist she moved to become a manager in a chemical laboratory that made a profit by synthesizing and selling chemicals to U.S. and French pharmaceutical companies. Yet, while these facts had little bearing on Natalia Konstantinovna's overall judgment of the decade, it was hardly because they were underappreciated. Rather, they were perceived to be unrepresentative—fragile exceptions rather than endemic elements of postsocialist reality. Focusing attention on them, therefore, would be considered equal to misrepresenting the true state of affairs.[18]

The same notion of a profound crisis underlying individual ruptures of postsocialist order was exactly what allowed Karina and Nelly Romanovna to make similar rhetorical moves in their discussion of urban disorder and moral decline. There, too, disconfirming information was relegated to a status of exception, unable to shatter the grim reality of an overall decline. A similar pattern can be read in Alena's description of her former workplace as a cemetery, although the "dozens of small companies" which reportedly sprang up in its place could, at least theoretically, make the imagery of renewal at least as likely.

Many other conversations followed the same trend. Successes and strikes of fortune were enjoyed and acknowledged, but largely as atypical exceptions. My interlocutors never failed to emphasize that the general developments in the country were far less positive than their own personal circumstances may have suggested: "I constantly have the feeling that I was lucky. Fate smiled on me and I found this job. It could have been worse, it all could have been a lot worse . . . I can't imagine how most people are carrying on . . ." (Nina Alekseevna, female, 51)

These appeals to the exceptionality of one's own personal and family situation as compared to the rest of the country may be partly explained by the fact that the standard of living and structure of opportunities for Moscow residents were (and still are) better than those for the rest of the country (Dubin 1997). However, as surveys suggest, evaluations of one's personal and family situation were uniformly and considerably higher than estimations of the situation in the country as a whole everywhere in Russia throughout the course of the 1990s (see figure 3.1).

Mass belief that one's success was always atypical pointed to the fundamentally a priori nature of the crisis framework. It suggested that, much as in political and media discourse, visions of deterioration in everyday conversations were not based on a systematic analysis of the available evidence. Rather, crisis was taken for granted and dictated the way in which particular experiences could be interpreted. Neither were the two spheres mutually independent—journalists,

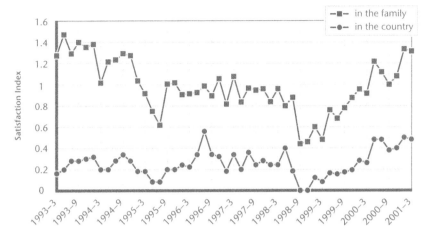

Estimates of the country's and the family's economic well-being

Figure 3.1. The upper line reflects the dynamic of the respondents' satisfaction with their family's well-being (calculated as the proportion of those who responded that they were doing "well" or "moderately well" to those who reported that things were going "badly" or "very badly"). The lower line reflects the same ratio when commenting on the goings-on in the country more generally. VTsIOM. 2001. *Monitoring obshchestvennogo mneniia: Ekonomicheskie i sotsial'nye peremeny* (Public Opinion Monitoring: Economic and Social Changes) 52.

politicians, and academics heavily relied on everyday discourse in making their case for the continuing postsocialist crisis, while individuals routinely drew on images of decline and despair provided by the media.

Selectivity of media coverage and its disproportionate orientation toward scandalous, sensationalist, and lurid events and materials has been noted and criticized by scholars working both in and outside of Russia (see McChesney 1999; Zasurskii 1999).[19] But particularly telling were the contexts in which Russian media references were scattered in the interviews. Apart from evocations of the media as the embodiment of venality, the only other relatively frequent references to the fourth estate were made to support the imagery of deterioration. Below is a peculiar example in which both messages, obviously contradictory, intertwine:

> Look at his [Yeltsin's] daughter, this Diachenko. She has her own bank already, and of course offshore. I mean, I don't know the details, I am not following this scandal, because I feel repulsed, and most of all I don't have time for all that. . . . But there are rumors, I mean not rumors but . . . by rumors I mean what they officially say on TV and in the papers. I just don't read these things closely, I quit reading newspapers a while ago because by now they're all nothing but mouthpieces. But they do report something like that, or I'd see a headline or something . . . So for me these are rumors. (Konstantin, male, 53)

Two inconsistent messages (one about reported corruption, and the other about corruption of the reporters) fit together seamlessly here, reconciled by the overarching imagery of deterioration. Mass media in this context functioned both as a site of moral and economical disintegration and as its impartial chronicler. In my conversation with Klara, a forty-five-year-old woman working as a registrar in a municipal health clinic, these two aspects of the media were quite apparent:

> I cannot stand these game shows like this *Field of Miracles* (*Pole Chudes*).[20] I mean, they are drowning in their millions, while at the same time there's misery all around. They showed recently, I don't remember, I think, in Yakutia somewhere, they had a flood, and these people, they lost everything, everything they had. And can you imagine—the federal authorities sent them this aid. Some ridiculous cereal, canned food . . . And they were distributing it to the family. Goodness, and they even were asking if they were satisfied with this aid, can you believe this? And these people said, "We don't need your aid, just give us work. So that we could earn money ourselves."
> AUTHOR: Why, was there some enterprise that fell apart?
> KLARA: Actually, I don't really remember now . . . You know, I didn't watch it so closely . . . I watch, sort of in between home chores . . . [Fervently] But then there was this, some city they showed, I don't remember which one. Everything fell apart there, too. They had some enterprise—a timber mill. And it closed—they're not working anymore. The only things open are a hospital, they showed a police station, and a prison. That's all! And everyone else just lives as it comes [*kto kak*]. Mushrooms, berries, fishing—that's how they are living. There's no work. (Klara, female, 45)

While Klara's narrative did not explicitly name the agent responsible for the lamentable conditions she was describing, her solidarity with the flood survivors' demand for work suggested that, much like them, she attributed the responsibility to the retreating state.[21] The overall logic of the argument and Klara's lack of interest in the specific details of the reported disasters would support the conclusion that she was interpreting the situation symbolically. Furthermore, in the context of what she perceived as total and invincible disintegration, Klara's own relatively worry-free life came across as a lucky exception.

Deciding what is common and what is exceptional requires some sense of statistical trends, and it could be that when my contacts asserted or implied that they were faring better than most, they were misled by the phenomenon Noelle-Neumann described in her "silence hypothesis" (1974). According to Noelle-Neumann, judgments about one's own condition are made on the basis of the individual's own experiences, while those pertaining to the larger picture are drawn from the information available through the media and reflect the biases and silences of the latter. In the spirit of this argument, my interlocutors' belief that they were relatively lucky, that (to use Nina Alekseevna's words) "fate smiled on them," could be explained by the consonantly catastrophic images supplied by the media, which made any good experiences seem atypical.

However, while this may be plausible, the image of a benign routine did not hold when our conversation moved from the condition of the country at large to the details of people's everyday lives.

Discussing their own recent experiences, Muscovites affirmed the exceptionality of their success just as stringently, but with a different implication. While in the context of comparisons with the population at large my interlocutors usually evaluated themselves as rather fortunate, the assessment they gave to their lives when talking about their daily routines did not support this optimistic conclusion. In other words, somewhat oxymoronically, they often portrayed their successes as highly atypical not only for the rest of the population, but also for themselves. The following quotation illustrates the way in which many of my contacts tended to understate their achievements:

> I'm telling you, ever since 1991 I can only afford the most miserable purchases, like socks and underwear. Nothing major. We have to limit ourselves to the bare necessities with my son . . . Well . . . [catching me looking at an obviously new computer on an old, worn-out desk that certainly stood out in the otherwise modest layout of the room] . . . Well, one thing—we did buy a computer for my son. I decided he has to learn how to deal with it. (Nina Alekseevna, female, 51)

Further on in the discussion, Nina Alekseevna reluctantly remembered that there were two other major purchases—a new refrigerator and a combined TV/VCR system—that she acquired after 1991. Unwillingness to reveal their increases in financial fortune, however unsystematic, was typical. In contrast to the American convention of not revealing one's salary, my Russian contacts wore their salaries on their sleeve but were far more reluctant to unveil what they considered atypical and unsystematic (however, as it turned out, quite regular) cash infusions, as if in disclosing them they were misrepresenting their true economic state.

This reluctance to project an overly thriving image of oneself seems to contradict the frequent insistence on one's fortunate exceptionality vis-à-vis most of the population, but only superficially so. In both cases, the narrative is governed not by the law of transference and non-contradiction, but rather by the unstated "fuzzy logic of practical sense" (Bourdieu and Wacquant 1992). From within this logic, individuals juggled and selectively applied alternative frames strategically, moving between positions of lucky minority and ill-fated majority and back, in order to demonstrate what they perceived to be the ultimate reality of postsocialist decline.

The Dilemmas of Freedom, Legitimacy, and Competence in the Midst of Social Change

In *Outline of a Theory of Practice,* Pierre Bourdieu observed a "dialectical relationship" between the objective social structures (such as institutional arrangements, available channels of mobility, and structures of opportunity), and "the cognitive and motivating structures which they produce and which tend to reproduce them" (1977, 83), a relationship which in his later work was referred to simply as that between the *field* and the *habitus*. While Bourdieu's sociology is so often criticized for its static bias, this proposition has great significance not only for understanding dilemmas of upward mobility or generational conflicts, but also for situations of rapid social change, in which individuals' social environments typically transform faster than their interiorized dispositions. Bourdieu termed what happens in such predicaments *hysteresis of habitus*, pointing out that in these moments, individuals' assets may become liabilities, because "practices are . . . liable to incur negative sanctions when the environment with which they are actually confronted is too distant from that to which they are objectively fitted" (78).

This observation, which was fruitfully applied by Ries (1997) in her discussion of perestroika-era discourse, has further important implications when we turn it upon the first postsocialist decade. In the course of that decade, individuals who grew up under state socialism, with its relative income equality and social guarantees, were challenged on several interrelated planes. In practical terms, many skills they had developed to navigate the social context of late socialism became nothing but a burden when this social environment was replaced with one requiring assertively entrepreneurial behavior, a certain adventurousness, and a number of other qualities that were not a part of their cultural tool-kit.[22] One example of an individual caught up in what she herself recognized to be an outdated approach to work is provided by Nina Alekseevna, an environmental engineer in her fifties and a single mother of a teenage son, who at the time of our first interview worked at a poorly paying laboratory job:

> [My lab] wasn't a very initiative-encouraging place. You know, we were young specialists, full of ideas, wanted to improve all the practices, but most of the colleagues were quite inert, didn't want to move, to do things. So after a while of trying to push an idea through you just get apathetic, you stop wanting to do anything, you don't want to invent anymore. And nowadays the times have changed, and now the situation is such that you just have to be active—but by now you are like a mass of porridge. You don't want anything anymore.

While Nina Alekseevna seemed to think of her disadvantage in terms of the qualities she lost in the discouraging milieu of the institute, Bourdieu's notion of habitus as a generating structure runs deeper, suggesting that, apart from the specific tools valued at the postsocialist marketplace, Nina Alekseevna lacked the very *principle of generation* of appropriate responses. This formulation construes the problem of postsocialist agency on a wholly different epistemological plane. It suggests that socialism was a universe with its own cultural logic, which implied its own definitions of "the impossible, the possible, and the probable"[23] and, as such, different scales of priorities, principles of action, and ascription of meaning. But in the changed social environment, what used to be measures of individual competence suddenly became irrelevant. This would have been less of a problem had the framework of postsocialist transformation been made clear. However, given the absence of an overarching national agenda, or even of a meaningful categorical apparatus to grapple with the ongoing changes, the new standards of action felt alien and illegitimate.

In this interpretation, dilemmas of competence and legitimacy appear more profound, because (a) they could not be easily resolved by individuals simply adding to their "tool-kit" a new set of (culturally valued) tools, and (b) they had important consequences for the most basic notions of freedom and autonomy. This was made apparent in a passing comment by fifty-nine-year-old Mikhail Aleksandrovich, an avid reader of political satire and a public sector employee who, during communism, considered himself an independent-minded member of the intelligentsia and certainly not a Party supporter. Despite Mikhail Aleksandrovich's relative economic success and appreciation of the new freedoms of postsocialism (he was particularly happy about the freedom to travel and took any opportunity to join a charter bus tour to Europe), he did not recognize the contemporary period as his own time. In a conversation about the impact of changes on his personal life, Mikhail Aleksandrovich phrased it in the following terms: "Until fifteen years ago, I was doing the things I wanted to do, and afterward—the things I was forced to do by external circumstances."

Mikhail Aleksandrovich's distinction between doing the things that one wants and being forced by external circumstances could not be a better illustration of Bourdieu's concept of hysteresis of habitus. From the vantage point of the dialectical relationship between the field and the habitus, the line between an unconstrained desire and an undesired constraint is drawn according to whether or not an individual accepts as "natural" (i.e., compatible with her internalized dispositions) the logic of the field in which she functions. In Mikhail Aleksandrovich's case, the standards of judgment and action that he employed prior to perestroika fitted with his social field seamlessly and thus carried no overtone of social determination whatsoever. By contrast, his postsocialist behavior was experienced as forced (i.e., unfree), because there remained a disjuncture between what he felt himself competent in and the actions that the new sociopolitical situation required.

Mikhail Aleksandrovich was, as noted earlier, rather successful in navigating the postsocialist social order. Although administrative restructuring at the Ministry of Construction (his workplace of thirty-five years) left him formally unemployed and working under contract for a few years in the mid-1990s, he managed to return to full-time work in the Ministry under a different title. In his new capacity as head of a department, Mikhail Aleksandrovich enjoyed a good salary, and he made much out of the comical fact that after a forced two-year idleness he returned to work not only in the same organization but, in fact, at the same desk. But the knowledge that in the end he had fared well didn't provide him much comfort. He continued to sense a lack of fit between his former cultural capital and the skills he perceived to be essential for success in the postsocialist economy. This made him experience his occasional victories as random, as unexpected and unearned, since he was not convinced that he possessed the required competence to systematically reproduce them in the future. To Mikhail Aleksandrovich, tomorrow's developments could be as unpredictable as, and less kind to him than, yesterday's, and the dilemmas of competence, legitimacy, and autonomy in the postsocialist context remained acute despite personal advances. In this respect hysteresis of habitus could be compared to wearing a badly tailored dress or wrong-sized shoes, when every move causes discomfort and constraint regardless of whether our hypothetical fashion victim makes it to his destination.

As one may expect, younger Russians, those who were in their twenties at the onset of the transformation, found it easier to accept the emerging social order as their own. To use a distinction made by an older Muscovite, "The younger ones can adapt (*adaptirovat'sia*), while [the older generation] may only accommodate themselves (*prisposobit'sia*) to the situation." Another spoke of her generation (in their fifties) as those who "could not reform, but some succeeded in staying afloat." In both cases, the distinction alluded to the individuals' ability to transform the most basic dispositions of the habitus to fit the newly emerging field of practice, instead of learning to live with the disjuncture, as the older generation found itself doing.

But even those younger Russians who had succeeded in taking advantage of newly emerging opportunities found it hard to embrace the changing and unpredictable nature of mobility and of the postsocialist job market in general. Among them, too, the command of the new "cultural tool-kit" did not automatically render socialist-era notions of "the possible, the impossible, and the probable" obsolete. As a result, even they refused to embrace the postsocialist social order as fully legitimate.[24] When speaking about the vicissitudes of the job market, such people as Zhenia, or Anton, a thirty-two-year-old manager in a Western firm, chose to align themselves with the victims of the ongoing restructuring rather than with those who, like themselves, rode the wave of the post-Soviet economy. More precisely, instead of seeing themselves as in some way pitted in the race for success against their less successful fellow citizens, they aligned the two groups together in the social landscape of the 1990s facing an already familiar adversary—the illegitimate retreating state:

> Objectively speaking, the entire category of people in their fifties, especially women, they are hopelessly stuck. No one needs them—not in the old dying system, nor in the new one. And of course no one needs the pensioners. That is to say, enormous social groups have been completely cut off. And I really feel the pain of the people who *wasted their entire lives for the state*. These people, they are our fathers, our mothers, they gave their lives to work, and they worked in full force, many of them at least . . . And now the state is simply unable to pay them pensions and finance their healthcare. Similarly, particular professions have discovered that there's no place for them. Heavy industry is not doing well, and no one needs engineers either. So for this group of people, it is a catastrophe, a complete catastrophe, particularly considering that many of these people used to be breadwinners. (Anton, male, 32; italics added)

If the issues of autonomy and competence, as well as those of the legitimacy of the postsocialist order, were so problematic to those who managed to learn the rules of the postsocialist economic game, one may easily imagine how acute they were to their less fortunate compatriots. The reality of individual careers, of course, was more complex than that, although not necessarily more benign. Indeed, those who belonged to the categories Anton identified as being "cut off" typically had to abandon the sites of their socialist-era employment. But rather than becoming unemployed, this decision usually meant changing jobs, sometimes repeatedly in the course of the decade, moonlighting or working on the side to supplement their income.

As a rule, it was an economic push rather than an economic pull factor that was cited as a legitimate reason for leaving. And given the erratic nature of the postsocialist job market and the absence of a functional safety net, once an individual was forced to leave the site of her long-term employment, she could exercise little control over her evolving career trajectory. A job in the same professional domain remained more desirable than a position in an unfamiliar field, and a stable income of course preferable to an unstable one, but all too often such deliberations were seen as unaffordable luxury.

A characteristic employment trajectory for the 1990s, therefore, was propelled by tactical and not strategic considerations. A good illustration of this is Nina Alekseevna, whose discussion of workplace dilemmas I cited earlier. Unhappy with the meager income that her lab job provided, Nina Alekseevna actively pursued scattered opportunities as she saw them and in the course of my two-year fieldwork period had changed several side jobs, ranging from night-shift security guard at her institute to a menial job at a food-processing plant. Eventually one of her side jobs slowly replaced the lab as the site of her primary employment. The job was in the same institute, but it had nothing to do with physics, her original specialty—Nina Alekseevna transferred to an administrative position in the personnel office. Although the new position did not fit the area of her professional competence, Nina Alekseevna liked it better, in part because it was not as grueling as some of the other side jobs she had to hold over the years. In addition, not only did it pay somewhat more, but it also allowed for "a busier workday"—a welcome change from her work in the lab where she sometimes had to spend days doing nothing but was not allowed to leave the workplace.

The model of work change exemplified by Nina Alekseevna could be called sequential—a chain of occupations, one leading to the next, overlapping at times, driven by momentary opportunities and without an overall vision or career strategy underlying the transitions between professions. This was the type of mobility that was most familiar to postsocialist Russians. It was especially prevalent during the early stages of the transformation, when the educational system was unable to prepare adequate numbers of specialists for the emerging occupations, and jobs in the new sectors of economy were obtained basically by being in the right place at the right time. This created highly ambivalent professional identities, as a quote from Andrei, the engineer–turned–insurance company manager, demonstrates:

> One thing I can say about my [former] work at the research institute, and it's a fairly typical thing: not far from the Palace of Pioneers on Leninsky Avenue there was a department store called Moscow, and in the summer months during lunch breaks we could allow ourselves to walk around the store for four hours every day . . . [pause]. But back then [in the late 1980s] all these cooperatives started springing up, and many of our colleagues found work in these cooperatives. And I had an acquaintance who was earning some crazy money in a cooperative, while our institute was paying close to nothing. So he told me, I have a place for you . . . That's how I left.
> AUTHOR: So basically, you left hoping to increase your income?
> ANDREI: I left hoping for the income, because I was naïve. And when I started working, I realized that I was being blown off, that I shouldn't have left, but it was too late.
> AUTHOR: And then? . . .
> ANDREI: I left again. It was one of the few moments in life when I left with no plan in sight (*ushel v nikuda*). There was little money and a whole lot of time. . . . But a moment came when I finally had to find a place, and I got a position on the advice of one of my acquaintances in a certain joint-stock company called Akveduk, and its line of business was [smiling] pretty much everything. . . .

Drifting through various milieus with nothing but serendipity to inform one's choices was hardly a desirable strategy. However, a more intentional and deliberate approach to changing jobs yielded even less results during the 1990s. When some Muscovites invested in purposeful reconversion to professions which, as they expected, would allow them to enter the forming economy with greater ease, they soon discovered that the project of finding a job involved much more than a "market-oriented" profession, and that they had under-estimated the many contingencies that go into the process. As a military man who tried unsuccessfully to go into business put it,

> I even completed training courses, have a small and middle-level entrepreneur diploma. And I have nothing against commerce, it could even be interesting to try, but no one will let you enter this field so easily. Second, I have no starting capital, and without this capital, there's not much [that one can do] . . . (Alexei Ivanovich, male, 46)

As a result, having received the diploma, Alexei Ivanovich decided to stay at his military base, supplementing his income with a part-time job at a cell phone service center he received through a colleague and postponing his dream of starting a small business until retirement.

Apart from merely practical issues of subsistence, economic pressures also impacted worker morale. As the wages at many enterprises lagged behind rising prices and the volume of work decreased, the value of employees' skills and qualifications had to be reexamined. Victor Vladimirovich, a fifty-six-year-old lathe operator, remembered the decline of the workload at the plant where he had worked for eighteen years, up until 1993:

It wasn't so much scary to leave the plant as it was hurtful (*obidno*), after you've become an integral part of the collective, after working there for eighteen years, well, it was hard to part with this collective . . . It's not that we felt any anger, but rather, some kind of apathy. That is, here you are, you have the same hands, and the same head, but there's no application. No worthy application. Before, it used to exist, and all of a sudden it doesn't.

This unexpected obsolescence of once-valued skills and talents was experienced all the more sharply because socialist-era enterprises were seen as parts of a nationwide interconnected system in a way that the newer companies and firms were not. As a result, the move from the former to the latter often carried with is a sense of exclusion from a larger meaningful network. Roman, a stout forty-four-year-old man working for a construction company, recollected his initial reluctance to abandon the site of his original employment (an equipment-manufacturing plant) for a metal casting workshop in the following terms:

I studied for my job. The reason I chose my trade school was that I was interested. I graduated, worked at a plant, with aviation equipment, with space. Then I flew planes in the army, then came back. It was interesting. I always knew when the next satellite would be launched. It wasn't announced on the radio yet, but I knew that tomorrow, or the day after, or next week it would take off . . . All the workers knew. We all had to sign the form against unauthorized disclosure. There was information . . .

Although in a practical sense Roman believed he had made a responsible choice when he decided to leave the failing plant, his comments revealed a nostalgic sense of having participated in an important and useful mission, of having played a part in a project of great scale and significance.

Victor Vladimirovich's and Roman's comments highlight an important implication of industrial decline and economic restructuring. Not only did individuals have to witness the breakdown of their habitual work collectives as workers one by one escaped the sinking enterprise, they also were confronted with losing markers of status and forgoing institutionally supported identities and signs of group membership. In cases like theirs, the dilemma of competence was thus both subjective (in the sense of hysteresis of habitus) and objective, embodied in tangible status pains.

The problem of losing the status that went with one's professional group was compounded by the impossibility of avoiding this simply by sticking to that profession against the odds, since the hierarchy of professions did not remain fixed either. In a sense, the game was impossible to win—those who abandoned their professional group had to rethink their professional identity on their own, whereas if they stayed, they had to undergo the vicissitudes of status mobility along with their group of affiliation. A classic example in this respect would be the numerous groups of technical intelligentsia (engineers, applied scientists, researchers, and so on) who were considered an elite under late socialism but who, in the course of just a few years of post-Soviet deindustrialization, entered the popular discourse in a new quality: as symbols of powerlessness and social irrelevance.[25] But hard as it was to watch one's social status plummet, it was the decision to navigate the job market on one's own that brought the most uncertainty and status pain—although often a greater economic reward as well. In these cases, attempting to preserve the bases for self-identification, individuals often combined their for-profit employment with activities that allowed them to symbolically articulate their unwanted cultural capital. Konstantin, who repeatedly changed occupations during the past decade, considered the few years he spent as a salesperson at a local market to be the toughest ones psychologically:

> A person who spent all of his life with technology, to be just standing like this. I don't know how these Azerbaijani traders[26] do it. They just stand all day, and they don't mind. And to me, it was morally hard. I needed to occupy my head with something, to exercise it.
> AUTHOR: So how did you deal with it?
> KONSTANTIN: I composed crossword puzzles, tried to write something, but this is practically impossible to do when you stand out there . . . Chart something, work on some radio circuit diagrams. Say, these TV sets break all the time, they are very old. Things break constantly, so there is always a need of work being done . . .

Konstantin's resentment had at least as much to do with the prosaic and mercantile nature of the job as with the forced idleness that it entailed. In the Soviet-era moral economy, profit-seeking was seen as deeply suspect. Institutional financial issues were separated from the sphere of everyday concerns of the Soviet intelligentsia rank and file, and monetary relations between enterprises were largely invisible (a theme raised by Karina in the beginning of this chapter as well). The very idea that one's professional worth now had to be measured by strictly economic criteria (as opposed to the level of education and the complexity of the tasks one was qualified to perform) came as a shock both to those who, like Konstantin, switched occupations, and to those who chose to stay in their fields and saw the logic of their operation transform in front of their eyes.

For the latter, the lack of prior experience with self-financing made it difficult to adapt to the new demands of the workplace. Under socialism resources came directly from the state budget, and their transfer did not require any conscious effort on behalf of the individual worker. The sudden withdrawal of guaranteed financing in the 1990s was, as a result, widely interpreted as yet another instance of the state retreating from its obligations to the citizenry.[27] I met with Evgenii Alekseevich, a stately sixty-three-year-old man, in his apartment located in a prestigious section of Moscow near the Moscow State University. Evgenii Alekseevich spent many years working in the same research institute doing what he described as "basic research," but it was not until the late 1980s that he had to split his time between theoretical research and administrative budgeting issues:

Right now, you have to pay for everything. Even for the telephone we have in our institute, we have to pay for it ourselves. From the funds of our lab, that is . . . And a lot of things have to be covered from this fund, which is basically what remains from the grants, what we have allocated somehow ourselves *from our own earnings* [italics added].

The new administrative responsibilities went against Evgenii Alekseevich's deeply held assumption about what an academic should and should not be required to do. He considered the time spent on the administration of his own grants to be wasted time, and the money earmarked for administrative expenses to be unfairly spent. The logic behind the change in his academic routine was also a familiar one—the logic of the state retracting from the spheres it previously oversaw in a move that was neither legitimized ideologically nor justified to Evgenii Alekseevich practically. In addition, the new work routines reformulated the standards by which his competence could be measured. Not all of Evgenii Alekseevich's professional colleagues managed to master the conventions of grant writing and administration, and as a result their symbolic weight began to transform in ways that they could not control. Nina Alekseevna, whose meditation on the changing times opened this section, found this to be true for her as well:

> . . . While in past years you had to go around, to build contacts, these days you have to pay money. If you pay money, your work will go fine, and if you don't . . .
> AUTHOR: Even at work, you have to pay? . . .
> NA: Yes, even inside the institute, every laboratory has its own money and its own balance, and if you have to use somebody's resources, you have to pay, you have to fill in forms, ask for grants, all that. Even if you objectively need to have something done, and everyone agrees that you need it, but still, if you don't have money the things won't move. So those labs that can earn on the side, sometimes with foreign companies or something—they have the currency, they can buy good equipment, have certain research programs, and if they need something, they'll go with their money and things will get done.
> AUTHOR: So what does it depend on?
> NA: On the lab profile, mostly on the profile.
> AUTHOR: So what kind of profile should one have in order to have money?
> NA: I don't even know . . . In our institute, you mean? [a bit puzzled]. It's hard to say . . . I really don't know, because I don't know who does what in our institute. There are some curious people who are well informed, but I'm not one of them. I only know what our lab does—we measure the condition of the environment, the purity of the air, etc. So we are paid for by the institute, by the other laboratories. I mean, we are useful, no one will fire us because the institute has to make sure that it doesn't harm the environment, and they pay us for that. But we can't earn anything on the side. In order to buy a new piece of equipment we have to ask the institute . . . So we have to live on what we have.

The postsocialist period, therefore, contained a set of challenges to the previously taken-for-granted ways of viewing one's relationship with oneself, with others, and with the world. While the economic dilemmas of the period took an unequal toll on different sectors of the population, the more fundamental transformation in the notions of control, autonomy and practical competence affected all the post-Soviet subjects.

This transformation had two interrelated manifestations. The first, readily apparent in the accounts cited so far, was the easy susceptibility to crisis imagery, which was experienced as the most intuitively accurate definition of the situation even by those who had managed to stay afloat and prosper in the post-Soviet economy. Indeed, in the course of the first postsocialist decade, Russian citizens faced a rapid restructuring of social forms that were previously taken to be immutable.[28] This restructuring was unaccompanied by a legitimating rhetoric of national liberation frequent in the former union republics and countries of the Eastern bloc (or, for that matter, by any other meaningful account of the goals and purposes of the transformation). As a result, postsocialist Russians experienced it as a form of betrayal and loss, which was all the more distressing because it meant parting with something familiar and meaningful for the sake of something vague and undefined.

The workings of crisis as an interpretive lens for understanding the postsocialist condition were apparent in the language used to describe recent political, economic, and sociocultural transformations. For example, while my interlocutors frequently evoked the image of the premises of their former institutions being taken over by small private firms and businesses, they saw it as evidence of disorder and destruction, rather than of a nascent market infrastructure. Alena, whose meditation on the cemetery-like feel of her former institute we encountered earlier in this chapter, concluded her discussion by posing a rhetorical question, the answer to which can easily be read between the lines of her account: "I don't know, maybe I'm judging too harshly, but recently I saw a leaflet inviting visitors to a furniture workshop, which is located in my former institute. I called the people who stayed there, and they confirmed that yes, a furniture salon now occupies the first floor of our building. Is this normal?!"

If it seems hard to grasp what precisely struck Alena as abnormal in the fact that a store moved into a prominently located building in the center of the city, this is because in the contemporary Anglo-American economic tradition dominated by neoliberalism, the role of the meaningful integrating framework belongs to the market, not to the state. From this vantage point, developments that Alena described in apocalyptic terms could be celebrated as the formation of a market infrastructure. This interpretation, however, would go against the spirit in which the ongoing restructuring of the economy was experienced on the ground, where it was perceived through the lens of loss and retreat, rather than in the more adventurous terms of renewal and emerging opportunities. This does not mean that people were blind to the opportunities that the opening economic system offered to many of them, but these opportunities were perceived either as unavailable to rank-and-file Muscovites, or (in cases when the speakers themselves or their immediate family members proved beneficiaries of the change) as untypical, undeserved, and fleeting. Alena's example is a case in point here, since the promising career of her twenty-four-year-old daughter (who was working as an interpreter in a French pharmaceutical company) did not have a redeeming effect on Alena's evaluation of postsocialist reality. It was the arguments she had with her daughter, the latter's perceived selfishness and excessive interest in consumption, that were considered by Alena to be a sign of the times. In other words, even if one's personal situation improved in the course of the 1990s, this victory was still experienced as local, and hence inevitably insignificant, while the losses were spoken of on a global scale.

The second manifestation of the post-Soviet hysteresis of habitus was the frequent emphasis on the fundamental uncertainty of the postsocialist condition. This uncertainty had many dimensions, from the often unpredictable transformations of property forms and institutional arrangements to the more intangible uncertainty regarding the appropriate modes of acting and thinking in the midst of social change. But a particularly poignant expression of this sensibility could be traced in the recurrent references to luck, chance, and games that were scattered through the interviews.

The imagery of games figured prominently in discussion of "games with the state" (*igry s gosudarstvom*). "Dirty game" imagery was prevalent in conversations about politics, and I often heard it said that participating in politics without knowing the hidden rules of the game was equivalent to playing cards with a card-sharp. But everyday occurrences were often viewed through the same lens as well. The risky character of many postsocialist projects, such as financial pyramid schemes or other shaky kinds of investment, made them especially conducive to being viewed through the prism of a game, usually a game with a trick or a catch.

While small tactical victories in games with the state were possible and could even bring their own enjoyment, this did not change the fact that participation in the game was often not voluntary, the course of play was precarious, and the possibility of an absolute and final victory questionable. Speaking of his reservations regarding the possible implications of the double accounting practiced at his office equipment repair shop, Gennadii said:

> I just keep thinking, what if some audit comes all of a sudden, and God forbid, the numbers won't add up correctly, and they'll just disband us all. Or even worse, make us pay something, I mean I don't know, because I don't get too much into our books and all of these financial matters. I just feel that such a moment could come. [Laughs nervously] Because they are happening, these checks by the tax police, and all. Of course we understand that we are small, you know, just six people, we don't really earn the same volume as . . . You know, as the ones who make real big money, the ones they really look into. But one day, they'll make it to our company too. [Laughs, then grows serious] Yeah . . . So in this respect, there are fears that we may get disbanded. That's what's unpleasant, that you feel that, yes, you are playing, but can you really win, playing with the state?

The theme of fate and luck went hand in hand with that of the game. Speaking of his turbulent work history in the 1990s, Sasha, a thirty-year-old entrepreneur and jack-of-all-trades, summarized it as follows:

> I do believe in fate, not everyone is allotted a carefree life. Some people get everything, some not. And of course, one has to use intellect, and one's own hands, but whatever you say, in order to achieve something, you need a chance. And chance, it's the same old fate [*A sluchai—eto ta zhe samaia sud'ba*]. Without a chance, yes, you can do something too. But in one way or another, a chance always comes along.
> AUTHOR: Do you have any examples?
> SASHA: Well, of a chance? Say, after I graduated from the institute, a while ago, I used to do car repairs. And I repaired a car for this one guy, and then he asked me about his acquaintance, he needed help with his car as well, and some other things, I don't remember exactly. But it was an absolute chance: I went to repair this guy's car, and we met and I became, basically, a partner in his business. Just by chance. And the business was handwoven carpets, which were exported abroad. He had his links and connections. But at some point this business died. And again, it wasn't my fault or anything. But I had to leave. What was it? A chance again!

At the time of our meeting, Sasha was working selling medical equipment; prior to that he had imported plastic dolls from China and worked as a driver for a foreign journalist. His entire occupational history, in other words, was almost completely shaped by chance encounters and random opportunities. But for others, the imagery of chance, game, and luck had more of a metaphorical significance. On the one hand, it underscored the unpredictable character of the times and thus helped normalize disappointments and misfortunes:

> ... My neighbor, he got huge sums of money [out of financial pyramid schemes]. But me, I realized right away that all these things are just a game, because otherwise, how would anyone get such unbelievable money? So in my understanding, this is the type of game where someone will win, and I will inevitably lose. (Nina Alekseevna, female, 51)

On the other hand, as demonstrated by numerous examples above, references to luck served to integrate discrepant evidence into the overall belief in a nationwide crisis. In this respect, luck and fate offered an unlimited rhetorical resource for having one's cake and eating it too: for sharing good news with one's interlocutors without disrupting the shared belief in the underlying societal crisis. But most importantly, the vocabulary of game and luck was true to the lived experience of the postsocialist transformation in that it highlighted the lack of ownership people felt toward their own successes and prospects for the future.

Perhaps the most poignant impression evoked for me by the Muscovites' narratives of change was a feeling of rupture, of a gulf between the first postsocialist decade and everything that preceded it. One can pinpoint particular manifestations of this rupture: in politics and in the economy, but also in personal career trajectories and in interpersonal relations, to name just a few key spheres. The disconnect separating the post-Soviet subjects' habitual skills and dispositions from the logic of the social world in which they had to operate impacted the ways in which they viewed their individual competence, experienced freedom and determination, and assessed their performance in a changed environment. In their own turn, the individuals took part in transforming their social worlds further as they responded to these challenges along lines that I will discuss in the second part of this book.

But while the logic of hysteresis of habitus accounted for the dramatic vision of the postsocialist rupture, it was also paradoxically at work in making the decade of the 1990s appear peculiarly devoid of substantive transformations. Indeed, in a striking contrast with the sea change my interlocutors reported having experienced in the late 1980s–early 1990s, their memories of the "crisis decade" itself seem relatively undifferentiated. This was hardly because their lives became devoid of disruption at that point. Quite the contrary. Occupational fields, income levels, and political concerns continued to be in a state of perpetual flux for most members of my sample; less than one-fourth of them entered the year 2000 working in the same enterprise and in the same capacity as they had in 1991. For most of the rest, a change of employment also entailed a change of field, professional identity, collegial relationships, and income.

In the light of such an intensely eventful chain of developments, it seems striking that people typically had trouble identifying the exact timing of this or that event occurring in the course of the 1990s, and even establishing the order of events that happened one after another. It was not uncommon that, after an attempt to recollect exactly in what period a particular development took place, my interlocutor would admit an inability to do so, often with a comment like the one I heard from Alena: "I don't remember anything anymore with all these reforms and reorganizations (*s etimi reformami i perestanovkami*)." This sensibility, affirming the essential sameness of all of the decade's developments, was hardly historically accurate. However, it does suggest, rather puzzlingly, that every change after 1991 was subjectively and retrospectively conceptualized not as a profound reordering of the existing routine, but rather as "more of the same." In what follows, I explore the ways in which the concept of hysteresis of habitus can be brought to bear on this undifferentiated rhetoric, and suggest that the dramatic vision of the 1990s as a perpetual crisis may have been not only an outcome of, but also a solution to, the many challenges of the times.

4 The Routinization of Crisis, or On the Permanence of Temporary Conditions

> Crises can happen on all possible levels, not just in politics. For instance, if you are riding a trolley, and someone steps on your foot, in your soul a crisis takes place.
>
> —Comment during a student sociology conference
> at Moscow State University, October 2000[1]

One objection to taking the notion of postsocialist crisis in good faith could be the fact that in the course of the 1990s, this notion was applied simply too broadly to be useful. To an extent, this criticism is accurate. After all, not only was *krizis* a term of choice for describing one's immediate experiences, but it structured the very logic of assessing separate events—from something as minor as a street quarrel to major disasters such as plane crashes or outbreaks of disease (and everything in between)—as indicative of one all-encompassing societal disorder. In this respect, the term itself did not even have to be evoked for the sense of a total crisis to come across.

But even if the catch-all rhetoric of a total crisis concealed more than it revealed, to the extent that it made diverse events seem analogous—not illnesses in themselves, as it were, but symptoms of a larger disease—and even if it was sometimes deployed in a contradictory and inconsistent fashion, it was nonetheless significant, because it quickly became a social fact in its own right. In some ways, its dogged persistence belied the connotations of extremity that the notion of crisis was meant to represent in the first place. After all, the emergency state inevitably loses some of its acuteness when it is announced for the umpteenth time. But it was precisely this routinization of crisis that made it such a significant force in shaping the mental horizons of the postsocialist life. In what follows, I argue that the perceptions of permanence and eternal return of the postsocialist crisis were closely connected to the dilemmas of freedom, legitimacy, and competence described above, and also linked to larger shifts in conceptions of temporality and history that the postsocialist transformation engendered. But the habitual gravity of a chronic crisis was not just a disabling condition. It was also a rhetorical resource that could be strategically used for building rapport, creating solidarities, and asserting one's practical competence in everyday interactions. In the moral and symbolic economy of the late 1990s, the image of a chronic crisis became a building block for many cultural performances, large and small.

Permanence and the Eternal Return

What does one mean when, in the midst of what was just proclaimed to be a severe crisis, one says, "There's nothing new"? There are several levels on which the imagery of permanence made more than a little sense in everyday conversations. On a macro-level, it was connected to the general vision of the political process as essentially futile and unproductive. In a sense, people dismissed political life as an endless process of changes that were invariably skin-deep:

> [In response to the question about her attitude to the recent change of prime minister] Well, for one, we are all *used* to things *changing* all the time. Here . . . the Duma, what does it do? It doesn't think about proper matters, but instead solves issues like . . . every six or three months demoting someone, looking into his biography . . . And it takes forever to do it, to discuss every little detail of his life, what he did, where and why. And it goes on. In half a year they take another one. In our Duma, as I say, what do they talk about? Only about someone's personal matters . . . (Kseniia Anatolievna, female, 43; italics added)

On a micro-level, the same message of permanence resonated in the detailed descriptions I received of the past months and the changes they brought (or did not bring) into the lives of my contacts' household members. While it would be hard to doubt that certain events that occurred during the late 1990s forced Russians to reorganize their lives (an obvious example being the economic breakdown of 1998), the imagery of cycle and succession curiously coexisted with the motif of deterioration:

> I had no panic in August [1998], or any special anxiety that, you know, I won't be able to feed the family or something. These times, of the Great Depression, or this crisis in the 1930s that they had in America, like they showed us on TV—with suicides, and all that—it makes me laugh. Someone went bankrupt. So what, he went bankrupt. I don't know. For Russia . . . In Russia, . . . we've been living that way for the longest time. (Konstantin, male, 53)

Implicit in this comparison between Russia in the 1990s and the United States in the 1930s was that, while a sudden economic breakdown may come as a shock to the unsuspecting and unaccustomed, such a breakdown would not affect a community exposed to a chain of equally grave developments over a long period of time, which had managed to develop an entire infrastructure to withstand similar shocks. This postulation of the repetitive character of turmoil was highly important, not only because it "normalized" the resented condition, but also because it indicated the direction in which one's practical efforts were to be channeled: toward developing infrastructures whose permanence would match the permanence of the crisis and prevent it from disrupting one's life.

There were several ways to interpret the persistent affirmations that someone's situation remained largely unchanged during the 1990s. On the one hand, this was the permanence of deviation from what was considered normal or appropriate. On the other, the sheer recurrence of aggravating circumstances made them normal in a statistical sense. Finally, the postsocialist sense of time and history catered heavily to a vision of history as repetition and eternal return.

Normative Sameness

There is a telling turn of phrase in the long quotation from Natalia Konstantinovna, the lab manager whose frustrated perestroika-era plans were discussed in the preceding chapter. When recollecting her dreams of opening a private pharmacy with her colleague, she chuckled at her naïveté and said, "We imagined it the way it would be in a normal country, where you can apply your knowledge productively." Natalia Konstantinovna's use of the idea of normalcy, or "normal life" (*normal'naia zhizn'*) is paradigmatic, and it goes a long way in explaining why so much of her experience with the 1990s felt like merely more of the same.

It is paradigmatic, first and foremost, because the imaginary normalcy with which Muscovites unfavorably contrasted their drab postsocialist existence was rather vaguely defined. Indeed, returning to Natalia Konstantinovna's comments, we will remember that the "normal country" she longed for was not exactly capitalist (hence her disdain of short vacations and exploitative work schedules), but also decidedly not socialist (otherwise, how would her private pharmacy business be possible?). The "normal" for which she longed was a postsocialist, or rather a socialist-era, utopia of what life outside of socialism *should* be—a utopia that resisted being pinned down to a specific exemplar, one whose vagueness did not tarnish but rather intensified its appeal.[2] Faith in the advent of such normalcy was conceivable only during the era of late socialism and was an integral component of the socialist-era habitus and the fantasies it made possible. Now that both the socialist-era habitus and its illusions were long gone, the actual variation of postsocialist life often meant less than its frustrating deviation from the unachievable and foregone ideal. Thus, as long as "normal life" performed the role of the yardstick against which individuals measured their circumstances, the internal variation in these circumstances was meaningless. What mattered more was the fact that their actual predicament was different from the normative ideal and hence always deficient, and in that way always essentially the same. For no matter how diverse their experiences at different points in time, these differences were far less relevant than the gap that continued to exist between the desired and the achieved.

Statistical Sameness

Statistical sameness was more obviously compatible with the imagery of permanence since it was based on accentuation of the routine and repetitive character of social, political, and economic tribulations. It also appealed to normalcy, but in the statistical sense of recurrence. In this respect, "normal" referred precisely to things *ab*normal in a normative sense: political corruption, continuous economic uncertainty, frequent political shake-ups. Their statistical "normalcy" did not automatically make these developments legitimate; it merely meant that they had ceased to surprise. Moreover, they all shared something in common—namely, they embodied the reasons my interlocutors no longer felt in control of their own lives, and so they all were perceived as essentially identical.

Statistical normalcy was reinforced in the particular context of my project by the repeated character of the interviews themselves. Recollections of the discontent and criticism voiced during previous interviews prompted my interlocutors, at our later meetings, to switch gears easily, moving back and forth between the framework of deterioration (of the actual circumstances) and that of continuity (of this deterioration and of their discontent):

> Prices are getting higher little by little, one doesn't keep track sometimes, and suddenly you look, and everything's almost twice as expensive. Maybe they'll raise our salary, but it doesn't keep up. What is it, a hundred ruble raise . . . And in the meantime, the rent has gotten higher, and the electricity will follow—do you think it won't show? [Laughing] I know you've heard it all . . . Nothing is changing here . . . (Valentina, female, 31)

Could it be that the shocks of the late 1990s simply faded in comparison with the magnitude of economic and political turmoil that preceded them? To an extent, this is possible, given the scope of changes lying outside the time frame of the project, from the breakdown of the Soviet Union to the financial pyramid schemes and the multiple inflationary spikes. But the way in which Muscovites discussed more remote historical events suggested that their vision of recent years was part of a larger optical shift.

Historical/Temporal Sameness

Recurrent in my conversations with Muscovites was the theme of history as repetition, as a flow that brought not development, but eternal return of the same:

> You see, history in Russia is something that repeats itself all the time. They [the narrow group in power] used Brezhnev to cover their deeds up—Brezhnev who could hardly talk, and Yeltsin has been used in just the same manner. Do you really think that he left power by his own will? All of a sudden, he decided to present the people with a New Year's gift?[3] What are you talking about?! . . . (Nelly Romanovna, female, 57)

Historical parallels designed to demonstrate affinity between disparate traumatic periods did not necessarily limit themselves to recent history, but spanned a wide spectrum of Soviet and even pre-Soviet developments. In all these instances, the eternal return of a set array of scenarios was considered the back-bone of the entire historical process:

> He [Yeltsin] keeps shuffling the people around him: Primakov, now Stepashin, and I don't know what is to come next. And it means that he doesn't have a clue, he is not professional, and the only art he has acquired is to turn his immediate aides into enemies of one another. It's an old art, take any historical novel, how some Catherine, to protect herself, would set all her retinue against each other, so that they all fight among themselves, and I will be their queen and protectress. That's exactly the way he's doing it now. (Dmitrii Kirillovich, male, 54)

This affinity between disparate historical periods stemmed either from characteristics seen as universals in the nature of the Russian people ("Russians always fall into extremes," "We are always the tsars in our own kitchen") or from their mysterious destiny ("It is a kind of fate, I guess, from above, that we've been a country of experiments. Always trying, trying, but never achieving anything"). The exact reasons, however, did not seem overly important, and my interlocutors often oscillated freely between these common explanations and rarely insisted on them. Far from being strong convictions, these factors were used rather randomly as available rationalizations of the widely shared sense that Russian history had no developmental trajectory and that its new episodes represented merely "more of the same."[4]

This undifferentiated, almost ahistorical sensibility built on selectively and tendentiously interpreted historical evidence was discussed by Boris Dubin in his review of the recent boom of historical fiction (2001, 254). According to Dubin,

> ... for the consciousness promoted by historical-patriotic novels, ... only the aspects connected by symbols of repetition and exchangeability of existence can be considered history ... Hence, history as eternity is all that repeats itself and can be recognized only in this repetition. "History" in the described novels is all that into which we "got ourselves" and have been getting ourselves "always": in Russia, there is always disorder and favoritism, always theft, always bad roads, and so on. Repetition certifies the importance of what has occurred, and the other way around: the occurrence not only repeats itself because it is important—it is important because it repeats itself.

For Dubin, repetition is a symbolic mechanism that "makes the individual a part of a special action, communal by character and integrative by meaning and effect" (255). In other words, it is a means of situating one's identity within the larger frame of a holistically interpreted culture. Without denying the plausibility of this claim, I would suggest that it only begins to address the complexities of what we may call a sensibility of the eternal return. More importantly, it fails to address a more burning question: why and how did this sensibility become so prominent during the 1990s?

In her book on postsocialist change and the politics of reburial, anthropologist Katherine Verdery reminds us of the connection between the changing structures of social life and the individual's conception of temporality, writing:

"Among the more unsettling aspects of postsocialist transformation, I believe, is the possibility that the temporal experiences and conceptions familiar to people during the socialist period are being changed . . ." (1999, 122). While Verdery's discussion located this change among the postsocialist elites, there is every reason to suspect that the shift in ways of experiencing and imagining time was more pervasive. Indeed, the collapse of the socialist order triggered a profound restructuring (or collapse) of the very institutions of education, employment, "organized leisure" (i.e., summer camps, enterprise-sponsored recreation trips, etc.), and other systems involved in providing what Anthony Giddens (1990) called "ontological security."[5] This evaporation of social security arrangements and protective mechanisms also meant the collapse of the linear temporality associated with the socialist developmental trajectory. Those who, to quote Natalia Konstantinovna, "all knew what was in store for [them]" and "what [their] retirement would look like," suddenly discovered themselves without a clear conception of even a minimally distant future. Their social worlds, clearly demarcated for them by the socialist system into distinctive periods of "school," "institute," "work," and "retirement," each following one another in strict order, started to crumble. It became entirely possible that "retirement" may mean a need for new schooling and a new job, and that education may become impossible without a simultaneous side job. In its turn, this side job could easily supplant schooling and grow into a full-time activity, leading one to a career totally different from the one initially selected. Nothing was stable, and nothing could be predicted in advance.

During the late Soviet period, the sense of linear temporality and ontological security in both personal and collective terms was fostered through a number of institutional means, starting from standardized history textbooks and finishing with the nationwide project of "reaching and surpassing" the capitalist countries. The uniform and non-debatable concept of history and perspectives of future development provided an ideological counterpart to the more practical measures of time—standardization through five-year plans, Party congresses, and national holidays such as Labor Day (May 1) or the Day of the Great October Socialist Revolution (celebrated, contrary to what the name would suggest, on November 7). On a more accessible everyday level, the sense of a secure future was buttressed by practically guaranteed employment, as well as the many welfare networks of late socialism:

> When we worked in our research institute, and it was a prestigious organization, we received decent salaries, we could afford to go on road trips in winter and in summer, we've been all around the European part of Russia, in the Baltics, in Ukraine, in the Carpathians. Back then, we all thought we'd be living that way forever. That with our two retirement packages we'll get by well enough. If I'd known the way things would come out, I would never have left my job . . . (Lina, female, 55)

Soviet Russia was not unique in its function of structuring both the *longue* and the *courte* (short) *durée* of its subjects. As David Gross (1985) points out, all modern centralized states shape their citizens' conceptions of temporality through the means of mass education, as well as through their tendency to organize a national calendar predominantly along a "civil-historical" timeline, rather than according to religious events and ancestral customs. The uniqueness of the Soviet state was only proportional to the degree to which it was centralized. In this respect, Soviet institutions of education, employment, and organized leisure had few precedents. Ordered and standardized on a national level, both past and future were experienced by the late Soviet subjects as set in stone.

It was in the end of the 1980s that the situation started to change. The restructuring and collapse of many security-granting institutions, such as the ones referred to by Lina, did not come alone. Accompanying them was the lack of a clear vision of the future on the part of the ideologues of the transformation, and a chaotic array of revisionist readings of the socialist past. This fundamental ambivalence about both the certainty of individual futures and the trajectory of the society as a whole was reflected in a profound confusion over the meaning of national holidays. Constantly revised and updated, new holidays not only failed to generate their own invented traditions but frequently remained "white spots" on the calendar. A characteristic example is the Day of National Independence (June 12), a federal holiday instituted to commemorate the adoption of the declaration of Sovereignty of the Russian Federation in 1991. Its yearly occurrence throughout the decade was unfailingly accompanied not by celebratory rituals, but by newspaper and magazine articles satirizing the ignorance of the Russian citizens concerning the meaning of the holiday and the event it was supposed to commemorate.[6]

Former certainties had also proven illusory. As Lina's comments demonstrate, the ultimate loss associated with the 1990s was not only a sense of institutionally sponsored optimism about the future, but also clarity about the past. Indeed, the very nostalgia for the late Brezhnev era was fueled by a realization that the much-praised "sense of stability" of that time was deceptive. Even more compromised were the perceived socialist-era historical truths, from the interpretation of the revolution to the conventional developmental benchmarks of five-year plans.

Historical politics is a fascinating topic in its own right.[7] But it has a special value for understanding the relevance that the notion of eternally recurring crisis had for many postsocialist Russians, for it highlights the *symbolic* dimension of the predicament that we have thus far examined only in its *practical* aspect. We already know that at the heart of the postsocialist crisis was the gap that existed between people's skills and dispositions on the one hand, and the evolving field of practice on the other. But at the same time, postsocialist dislocations also eroded the temporal coordinates in which this change could be recorded and comprehended.[8] As a result, the multiple postsocialist aggravations discussed in the media and rehashed in daily conversations started to look timeless and permanent, and to demand equally permanent solutions.

Crisis as a Moving Target

From our examination of how the imagery of stability functioned in conversation, it becomes clear that it was part and parcel of the deterioration rhetoric and could exist only as an extension of the latter. In other words, far from denying the profound decline in multiple spheres of life, statements of stability merely postulated the continuous character of this dramatic decline. The seemingly contradictory messages of deterioration and stability were thus essentially tied into the same interpretive framework. This broad interpretive framework, within which the messages of drastic deterioration and extended stability safely coexisted, is what I will call in this work the framework of the total crisis.

The remaining chapters of this book will discuss how this definition of the world was articulated and developed in specific postsocialist sites: in stores and open-air markets, in individual apartments and clinics, in public transport and on the streets of Moscow. But the discussion would be incomplete without a clear understanding of what made this discourse special. In the rest of this chapter I will highlight three main points. First, the framework of the total crisis functioned as a loose interpretive system that could accommodate an infinite number of periods and situations. In fact, this flexibility was precisely what made it so powerful. Second, this framework was not only an expression of the hysteresis of habitus discussed in preceding pages but, paradoxically, also a form of its resolution. Precisely because of its perceived permanence, the crisis itself represented a new habitus in which particular and unique skills could be honed. In other words, this lingering definition of the situation offered many Russians a new language for imagining themselves and articulating their relationship to the world. And finally, the perceived permanence of the crisis was an important factor for how its navigation was conceived. The continuity and permanence of deterioration were matched by efforts to create equally permanent arrangements through which this crisis could be excluded from daily life, and individual autonomy, violated by the postsocialist change, could be restored and preserved. And the association between the crisis and the retrenchment of the state suggested that such restoration could be achieved specifically through creation of parallel structures and institutions. Too overpowering and final to be challenged or changed, the crisis implied that the only reasonable approach was defensive and compensatory.

Flexibility and Uses of the Total Crisis

The flexibility of the total crisis framework meant that every liminal event could receive an interpretation in terms that made it seem grave but not unusual. It also meant that, at least theoretically, any event could be described in crisis terms—a twist that only contributed to the pervasive sense that repetitiveness of crises was the only reliable feature of the postsocialist condition:

Right now we don't believe, as we may have before, that anything will ever change. I mean, how many times have we had this [situation], when things started to improve and then—bang!—this crisis, or a coup, or what not. Where do they come from? You only just start getting better, and all of a sudden—here you go, another mess. Take this recent one, the peak of the crisis. Some things were starting to work, little by little, even perhaps some trust was appearing toward these [political] leaders, and then again, this collapse, and again you remember all of their old sins and tell yourself, "What the heck? . . ." (Gennadii, male, 43)

But there remained the question of what was to be judged a crisis. Gennadii's quotation pointed at the difficulty of identifying it clearly. He referred to the same economic meltdown as a crisis itself ("this crisis"), and as a highpoint of a larger-scale crisis ("this recent one, the peak of the crisis"). When examined across multiple contexts, the total crisis framework rarely rested on a stable positive referent from the recent past. Instead it spontaneously emphasized the dramatic aspects of each historical juncture, making every period worse than the preceding one. For that reason, when asked to offer an example of a stable non-crisis period from recent personal history, many of my interlocutors felt puzzled and distracted from their line of argumentation, perceiving such a request to be inappropriate given the logic of their narrative. Alena's first interview provides a case in point. At different points in the narrative, she characterized a number of periods in her life as exceptionally hard, but in different ways—ideologically (the "tumult and hopelessness" of the mid-perestroika period), psychologically and organizationally ("the awful shock and problems in the institute" during the early Gorbachev period), and financially ("desperation and poverty" of the 1990s and "the dire straits of being a young mother" when, in the early and mid-1980s, she was forced to work several jobs and to sew at nights to make ends meet). When, toward the end of the interview, Alena's circular narrative returned to her current circumstance, which she described as "increasingly tough," I asked her what period of her life she considered relatively benign. This question, which probably wouldn't have puzzled Alena if asked in the beginning of the interview, made her pause; by applying various criteria for judging the preceding periods, she had discarded all of them from the potential status of the "golden age." Hesitantly, she said, "I guess, when I studied in the institute [late 1970s–early 1980s], this was a good time for me." Later, when the tape-recorded part of the interview was over and she was showing me the family album, she suddenly smiled, and said: "You know, looking at these [baby] pictures [of her older daughter], just . . . all of these things she is wearing, I remember how I was making them, from someone's old coats and pants . . . I doubt it was such a great time. I don't even know when was a time I would consider benign."

The point, then, is not that the total crisis framework was not built on the notion of a "golden age" that preceded it, but that the golden age itself was unfixed and could always, on close inspection, turn into crisis itself. In the course of such assessments the lines of comparison could change, and the events that may have been regarded as crises earlier in the conversation would blend into the positive background against which later developments could be bemoaned. The ambiguity of what exactly was to be judged as a crisis, and against what background, becomes apparent in the following exchange:

LINA: . . . Of course, when reforms are taking place, any more or less educated person understands that these reforms will bring about some changes. But to imagine that our country will come to such (pauses) . . . I had no idea that our country could come to this, to such a horrible state, I could not foresee it. If I had only known, I probably wouldn't have supported Yeltsin the way I did . . . Because, of course, I could not expect that he would cause the majority of the population to fall below the subsistence level in a matter of years.
AUTHOR: When did you first feel that things were declining?
LINA: Right after the Pavlov reform of 1991–92 [*sic*], when people lost all their savings. The state took them, you can't say it any other way . . . The pensions shrank, and so did salaries. It was a little better than this time, after August 17 [1998], but it was also very, very hard. But after a few years, it normalized again, they added salaries and pensions, and, until this recent currency plunge, our combined family income was relatively sufficient. Granted, we couldn't afford any huge purchases, but some daily things we could, even durables here and there. And now [after the August crisis], they've forced us into such a circumstance that we have to figure out how to cut expenses. Because, de facto, our pension has shrunk threefold compared to prices . . .

In the course of her narrative, Lina shifted in her description of the decade from the generalized image of a ten-year-long grave crisis to the more differentiated image in which periods of crisis and improvement succeeded one another. Interestingly, this shift of optics occurred as her narrative moved from a generalized discourse regarding the state of affairs in the country to a discussion of the well-being of Lina's family in particular. I have mentioned that Muscovites tended to view their personal lives in a somewhat more optimistic light than the general state of affairs in the country. This is not necessarily to suggest that crisis imagery played no role, but rather that the immediate environment was more likely to be talked about as a chain of smaller-scale crises alternating with periods of relative improvement, while the wider context lent itself more easily to the "wholesale" crisis label.

The boundaries of the crisis could shift not only within a given narrative, but also between successive narratives of the same individuals. This was driven home to me when I returned to Moscow in the winter of 1998–1999. Only six months had passed since my first wave of fieldwork, but the distance felt like years, because so much had happened in Russia over that period. The rapid currency collapse of August 1998 triggered a sequence of price hikes for everything from bread to real estate, and pessimism about the economy was in the air. Added to the economic was political instability. In an effort to externalize blame, Yeltsin dismissed the government of the young prime minister, Sergei Kirienko (who was shortly thereafter wittily nicknamed *Kinder-Surprise* in tribute to the default), and replaced it with the cabinet of Sergei Stepashin, who had to learn the ropes in an increasingly complex situation with further inflation looming. Given the circumstances, I expected to witness much more intense distress when I was making arrangements to meet with my contacts again. But it turned out that I underestimated the "absorption capacity" of the crisis discourse.

In the summer of 1998, Russians articulated their rather emotionally expressed and widespread frustration with the economic realities of the day in two forms. On the macro-level, there was a loudly voiced opinion that the reforms had failed as far as people's expectations were concerned. The situation in the country was widely affirmed to be not what people had expected when the transformation was only beginning. On a more micro-scale, people consistently maintained that while they were predominantly successful in making ends meet, they were doing so out of their last resources and with an enormous amount of luck. The government received no credit for whatever successes the citizens were enjoying in their private lives. On the contrary, it was perceived as hostile and responsible for the dramatic situation in the country:

> I thought that when the democrats came to power they would establish rules like other civilized countries have. So that those who work would get fair compensation. But here it has all worked exactly the other way. They did raise prices to the world level, but they failed to do the same with salaries . . . (Dmitrii Kirillovich, male, 54)

> The ones in power, they're the ones who cheated everyone, who have a lot, and that's why, I think, they don't punish the others who steal a lot, but prosecute those who are lacking basic necessities . . . My question is, how could this have happened? (Nelly Romanovna, female, 57)

Given the crisis-ridden rhetoric of the summer 1998 interviews, it is fairly clear why, as I was coming back to Moscow in December of that year, my expectations were mixed. On the one hand, the mistrust and dissatisfaction with the government and political elites had been so prevalent already in the summer that one could expect further worsening of the situation to result in mass protests. On the other hand, since many of my contacts consistently complained about material deprivation and impoverishment in the summer, the sharp rise in prices could be expected to produce unrest on the economic grounds. What I witnessed, however, was not protest activity but a few subtle shifts in rhetoric allowing people to meaningfully incorporate the fact of the breakdown, and its consequences, into the total crisis framework.

Specifically, the experience of the recent anguish associated with the financial crisis made a new interpretation of the preceding few years possible—as those of relative well-being. While the macro-scale assessment of the postsocialist decade remained as critical as ever, the recollections of recent personal circumstances became almost uniformly benign. In the winter of 1998–1999, individuals who a few months back confessed that their "finances [were] exhausted," and who saw "no perspectives for the future," referred to the preceding two years as time of "relative stability" when they could "at least afford the basics." Another rhetorical shift concerned the hypothetical trajectory of the crisis. Prior to the economic collapse this topic was hardly ever raised spontaneously, since the crisis was understood to be lingering and relatively unvarying over the years. After the breakdown, however, when references to the crisis situated it in a much more narrow and specific context (limiting it to the events connected to the financial collapse of 1998), the future trajectory of the crisis became a much discussed topic, and the gravity of future developments were typically expected to overshadow even the initial shock of the first months after the collapse. To put it differently, a sense of disappointment with the course and outcomes of the reforms, with "things not being what one hoped they would be," was superseded after the breakdown with a fear of "things getting worse than they are," thus shifting the reference point for the crisis, and, at the same time, contributing to the acceptance of the fragile status quo.[9]

There was yet one more way in which the crisis rhetoric, seemingly conducive to breeding greater discontent, functioned as a pacifier in everyday talk. Through framing the recent developments as indicative of a broad social crisis, my interlocutors automatically incorporated them into the row of crises that preceded it, thus normalizing their experiences by linking them to something people have managed to deal with in the past. Among the most oft-evoked instances of past crises were the monetary reform of 1991 ("Pavlov's reform"), shortages of the late 1980s–early 1990s, the confrontation between Yeltsin and the Parliament resulting in the Parliament's dissolution in 1993, as well as the historically more remote years of revolution and of World War II. When viewed on this comparative plane, the hardships and disappointments of the current crisis appeared stark, yet not unbearable; as one Muscovite put it, "we still have bread and milk to survive." Moreover, past crises could also be interpreted as proof that active expression of protest and discontent were actually detrimental:

> So what should we do, rebel? I think our history is packed with evidence that rebellions never improve the situation, but only make it worse . . . Anything is better than civil war, and that's what will happen if people get militant . . . (Andrei, male, 38)

The framework of total crisis, then, provided people not only with a rhetorical tradition in which to articulate their grievances, but also with a meaningful structure within which these grievances could be comprehended and endured. Far from being implicated in one stable version of ideology, it functioned as a stretchable frame enabling speakers to justify different periods of the past and different coping strategies, and to create alternative images of the future. At the same time, this stretchable character of the total crisis framework made it difficult for an observer to assess the exact degree of deprivation at each particular point in time, since the speakers drew on different references at each historical juncture, routinizing the very concept of the crisis and creating a perpetual impression of liminality of the unfolding events.

The fact that crisis discourse was far from a uniform set of propositions is important, because it pointed to the sources of the framework's vitality. Due to the multiplicity of evidence one could invoke, as well as the variety of rhetorical styles, total crisis narratives could be used at the will of the speaker in multiple contexts, referring to anything from an increase in crime to political instability, and from discrete upheavals to the entire decade (if not centuries) of Russian history. Depending on the amount of control an individual felt (or desired to communicate) over his or her environment, these accounts could be more or less emotional and involve varying degrees of role distancing on the part of the narrator. Similarly, political conclusions drawn from such discussions could vary across the entire political spectrum. Much like big political players, ordinary people easily used the notion of a total crisis to buttress various ideological stances. Yet all of these forms shared the underlying interpretive schema in which dramatic deterioration was presumed to be lasting and unavoidable. In this sense, the existence of a dramatic yet permanent decline could be considered *doxa* in Bourdieu's definition, "that which is taken for granted" and which constituted a common denominator for an entire range of further opinions (Bourdieu 1977, 166).

It was precisely this flexibility of the total crisis framework that allowed it to function as communicational currency in routine encounters and to bridge ideological gaps between the exchange participants. I had the occasion to observe numerous instances in which potential hostility in an encounter between strangers was successfully mitigated by a timely invocation of "the crisis" or its institutional counterpart, "the [postsocialist] system." Particularly in communication across class barriers and when the political position of one's interlocutors was unclear, a generic invocation of a crisis functioned not unlike the ritualized discussions of weather in a stereotypical British conversation.[10] In most cases this invocation was explicit; a cynical commentary on universal corruption could elicit a chuckle from fellow travelers sharing the same compartment or provide for a smooth elevator ride between a manager and a secretary. Other instances were less explicit. I recall buying knitted mittens in a subway crossing and asking the salesman, a robust man in his late forties, about their origins. "I made them myself," he responded with a grin and, catching the expression of disbelief on my face, continued, "No, really, I did. I learned to knit a while ago. Boris Nikolaevich [Yeltsin] taught me how."

This stranger's joke crystallizes many elements of the postsocialist situation discussed above—the experience of economic uncertainty, social dislocation, and downward occupational mobility, the personalized vision of politics, the retrenchment of the state. In just a few words, the economic and social crisis became an insider's wink, designed to elicit solidarity based on the shared framework of reference. Through this wink, my chance interlocutor signaled to me (as he did, no doubt, to his other customers who must have heard the joke as well) that he recognized me as a fellow-sufferer who, like himself, occupied a position of vulnerability in the postsocialist field of power. Thus, evoking the image of the crisis (which could be done just as easily by saying confidingly "In this life of ours . . .") became a means of insuring a smooth interaction and an atmosphere of mutual understanding.

The crisis talk fulfilled other important functions as well. On a rhetorical level, it allowed for smooth transitions between topics and provided speakers with an easy way to account for the events under discussion. But it also had more instrumental applications, often serving as a means of help-seeking. The social acceptability, if not anticipation, of a crisis narrative in the course of the conversation opened doors to the possibility that misfortunes and dilemmas could be brought up without the risk of negative sanctions. Since speaking of one's problems did not violate any conversational rules, this topic was raised frequently and often productively. It could easily turn out that the other party had connections or information that could be of help and was willing to offer her knowledge or services in the spirit of informal exchange. Muscovites' healthcare problems were often resolved in this fashion; the same was true of educational or employment concerns. Vera Vladimirovna, a forty-three-year-old cleaning lady who was the main breadwinner for her family of four, found a job that way:

> There is this woman, she also works in the courthouse with me, also cleaning . . . and her daughter, I don't know how, but she found a job at this Miranda's [an elite furniture salon] as a personal assistant to the director. And they had a need for a cleaning lady there, because the one they had there for some reason wasn't satisfactory and they practically fired her. So this woman, the one working with me, we were talking once about how difficult life had become, and she offered the job. Actually, she didn't offer it just to me, but to two other girls who were there as well, but they said no right away, and I jumped at the opportunity because I've been looking. And I even had some other options at the time, but they all paid less than a thousand,[11] and I wasn't happy with that, because it was too little. And here she offered hundred and fifty in dollars, and a part-time schedule, so I said yes.

Apart from practical help and advice, another form of assistance was frequently sought by those who shared their discontent—namely, the psychological one. My informants were often aware of the fact that by exchanging crisis narratives they were pursuing emotional relief, and in several cases they spontaneously compared the effect of such talk to a psychotherapeutic or stress-relief session. Such a perspective was particularly characteristic of women, whose crisis narratives tended to be more verbose and dramatic.[12] After my interview with Konstantin, his wife offered the following interpretation of our conversation:

> We are not accustomed to going to a psychologist. But we can talk to one another, communicate, and next thing you know—someone is feeling better. At least the one who wanted to speak out and get relief that way. I use it myself sometimes.

Similarly, another woman said,

> Sometimes, we'd meet up [with girlfriends], talk the evening away, spill it out, as they say. Pour it out into the open, let the steam out. Because otherwise, of course, there is a lot of indignation. So . . . yeah, just pour it all out, not keep it inside. As they say, the more you keep in your head, the more you have on your head. Gray hair, that is. And I have enough gray hair as it is. (Kseniia Anatolievna, female, 43)

Crisis talk, hence, could function as a cathartic ritual through which the tensions of everyday life were lived out and transformed into narrative. Ordered and organized, the narrative form gives the speaker a sense of control even in those cases when the narrated events are uncontrollable.[13] The phenomenon of crisis talk in this respect was not unlike the interviewing process itself. The fact that often, after the interview's completion, my interlocutors reported that it had a therapeutic effect on them, made me all the more aware of the power of narrative to alleviate stress.

Imagery of the total crisis functioned as a means of a psychological defense on three further levels. On the one hand, when needed, it provided material for social comparison through which even the least fortunate could differentiate themselves from those who were, to use the words of Loïc Wacquant's informants, "doin' *worser* than me."[14] Media images offered especially rich data in this respect, and they were frequently evoked in conversation as evidence that the speaker's circumstance was not the worst one imaginable. On the other hand, the imagery of crisis could be used not to differentiate oneself, but on the contrary, to emphasize the commonality of the people's predicament. In other words, the speaker found safety in numbers. The fact that strenuous circumstances became the lot of the majority served in this context as an assurance against the possibility of a uniquely personal tragedy. And, while this strategy may appear contrary to the one above, in practice they often intertwined:

> What can you do? My thinking is, I'm not alone in this. How many of us people there are! And everyone is going through this. Still, in one way or another, people will find a way to live. Of course, I sympathize when they show on TV that people don't get paid. These people they show, in the provinces, where the miners are. How do they live, poor things! How can you survive? Families, hungry children. Of course I feel for them. (Tatiana, female, 68)

Another mode of using the crisis rhetoric in order to make the present psychologically more acceptable had to do with predictions for the future, which were usually cast in a gravely pessimistic light. Among the events I heard anticipated in the nation's immediate future were civil war, famine, dictatorship, the breakdown of the Russian Federation into a multiplicity of independent states, and the end of the world, not to mention fiscal disasters, such as astronomical tax increases or an avalanche of financial breakdowns of the same scope as the one that occurred in August 1998. The following quotation illustrates the spirit in which such predictions were made:

> MIKHAIL ALEKSANDROVICH: Let's say they are planning, at this very moment as we speak, to raise taxes, and it will probably evoke a certain hue and cry, and may even bring people to hysterics, if they put their efforts to it, because it looks like they are planning to collect money predominantly through [income] taxes, while RAO ES or Viakhirev[15] will not be even touched. Everything will be collected, as always, at the expense of the people, it's easier, isn't it, so many people out there for them to rip off.
> AUTHOR: Did you hear about it recently?
> MA: Well, they've been wanting to for a long time, and they keep shaking up the tax system, planning to change it again and again and again. They want to introduce a

higher property tax. Just recently they forced everyone to privatize their apartments, and it was covered at 0.1 percent I believe, and now they want to make it up to 3 percent, and this comes out to be almost $1,000 from a person per year.

AUTHOR: But where do they expect people to find $1,000?

MA: Well, this doesn't bother anyone. You can't pay? Then sell your apartment, get yourself a smaller one, live where you can, leave Moscow for Riazan or God-knows-where, and if you can't even pay there, this doesn't bother anyone either. I am telling you, our government has no interest in the people whatsoever, they are busy with their own business, and people are just left to tend for themselves.

AUTHOR: How likely would you say it is that they'll introduce such an outrageous tax?

MA: Why not? Of course it's likely. Nobody knows what will happen in the future, and how. Because the Duma only thinks about itself, they only care about themselves, they are procuring apartments and salary, and all the money they can get, wherever they can grab it, through everything, through interviews, through middlemen, through everything. Of course they won't part with their own for tax purposes, but why not rip people off again? (Mikhail Aleksandrovich, male, 59)

Mikhail Aleksandrovich's prognostication was hardly realistic at the time, for its fulfillment would have led to a mass exodus of practically the entire city population into the provinces. However, it was not precision of forecast that mattered. Through this form of crisis talk, by voicing his disbelief in the integrity of the government and conviction that things could get worse, Mikhail Aleksandrovich was achieving several interrelated goals. First, he made the current situation seem simultaneously lamentable and acceptable by contrast to what could come next, and thus rationalized the present-day political passivity without dropping the possibility of the "hue and cry" in the future. Second, by describing the prospects in a negative light, he insured himself against any disappointment that he might have encountered should his plans for the future have been more optimistic. Hence planning for the worst served as a form of psychological self-defense through damage control.[16]

Total Crisis as a Postsocialist Habitus

The multiplicity of uses that total crisis served in everyday discourse suggests a new way of looking at the predicament I have been discussing under the broad label of hysteresis of habitus. Thus far I have looked at the popularity of the total crisis framework as an expression of, and a reaction to, the multiple dislocations associated with the postsocialist era.[17] But while the concept of hysteresis of habitus sheds light on the reasons for crisis rhetoric's wide popularity, it stops short of explaining its consequences for the organization of daily life. It posits the problem, as it were, but does not look for answers. Since it does not presume that people are sufficiently creative to substantially reconfigure their social environment, it has little interest in how these people deal with the notorious lack of fit between their cultural resources and the social reality around them.

A reevaluation of this assumption does not require much more than supplementing the old question of "What does the total crisis framework express?" with an additional, equally important one: "What does it make possible?"[18] The preceding section already began to address this question by looking into the things achieved through daily perpetuation of this rhetoric, from purely practical (such as emotional release or pursuit of new opportunities) to less tangible ones (cognitive mastery and damage control). To these I would add another key function of the total crisis framework: the centrality of crisis imagery to the task of displaying practical competence in the postsocialist context.

After all the discussion of threats that the reforms of the 1990s presented to the individual's sense of practical competence and autonomy, this assertion needs to be qualified. Being a part of what Berger and Luckmann (1967) call the "common stock of knowledge," practical (or pragmatic) competence is crucial to the individual's sense of identity, both in terms of membership in a community that shares the same ideas about the mastery of routine problems, and in terms of boundary maintenance from those who fulfill this task less successfully. But the task of demonstrating practical competence requires clear institutionalized "rules of the game" to structure the competition. These were precisely the matters that the process of the transformation unsettled. However, while criteria of professional success or channels of communication with administrative bodies may have become obscure or lost their universal legitimacy, the definition of the situation in terms of a total crisis remained a widely shared reality of the postsocialist years.

Given the extended period in which total crisis functioned as a master frame in the postsocialist context, it makes sense to view this framework not as merely a symptom of hysteresis of habitus, but as a new form of habitus itself.[19] The very temporality of the total crisis framework suggested this as a possibility; it accentuated the permanent and timeless nature of the postsocialist decline, implying that those caught in its midst had every incentive to restock their cultural tool-kits and equip themselves adequately for the predicament which, they were convinced, was there to stay. "Competence" in this new context could refer only to the knack for expertly navigating the crisis environment. It was in this task that individuals could, and indeed did, strive to excel, and it should come as no surprise that such excellence came at the implicit cost of further solidifying the total crisis framework.

The discussion by Mikhail Aleksandrovich of possible tax reforms bears the imprint of this dual act of decrying the corrupt nature of postsocialist politics even while relying on it for one's own self-image. But I would like to discuss here another instance in which the mutual dependence between practical competence and the total crisis framework became evident.

I first met Sergei Mikhailovich in his office at the institute where he spent twelve years of his life working as a geologist. The building, which was located in a residential area of Moscow, had a haunted feel to it—the corridors and stairs were virtually empty and looked uninhabited. Despite the fact that I came at 11:00 AM, the large windowless room where Sergei Mikhailovich had his desk was virtually empty. The only one of his colleagues working was a woman in her late forties whom he introduced as Liudmila Ivanovna. The room was furnished with tables and chairs that seemed to have been there since the Brezhnev era; hanging on the wall was a faded-out work schedule from 1991. The only relatively new object in the room was an electric kettle, but even it looked untidy and worn out.

Our conversation took place in the middle of Sergei Mikhailovich's work day, which did not bother him or his colleague since, as he informed me, their working group had recently finished and submitted a contract and had no new projects at the time (this also explained the emptiness of the office). But despite the fact that Sergei Mikhailovich was not in a rush and had nothing better to do, the interview was not going well. Sergei Mikhailovich's demeanor communicated a mix of reservation and resentment; his answers were curt and minimal. What seemed most puzzling was the incongruity between his manner of speaking—calm, unhurried, deliberate—and the content of his responses. In his confident and measured manner he was predicting that Russia's most immediate future held imminent impoverishment and famine, years of instability, and a civil war that would bring the country to ultimate dependence and turn it into what seemed to denote for Sergei Mikhailovich ultimate failure: "the United States of Mexico in Russia."

When I expressed disbelief at Sergei Mikhailovich's resignation in the face of the prospects he was just describing, he smiled with a touch of irony: "What should I be doing? Running in circles, screaming? Perhaps we shall get used to that poverty, that third world existence." Sergei Mikhailovich shrugged his shoulders, indicating the absurdity and inappropriateness of panic in the face of the crisis. And yet, in just a few minutes, he erupted in precisely the kind of outburst that he earlier dismissed as inappropriate. But it was not my comment that elicited it. At some point of the interview, Liudmila Ivanovna, who was visibly bored at her desk, interjected some minor comment into our conversation; this triggered Sergei Mikhailovich's outrage and elicited the following tirade, which clearly was a continuation of lasting political disagreements between Sergei Mikhailovich and his colleague:

> All this drivel that I hear about, all this "let's nationalize this back and that back," this is just ridiculous! The state owned all of this for seventy years, and what do we have?! We have today's situation! Do you think anything would be better if this seventy-year-long nonsense continued? There was no life! And these supposed high morals of socialism, where are they now? What are all of these highly moral people doing? In just five years they all turned into bandits! All of these bandits grew during the Soviet era!

After an uncomfortable pause, in the course of which the communist sympathizer Liudmila Ivanovna retreated to her desk and buried herself in paperwork, Sergei Mikhailovich resumed his air of detachment and calm, although now he was visibly embarrassed by his outburst. He was eager to wrap up the interview, and in his eagerness he seemed not to care any more about the consistency of his predictions. His confident and slightly detached tone became ironic as he informed me that, in thirty years' time, Russian life could prosper if the children of today's bandits could turn back into Pioneers again. After a few more minutes of small talk, what seemed to me at the time to be the most perplexing field encounter I ever had finally came to an end.

It would be a futile endeavor to try to reconstruct Sergei Mikhailovich's political philosophy from this encounter. But it would be equally wrong to dismiss it as uninformative. For, evasive as he was about his take on postsocialist realities, there was one element of the interview in which Sergei Mikhailovich was quite consistent, if not insistent. This element was the projection of a particular persona: calm, deliberate, and unshaken by the gravity of the postsocialist crisis. The rupture of this projection amounted to an embarrassing loss of face and was quickly neutralized by irony, as if the fact that Sergei Mikhailovich actually cared about the fate of his country could somehow compromise him in the stranger's eyes.

The intensity of Sergei Mikhailovich's emotion was understandable: his was the despair of a person who, despite his perestroika-era hopes, could find no better place for himself in the postsocialist system than his conservative-leaning colleague (who remained separated from him by an ideological gulf). This reaction made more than just a little sense from the hysteresis of habitus point of view. His distaste for socialism was embedded in the ideological, political, and moral commitments of his past, which proved, however, to be poor allies in the postsocialist era. Initially a supporter of the transformation, he had to watch it eliminate his very own social niche. In this respect he was in a more difficult position than his colleague. Like her, he had every reason to decry the postsocialist order, but unlike her, he had trouble reconciling his disappointment with his earlier views.

But Sergei Mikhailovich's emotional distance indicated that the total crisis had also become an important element in how he presented himself. The gruesomeness of his predictions stood in sharp contrast to the demeanor and composure by which he signaled his ability to control if not the postsocialist developments, then at least his response to them. The total crisis became the background against which his calm and dignity could become apparent.[20] It provided Sergei Mikhailovich with a crucial means of self-presentation: he was keen to show that the total crisis had become a part of his habitus, an immediately familiar reality with which he had every ability to deal.

But while Sergei Mikhailovich *rhetorically* separated himself from the dramatic condition he took for granted, others highlighted their *practical* ability to resist the crisis. Remembering the financial decisions she and her husband made prior to August 1998, Lena, a thirty-seven-year-old cleaning lady and jack of all trades in a private company, said:

> You know, my husband did suggest once that we should open a ruble bank account, it was called a "Christmas Account" and yielded better returns in one or two years, I even made my calculations. That would mean changing our dollar savings into

rubles, and it had to work, but I still said no. I did consider it though for a while, made estimates, because dollars [the exchange rate] grow slowly, these are just kopecks, so we might have won if we did it, at least a bit, but I just didn't feel like all this deceit.[21]

AUTHOR: Why do you say "deceit"?

LENA: You know, I am just used to the fact that we are always being deceived. [Laughs] So I said, "You know, Sashka, I don't believe it." [Smiling with satisfaction] So we just let it rest, and recently, he said, "Good thing we kept this money [in dollars]." Had we changed them into rubles—we would have lost out. . . . And you know, somehow, we've been swindled and deceived so much that, whatever forecast they throw out next, people won't buy it.

Lena's comments suggested that there was a certain sense of fulfillment and self-appreciation involved in playing and winning the "games with the state" (in the context of her comment, it was clear that a wise refusal to play the games in itself constituted a moral and a practical victory). What brings her comments together with Sergei Mikhailovich's is the fact that both of them relied on crisis imagery in order to construct their presentations of self. For both, their achievements were inconceivable in isolation from the gruesome context in which they were made. And because the context was there to stay, it made perfect sense that one's abilities and skills were to be tailored to it.

Autonomy and Living Day by Day

If habitus is defined as a system of skills and dispositions, what were the skills and dispositions needed in order to carry on in the midst of a permanent crisis? The answer to this question largely follows from the most oft-cited charge against the postsocialist era—the disorderly breakdown of familiar institutional structures, and the retreat of the formerly paternalistic state. Given the frustrations regarding the loss of control over one's life and future that these developments engendered, it is hardly surprising that a competent response to them entailed an attempted reconstruction of this control. Control here amounted to an ability to cultivate such self-sufficiency and autonomy that further crises would leave oneself and one's immediate environs unperturbed.

Such a narrow interpretation of what could and had to be done in the face of the postsocialist disorder was predicated on the absence of alternative frames for collective mobilization and of institutionalized mechanisms that could facilitate formation of distinctive communities of interest. But on another level, it was inspired by the ubiquity of the crisis imagery itself. Indeed, in a world where everything from housing stock to public morality was seen as caught in a perpetual process of decomposition, it seemed naïve and idealistic to hope that any steps whatsoever could comprehensively address the situation, since every such step would necessarily entail reliance on some other element of a social fabric itself in the throes of decay. The options that remained viable dealt with a restoration of autonomy on the more intimate scale of individual households. While a number of commentators decry this moderation as apathy,[22] we should keep in mind that the losses of the perceived socialist-era freedom to act "as one wanted to" (to paraphrase Mikhail Aleksandrovich) were also experienced on an intimate scale. Hence, the drive toward autonomy could be seen as an effort to preserve (or reconquer) that lost space of control.

One danger in using the language of autonomy to describe the postsocialist sensibility is that the English term is so deeply rooted in the heritage of Anglo-American liberalism. But the understanding of autonomous action one could deduce from postsocialist practices was far from the American tradition of conceptualizing autonomy as part and parcel of the culture of individualism, as described by scholars from Tocqueville to Bellah et al. (1996). Unlike the Anglo-Saxon autonomy, built on "finding [one's] true self independent of any cultural or social influence, being responsible to that self alone, and making its fulfillment the very meaning of [one's life]" (Bellah et al. 1996, 150), the autonomy aspired to in postsocialist Russia was far less introspective and individual-centric. Its unit (and simultaneously, the *sine qua non* for the successful attainment of this autonomy) was not an individual, but a household. Further on, autonomy itself was pursued not as a precondition for development or as a means toward an end, but as an end in itself, as a desired although never fully achievable state in which one's ontological security was unthreatened and the breakdowns of infrastructure were rendered unable to disrupt the order of things. Finally, while the American tradition shares postsocialist skepticism regarding the desirability of the state's intrusion into individual lives, it takes this position regarding *any* state, and infers from it the need for a clear differentiation between the duties of a government and those of its constituents. In late 1990s Moscow, by contrast, this sensibility was formulated as a grievance against a *particular* (postsocialist) state. Thus it was far from normative, and it arrived at an opposite conclusion: the responsibilities of the state should not be differentiated from, but should rather be reproduced by, the constituents on their own level, and not because this was desirable, but merely to safeguard oneself from the state's inevitable failures.

A poster advertising stress medicine that I saw in the Moscow subway in the winter of 1998 provides a graphic illustration of the peculiarities of autonomy in its postsocialist interpretation. The poster depicted a middle-aged man, dressed in office attire and virtually collapsing under the weight of what could easily be identified as sources of stress (figure 4.1). The pile on the man's shoulders included such universal stressors as "prices," "work," "sex problems," and "illnesses" (and also, somewhat incongruously, "husband," perhaps in indication that the image was directed to women as well as men). But mixed in with these universally familiar sources of aggravation were also others: "government," "president," "elections," "inflation," and at the bottom of it all, perched on the man's right fist, "crisis." The advertising slogan on the bottom proclaimed, "VITATRESS is stronger than stress!"

This image is notable for several reasons. First of all, it reduced complex political institutions such as the Russian parliament and elections to nothing more than sources of stress and aggravation, something on a par with the daily

Figure 4.1. "VITATRESS is stronger than stress!" Poster advertising stress tabs in the Moscow subway. OAO Veropharm.

hassles of failing health and financial problems. Furthermore, the fact that all of these multidimensional phenomena were indiscriminately piled up together on the back of an oppressed citizen speaks volumes about the perceived lack of mediating institutions and safety nets that are supposed to alleviate the adverse effects of political and economic processes. The advertising depicted all types of stress as identical in nature, thus implicitly suggesting that government and politics should ideally be kept at a distance with the same diligence as illness and poverty. Moreover, it explicitly acknowledged that those who had to confront trouble were ultimately on their own. And given the all-encompassing nature of postsocialist aggravations, self-defense from them had to be equally multifaceted, providing in advance for a plethora of potential problems, from large-scale (inflation or unemployment) to purely personal (health emergency or debt).

Autonomy, in other words, was hardly a moral and psychological utopia. Rather, it was a condition to which people felt condemned by the very postsocialist system from which they strove to separate themselves. A logical question would be, of course, what was this "system"? It was not easy to formulate a definitive answer to this question on the basis of the interviews, not because it did not exist, but because, much like "the crisis," its originating source, "the system" was an elastic concept, and it was applied differently in different contexts. On the most general level, the concept of the system served as a depository for all the negative features of the postsocialist situation—the site of chaos, disintegration, and inefficiency, the effects of which impacted people's everyday lives. But because imagery of the system was so closely connected with narratives of collapse, inadequacies, and vacuum, the very term is misleading, and it would perhaps be more accurate to speak of "the ghost of the system," since its criticisms more often dealt with the perilous absence of infrastructure than with is overpowering presence.

The protest against the system's ineptitude was always a protest against something external, the embodiment of disorder against the grain of which people were trying to organize their own, autonomous existence. The fact of one's own participation in the system was misrecognized, as was the fact that, imperfect as they were, its institutions created the context of one's achievements and facilitated them. It was this ultimate otherness of the system that mattered for the individual's rhetorical self-definition. Thus, when my conversation with Mikhail Aleksandrovich—himself a middle-rank government employee—elicited statements like "The government is on its own, the Duma is on its own, and the people (narod) are on their own," Mikhail Aleksandrovich's moral outrage was possible because it was narod that he associated himself with, not the government. The same is true for the man on the Vitatress poster, whose apparel marked him as a businessman or a mid-rank government bureaucrat. But even though this character belonged to a professional category whose upward mobility was part and parcel of the postsocialist system, the ad cast him as its oppressed victim. A similar move was routinely made in conversation by those whose professions coincided with the most widely agreed upon sites of disorganization and collapse, such as medicine, politics, education, or law enforcement. A teacher would illustrate her narrative of the systemic collapse with a case of corrupt medicine, a doctor would draw examples from the inefficiency or corruption of police practices, while a policeman's wife would concentrate on the "complete collapse of our school system," externalizing the site of the chaos and attributing to it the total and impersonal character that marks otherness.[23]

Thus, despite the profound skepticism regarding all aspects of the system, it was not a given that particular people who comprised it would be considered guilty by association. Everything depended on one's rhetorical ability to assert autonomy. This was particularly true for those who occupied an intermediary position between the system and the people—say, policemen or salespersons. Although during and after the economic crisis of 1998 some people blamed the salespeople for triggering the consumer panic that followed the price hikes, others—in particular those who counted some retail workers among their acquaintances—considered them their fellow-sufferers who were as affected and disempowered by the crisis as the rest of the population. In the latter case, the prerequisite for acceptance of the salesperson was the fact that she was also affected by the faulty system.[24] A similar logic affected relations with particular policemen (police in general were almost invariably considered thoroughly corrupt). Any policeman, so the logic went, from a traffic cop to a tax officer, existed in a firm hierarchy and could in many ways be seen as a hostage of the system as well. Successful negotiations with police depended, therefore, on how well an individual could convince the officer that the two of them existed on the same side of the people/system divide. This could be achieved by appealing to shared identities ("I'm a military man myself") or to shared definitions of the crisis ("You know how hard it is to pass inspections these days"). In the vernacular, achieving this effect of solidarity between the officer and oneself (and thus avoiding the otherwise inevitable sanctions) was designated as "agreeing in a human way" (*dogovorit'sia po-chelovecheski*), which implied mutual understanding and loyalty cutting across the bounds of duty.

This flexible logic of the opposition between the people and the system is instructive, because it allows us to see the fluidity of the symbolic adversary against which the project of cultivating autonomy was carried out. Maintaining a degree of defense against this shifting opponent could be a harrowing task—so harrowing, in fact, that many Muscovites claimed not to preoccupy themselves with systemic defenses at all, preferring instead to "live day by day" (*zhit' odnim dnem*). But while it might be tempting to view this strategy as incongruous with the task of maintaining everyday autonomy, in many ways it was constitutive of it.

Living day by day implied that in the conditions of uncertainty and unpredictability, a reasonable person had to concentrate on the immediate practical considerations of the moment. On one level, this was dictated by the practical necessity of keeping all of one's bases covered before considering any more long-term plans. On another, by forgoing more ambitious projects, people also felt paradoxically more immune to political and economic disruption, since they had fewer things to lose. By declaratively giving up the hope of achieving the utopia of full practical autonomy from the state, they claimed to achieve a measure of psychological autonomy:

I don't see any difference between August 17 of this year and 1993,[25] or all these Pavlov monetary reforms, when the retirees lost all their savings in 1991. There is no difference. Just, once again, the state has reached into my pocket. That's all. That's my feeling. Except that my personal pocket happened to be empty because I'd already learned the lesson of living day by day, during Soviet times. (Konstantin, male, 53)

However (and this is where the language of living day by day becomes misleading), it would be a mistake to take Konstantin's words literally and assume that he did not plan for the future, or that he had no savings. Far from an invitation to "seize the day," the motto of living day by day amounted to precisely the opposite: a recognition that the uncertainty of the postsocialist era had to be managed daily. In Konstantin's case, such management included meticulous budgeting, summer stints with a construction brigade, subletting a room to a tenant, and ensuring that his modest savings were either converted into hard currency or spent on the upkeep of the apartment. It was due to this scrupulous planning that his family made it through the currency crisis of August 1998 with minimal losses. In other words, the fact that the economic breakdown of 1998 did not catch him unawares was precisely due to his *not* living day by day in the most immediate sense of these words.

The motto of living day by day, rather than being taken at face value, is better viewed in the context of the detemporalized perception of history discussed above. Given the collapse of the legitimate socialist temporality and of the many institutions that supported it, it seems fair to say that post-Soviet subjects were almost forced to retreat into their present as the only temporal segment that they doubtlessly possessed. The present, of course, did not automatically grant any firm visions of the past or of the future, which became too amorphous and too undifferentiated to be thought or spoken about in concrete terms. At best, they could be imagined as mere extensions of the present, as the eternal repetitions of the particular features and dilemmas of today. By extension, everyday choices were to be made in the face of this eternal present, an endless chain of crises and breakdowns so naturalized that their recurrence seemed almost inevitable. As a result, every day of the day by day living was a compressed version of all past and future mishaps, and had to routinely include preventive arrangements against them. Instead of indulging themselves or enjoying the pleasures of the moment, post-Soviet subjects were relentlessly reliving the same expectations and fears without hope for their clear and final resolution.

As a result, the prevalent modus of control consisted of an interesting blend of self-reliance and fatalism. On the one hand, the very decision to circumscribe one's life plans by the immediate few months at hand was rationalized in terms of erratic fate and the uselessness of attempting to predict its turns. On the other hand, the activity developed in the course of living day by day hardly amounted to resignation. On the contrary, it consisted of holding a multiplicity of jobs and positions and generally staying active and open to economic opportunities—an orientation described by the Russian expression "*kak-to krutit'sia*" (somehow spinning).[26] This vibrant activity could be directed toward a continuous search for economizing techniques ("defensive strategies" in terms of Burawoy et al. [2000]), or toward exploring new forms of employment and earning ("entrepreneurial strategies," op. cit.), but in each case it was hardly compatible with the fatalistic rhetoric so frequently accompanying it. Thus, while one could bemoan the incomprehensible whims of fate as a retrospective justification of one's failures or an indication of limits to one's powers (a function which, as Michael Herzfeld [1992] suggests, fate shares with bureaucracy), they did not preclude trying further; rather, they morally obliged one to do so.[27]

5 Permanent Crisis, Durable Goods

To this point we have pursued a description of the total crisis framework in terms of rhetoric, but we should certainly not dismiss it as "just rhetoric." The manner in which people discussed and imagined the postsocialist situation mattered deeply. For one, it provided the context in which the need to think and speak of oneself as an autonomous individual became a part of cultural expectations, and of the vocabulary in which one was trained to think about one's choices. Since an opportunity to think of and present oneself as an autonomous subject was important for individual self-definition, the rhetoric of autonomy extended beyond the merely instrumental needs of making up for the gaps in the infrastructure. In other words, it had a morphogenic capacity: affirmations of autonomy gained a value of their own, and, just as with other identity discourses, they transformed multiple fields of practice, from political talk to choices of lifestyle, and spurred the formation of uniquely postsocialist institutional and organizational forms. And in their very proliferation they often enhanced the subjective experience of the crisis in which they originated.

What were the implications of crisis becoming the overriding metaphor for postsocialist condition? How did the ways of living and navigating through this crisis shape the post-Soviet world of practice? As the following chapters will demonstrate, the "totality" of the crisis framework can refer not only to its all-encompassing character, but also—as Mauss (1967) used this term in his essay on the gift—to its simultaneous expression in a multiplicity of social institutions, from economic to moral, aesthetic, and sociomorphological. This meant that traumas developed a routine quality and saturated the social order, so that analytic efforts to make clear-cut distinctions between traumas and the rest of daily life would be unsuccessful. But if all traumas had a bit of "everyday-ness" to them, the opposite was true as well: everyday activities always contained a reference to the crisis, and it was from this premise that they gained their logics, their legitimacy, and their meaning.

The three chapters that follow explore the linkages between the crisis narratives and the choices that individuals made daily as they went about living their lives in postsocialist Moscow. The themes I have identified in the previous chapters—the complexities and permutations of trust, the changed definitions of safety, autonomy, and practical competence—are traced here through a multiplicity of social realms, from consumption to health protection, and from leisure to political behavior. These behaviors were, in a number of ways, logical (although at times unintended) consequences of the changed attitudes I discussed above, but we should think about them as something more than mere corollaries of a rhetorical and attitudinal shift. In a more immediate way, the practices were just as important as the people's narratives in constructing the image of a world in crisis. In other words, they were performative statements in their own right, carried out through a different medium—through actions and objects rather than words—but directed toward the same end. The fact that they follow everyday rhetoric in my account is a practical choice, not an indication of their sociological inferiority in the real world where the two were intermingled in a way most unconducive to a linear narrative.

This being said, the fit between verbal assertions and practical behaviors has not always been self-evident and unproblematic. Many times I observed a discrepancy between what people said and what they did, and I was tempted to conclude that either the assertions were misleading or the behaviors erratic.[1] And while at times both possibilities might have been true, the larger issue at hand was that each of them individually represented only a part of the post-socialist "logic of practice." Instead of confronting rhetoric and behaviors, therefore, I looked for the logic of their interrelation—indeed, looked at behaviors as just *another kind of rhetoric,* and used practical choices and behaviors as further sources of insight into the meaning of words (as well as the other way around). It was through this constant negotiation that the realities that had initially appeared contradictory slowly and almost imperceptibly started to make sense together.

As an illustration of contradictory realities, consider a story told in 1999 by a colleague whose parents live in an industrial Siberian town. Nikolai's mother and father are retirees living alone in a three-room apartment they once shared with their son and daughter before the children moved out to start their own families. In the mid-1990s, Nikolai's parents surprised their children by deciding to purchase a second refrigerator, an ultramodern frost-free model. "We were a bit puzzled, since they live alone, and hardly even use one fridge," Nikolai said. "Plus, our kitchen is not so big, and the second fridge completely crowded it." After a while the old fridge broke, and Nikolai's parents moved it into the empty bedroom, purchasing at the same time a deep freezer, which they installed in the corridor. They insisted on keeping the old model "just in case" (or, as Russians say, "*in case of fire emergency*" [*na vsiakii pozharnyi sluchai*]), and so it was used as a storage space for about a year, after which they fixed it and left it to work in the bedroom. None of the cooling devices, however, liberated Nikolai's parents from the life-long habit of hanging frozen produce out of their windows during the long Siberian winters. Therefore, despite the abundance of refrigerators, the family news Nikolai received from Siberia remained full of accounts of produce spoiled by sudden thaws or frosts. Apparently, his parents never got to the point of actually using their expensive new kitchen devices to their full capacity. Indeed, as Nikolai quoted his mother, "Why overuse the fridge when we have the windows?"

If Nikolai's story comes across as absurd, it is because its heroes, the retired couple from Siberia, demonstrated hybrid consumer attitudes. On the one hand, they were sufficiently fascinated by the new household gadgets to stretch their modest budgets in ways that may seem unwarranted and unwise even to the most sympathetic observer, their son. On the other hand, they could not bring themselves to part with their old household possessions, thus belying all tempting allusions one could make to the corrupting spirit of capitalist consumerism. Furthermore, like many others who stretched their means to invest in their apartments, they saw their responses as directly related to, and not in any direct contradiction with, their sense of a total societal crisis surrounding them.[2]

To understand how the experience of total crisis manifested itself in everyday life, it is useful to explore the topic of domestic consumption, concentrating on the discourses and practices that surrounded the purchase and use of large domestic appliances as well as on the importance of home improvement ideology more generally. There is an ethnographic and a theoretical reason for launching the inquiry into the practical dimension of the total crisis from a study of consumption. Ethnographically, consumption is unique in being recognized by Russians as one of the few spheres of life in which postsocialist degradation coexisted with a measure of improvement from the socialist era. If the total crisis imagery was significant for practices forming in this sphere, we may have every reason to expect it at an even grander scale elsewhere. Theoretically, consumption provides a good entry point for observing the workings of the total crisis framework because, as Slater (1997) points out, consumer desires and needs are necessarily rooted in larger and usually taken-for-granted assumptions that govern daily actions. Among them are the shared definitions of "what constitutes good life in society, how we should live," as well as "the values in terms of which social action and institutions are oriented" (Slater 1997, 55). However minute and routine individual acts of consumption may seem, they give concrete shape to the understandings that are profoundly moral and political in their nature. Therefore, by examining the role that the total crisis framework played in consumption, one can begin to appreciate its contribution to practical action more generally and, ultimately, its role in the formation of the specifically postsocialist moral and cultural landscape.

The Family Cauldron

The importance of domestic consumption, and the share of resources people were willing to allocate for it, would be incomprehensible without an understanding of the role that the family unit had come to play in the course of the protracted postsocialist transformation. Muscovites' narratives of total crisis discussed in the preceding chapters firmly located the site of turbulence and instability in the public sphere—on the workplace, in high politics, and in the economy. By contrast, the private sphere of the family became subjectively more important during the first postsocialist decade precisely because family remained seemingly disconnected from the economic and political upheavals.[3] In a sense, it provided a safe refuge and a stable referent in a situation when most other referents, such as those pertaining to class, citizenship, and profession, were in a perpetual state of flux. This of course did not necessarily mean that family relations became any more loyal or loving,[4] but simply that they were experienced as more permanent than other kinds of ties. One could stop being a Soviet citizen or an engineer, but one still remained a daughter, a sister, or a wife. Aware of this persistence of familial connections in comparison with many other, more fleeting ones, Muscovites placed family in the very center of their personal narratives. While some did it explicitly (by stating, for instance, that they "have never accumulated valuables, because the main and only valuable is the family"), the majority achieved the same effect not by drawing on a self-conscious discourse of family values but by discussing their choices as first and foremost collective choices, something made by the family as a whole and with the family's collective benefit in sight. To interpret these choices as actions of independent individuals would be to miss the very point of the game, as witnessed by a quotation from Lena. Lena's "pre-perestroika" employment (in her own formulation) was as a hospital nurse, but she left it after she gave birth to her second child. She had since worked as a cleaning lady, a phone-survey interviewer, and a petty trader selling tea on the market. At the time of the interview she juggled two cleaning jobs, while her husband continued to be employed as a municipal policeman:

> Before perestroika, they [policemen] were forbidden to earn anything on the side, if only unofficially, and now they can. Now, though, there's another problem. The salary is now tiny, just kopecks really—one million.[5] My morning job right now, at the bank: I earn a million there—and then he earns a million, this is ridiculous! Our one hope, as I often joke, is retirement. He has two years left till retirement, and we are waiting for it in order to start earning. Only in our country such a thing is possible! [Laughs] To wait for your pension in order to start earning! . . . Because otherwise, it would be too bad to lose it [the pension]: I have none, and who knows what can happen, there is nothing stable in our country . . . All this could be abolished at any moment [meaning private businesses paying decent money], and in this case, at least there will be his pension, at least some kopecks, and we wouldn't like to lose that.

It is easy to see from this extract that the decisions Lena and her husband made heavily relied on each other's resources. At the time of our conversation, the family lived mostly on Lena's earning, yet did so in the hope of obtaining something Lena did not have—the security of a small but stable lifelong income in the form of her husband's pension. The resources that family members contributed to the task of collective navigation of post-Soviet economy were not limited to the economic ones. The joint stock of the family (or the family cauldron [*semeinyi kotel*], as Russians would put it, with "family" often encompassing rather distant members: great-aunts, uncles, in-laws, etc.) included all types of resources, serving as a kind of showcase for Bourdieu's types of capital. Many of these diverse resources (or assets, as Burawoy et al. [2000] call them) had been inherited from Soviet times but were put to work in the contemporary market economy. Rooms and apartments were rented out to supplement earned income, old acquaintances were mobilized in the course of job searches and information exchange, and skills and knowledge were applied both to cut expenses through self-provision and to increase earnings through secondary employment.

The creative arrangement of various resources into a patchwork enabling the survival of the household could be a one-person job, in which case the bread-winner of the family would juggle several jobs and draw heavily on network connections and other assets in an effort to balance out the demands for both stability and income. Much more frequently, however, getting by was a family matter and was treated, correspondingly, as a collective project. One family member's high earnings were matched by the retirement prospects of others; connections, access to information, or favors were reinforced by flexibility and time contributed by the retired or unemployed; pensions and special privileges associated with age or health status supplemented unstable income from moon-lighting and side jobs.[6] It was this fundamental complementarity of individual behaviors within the framework of the household that made it impossible to fully understand employment decisions unless one looked at them relationally, taking into account the distribution of roles and contributions within the cor-responding family.[7] To see how complementarity worked in practice, we can take the fairly typical case of Maria, a nurse in a municipal outpatient clinic (*poliklinika*). Discussing her work, which didn't pay well but satisfied her be-cause of working hours and convenient location, Maria said:

> In August our salary was delayed, and it was an enormous shock for me, I just couldn't understand: how is it that I am supposed to have a salary, but I don't. A month passed, then another, and I still didn't receive it. Can you believe, our tiny salaries, and they couldn't find the money to pay?! Of course, my husband is getting paid, but still, it does influence your outlook when you're not bringing anything home. My mother-in-law, her pension also helps, but still . . . I always say, we're mak-ing it just because of [my] mother-in-law, she's the one who helps us. She has the pension, plus she has discounted apartment rent. Because the full rent—it's practi-cally half my salary right there. But since she was involved with Chernobyl [she has discounted rates], it's a huge help for us. (Maria, female, 37)

The sudden arrears were evoked by Maria in the context of discussing re-gional differences in well-being, which was a topic she knew from her own ex-perience: her sister lived with family in a provincial town in Central Russia, in an area heavily affected by non-payments. The theme of arrears automatically triggered recollection of the security mechanisms that Maria had in place and that had managed to soften the blow of the non-payments in her particular case. Unlike her relatives who were confined to a much narrower job market, and hence had a lesser chance to "diversify" the household portfolio of eco-nomic activities,[8] Maria was lucky to have family members whose contribu-tions complemented one another: her salary and her husband's were relatively modest (about seventy dollars a month each), but hers provided her with some private practice in the evenings and opportunities of discounted vacation pack-ages, while her husband's job as a security guard in a private firm gave him enough free time to do odd jobs and to work around the house and on his sister's dacha. Both Maria and her husband have had times when they had to count on the other's salary because of arrears; as an emergency option, they sometimes borrowed money from the husband's mother who lived with them and made the household eligible for reduced accommodation and utilities rates.

The web of interconnections and mutual reliance had both enabling and inhibiting aspects. For one, the expectation that all family members, in one way or another, would contribute to the well-being of the family could be a heavy burden, especially if one of the members felt unable or unwilling to participate in this reciprocal exchange. It created grounds for tensions and conflicts around the distribution of activities, and justified potentially unrealistic expectations of personal sacrifices in the interests of the household's collective well-being. As a result, while it gave family members some measure of protection against the unpredictability of the job market and the economy at large, it also made it difficult to explore available options, since every change in the status quo jeopardized the delicate balance of mutual favors. In Maria's case, her thoughts of changing occupation were hampered by the fact that a new job could mean that the duty of caring for their teenage daughter would fall fully on the shoulders of her mother-in-law, something that Maria feared could be interpreted as an effort on her part to get rid of her share of household responsibilities. This is not to say that change was impossible, but rather that, in contemplating its possibility, people often had to take into account not only the direct pluses and minuses of available options but also how they would factor into the patchwork of the collective household economy.

My conversation with Maria offered yet another insight into the importance of the family and its implication in the project of navigating the post-socialist economy, one having to do with generational and gender roles. While her mother-in-law received credit for helping the family get along financially, Maria's recognition of the older woman's contribution did not end there. Apart from supporting the family with her pension and privileges, Maria's mother-in-law also contributed another much-valued resource—her experience in making ends meet in dire financial circumstances. This skill, considered to be an important asset of any Russian homemaker, was essential for families with restricted incomes, and the process of transmission of the everyday art of getting by bound together older and younger female (and due to the gendered division of labor, almost exclusively female) members of the household. In addition, this practice also helped normalize the situation by calling to mind predicaments that preceding generations had dealt with. Maria continues:

> My mother-in-law taught me a great deal about how to live . . . Things like, say, storing products . . . not stocking whatever, but how to buy something useful, economical. Not like I tend to buy, something that gets eaten in just one day, and then you have to go to the market again. But the real stuff, products you can cook different things out of . . . She taught me. Of course, she always says, we lived through war, and there was no money, and later on too, they lived on a small salary. So they always had to manage somehow.

The capacity of the older generation to transmit the "know-how" of decent poverty represented an important cultural resource, which somewhat compensated for what has been described as a major loss experienced by the "grandparent generation" during the years of transformation (Nikolaev 2000). Grandparents' household responsibilities during the late socialist deficits included the purchase of daily necessities, such as meat and dairy, which required a considerable time investment and was thus delegated to the non-working pensioners. In the late 1990s, when consumption required greater investments of money than of time, many seniors felt that their usefulness for the family had decreased, and ascribed all the greater importance to the resources they still possessed.

In the context of unsettlement of many "public" identities connected to professional and public spheres, it is hard to overestimate the importance of the idealized discourse of family. But different family members had access to different resources for self-reinvention through family role. While seniors and women had to bear the heaviest weight of expectations as far as their contributions (and sacrifices) to domestic well-being were concerned, they also had a more immediate access to this alternative source of meaning and self-respect. The men's situation, on the other hand, was more ambiguous. If they were successful and gainfully employed, their financial contribution entitled them to "have it all," that is, to enjoy professional fulfillment even as they maintained the status of provider for a family (or, as in the example below, several families). But in cases of unemployment, payment arrears, or low pay (in short, exactly in those cases when the domain of the family became the last resort for developing a meaningful identity), only a select few were sufficiently competent to contribute to family stability in other ways. The weight of what Ashwin and Lytkina (2004) call "domestic marginalization" was thus particularly heavy exactly for those men who had little access to meaningful identities outside of home.

It is hardly surprising that low-income households found themselves bound together by the idealized discourse of the family in a system of mutual support and reciprocal exchange. But those whose financial situation was more comfortable did not disconnect themselves from close familial ties either. On the contrary, they typically perceived it to be their duty to support as many of their less fortunate kin as possible, to the extent that it became a measure of one's moral worth:

> Clearly, certain professions just found themselves on the sidelines. Heavy equipment manufacturing, engineers—there is just no demand for them . . . And it is a tragedy, because oftentimes, these people were the breadwinners for the family. Say, me, because today I have five dependents. That is to say, in my circle, those who couldn't find themselves in this life . . . my wife's father, her mother (she has health problems). I mean, my mother-in-law, she's not very healthy so she will slowly turn into a dependent. My mother is retired, and she was a teacher. Consequently, she has a pension that's up to six months in arrears. Plus I have a wife and a child. So you have five people right there. And I, so to say, feed them, and provide them with some level of well-being. It's my job to provide for them. (Anton, male, 32)

Six months later, during a repeat interview, Anton spontaneously returned to the topic, this time widening the circle of his dependents to include his father, his best friend, whom he consistently provided with employment leads and work on commission, as well as "the second circle"—a more remote group of (as he put it) "approximately thirty people who know they can count on me with work, money, and anything else I can do for them." The emphasis he placed on his role in extending support to less fortunate kin and friends is particularly significant given his identification with the postsocialist economy, which, as he himself has pointed out, had caused these cases of downward mobility. Redistributing resources and funds he obtained from his professional activity among the members of his extended family, Anton has preserved the legitimacy of his involvement with the market despite his recognition of the harsh implications its advent has had for the majority of the population. Family in this context served as a moral justification and legitimation of the individual's economic behavior.

It should be clear that, while family relations and kinship identities were experienced as tokens of stability in an uncertain context, they were not at all disconnected from the larger political and economic upheavals. If anything, awareness of the centrality of the family often derived from the collective experience of navigating the 1990s, and the importance of kinship ties was narratively demonstrated by setting them against the background of what they were supposed to help one overcome. This mutual constitution of hardships and the family is evident in a statement made by Natalia Konstantinovna during a conversation in her two-bedroom apartment, which on that Sunday morning was full of people: her husband was busy in the kitchen, her daughter was tending to her baby son in an adjacent room, and the son-in-law was running errands in the neighborhood, periodically dropping by to pick up or drop off bags and papers and to check up on his son, his brief arrivals always greeted with enthusiastic barking of the family dog. "If there is no family, it's impossible to survive," she said:

> Take our situation: our grandson was born. Sveta, my daughter, used to have an income, but now that's it. So what do we have? The monthly benefit for a newborn is fifty-eight rubles,[9] let everyone hear this! Another two hundred and fifty was paid by Luzhkov,[10] as a one-time child payment. Her company was paying her during the first six months, and now that's over. And her husband [lowering her voice to make sure her son-in-law does not hear], he used to earn the equivalent of three hundred dollars, and now they are still paying the same sum in rubles, but now [after the crisis] it is worth a third of what it used to be.[11] So how is anyone supposed to make it? Only as a large family, helping one another. In some ways, his [the son-in-law's] mother helps out, she lives in Leningrad [*sic*], rents out an apartment and sends some money here. And all of us, we're spreading ourselves to the maximum. And otherwise I can't even imagine, say, Sveta asks me often, "Mom, how could single mothers survive before? All alone, just like this?" And indeed, it is impossible.

Natalia Konstantinovna's account makes another case for the importance of complementarity in distribution of roles and responsibilities within the family.

It also suggests an answer to the puzzling finding made by Braithwaite et al. (2000) regarding surprisingly high poverty rates among single-person Russian households in the 1990s.[12] Its general message, however, may be interpreted in two ways. On one level, it is a testimony to the pivotal role of the family in general, and a moral tale of the achievements of Natalia Konstantinovna's family in particular. On another level, it is not a story about family at all, but one about the economic pressures and injustices making independent existence practically unthinkable. The two themes merge together and feed upon one another, weaving an image of the family as simultaneously a refuge from and an integral part of postsocialist discontents.

Consumption—Another Face of Politics

If family was seen as both entangled with and differentiated from the political developments of the day, consumption was interpreted as essentially just another face of politics. The tendency to conflate consumption and politics, a habit older than the postsocialist era, can be traced to experiences under the socialist economy when, as Caroline Humphrey notes, "perhaps only a professional economist could separate out such an object as 'the Soviet economy.' For everyone inside, it was experienced as a *political economy,* that is, imbued at every point with politics and ideology" (Humphrey 1995, 46; italics in the original). Throughout the 1980s and 1990s political changes were invariably accompanied by changes in consumption, with the latter often providing grounds for criticism or evaluation of the political course.[13] Consumer experiences of the late 1980s and early 1990s, inseparable from memories of shortages and distributory policy measures such as coupons, closed enterprise sales, and "consumer cards" (*vizitnye kartochki pokupatelia*),[14] resurfaced in interviews on a regular basis. Such memories were particularly vivid among women, who were more prominently involved in provisioning the household.[15] Often, one probing question about the felt effects of the transformation sufficed to provoke a virtual outpouring of consumer memories, as was the case with Kseniia Anatolievna, a pleasant forty-three-year-old woman who spent twenty years working in a watch factory before she left the badly paying job in order to work part-time, first as a saleswoman at an open-air market and then as a cleaning lady. Most of her time she spent looking after her two school-aged sons and taking care of the house, while her husband, who worked in a construction brigade, was the main breadwinner for the family. My conversation with Kseniia Anatolievna took place in her neat living-room furnished with newly purchased armchairs and a sofa. The first several minutes of the conversation were relatively unanimated, until we unwittingly hit a virtual gold mine by opening up the issue of consumption:

> AUTHOR: I want to ask about changes in the big politics, how did they reflect upon your life, if they did at all?
> KA: Politics is politics, when a government changes . . . as they say, the new broom sweeps differently, right? So a government changes—it means new laws, some-

thing else changing here and there, new regulations . . . [pause] In 1990, you were in
school still, so you probably don't remember . . . There were these personal cards that
we had to use when shopping . . .

AUTHOR: Why, I remember, I even still have mine somewhere.

KA: You do? Well, then you know what I'm talking about. We would go to shop and
we'd stand in line for God knows how long—for hours. Even back when I worked at
the factory. We had a very nice supervisor, Masha. So we would be like, "Masha, this
and that is on sale in the store,"—"Well, OK, go get in line, then."[16] And what could
you do? You had to feed the family somehow. . . .

AUTHOR: So speaking of changes, do you remember how they started? Did you
notice them?

KA: The political ones? Starting from 1991 the price increases started. So the most
[central] one was 1991. Which was an insane year (*beshenyi god*) when we chased
and hunted for children's clothes, for whatever else. At work we got coupons for
Children's World[17] and we stood in line forever, almost for an entire night. At some
point, before the New Year, we had this coupon . . . So on January 1, or around then
anyway, it was an entire night, I mean, at five in the morning they would drive us
there in a car so that we could get in line before the store opened, before eight AM,
in order to get in and buy something . . . I knew I needed it, I had to dress two children, so I arrived, I stood there, I warmed myself at the bonfire . . . Afterward, things
started getting easier. But 1991 I remember really well. Later, things started to appear in stores, and you could buy something much easier. And I know because . . . if
I'm not mistaken, we even have some boots that I bought back then, ten years ahead
of time. Yes, size thirty-seven, I remember I bought them, I just don't know if I still
have them or we gave them away. Because I bought them for my son. And he grew
up, he looked at them and said, "Mom, are you kidding? I won't wear these." Whereas
before, we chased them, we grabbed everything we could for as long as the money
lasted. Everything. Now, there is everything in the stores, and there's no reason to
buy ahead of time. But back then, I used to buy five, two, several years ahead all the
time. By size. Let's say, he [the son] was size fifteen, and I could buy size seventeen,
or twenty. Just because we had no idea what was coming, and right now, everything
is right there in the stores, you can suit yourself . . .

The talk about the stores did not end there. Kseniia Anatolievna repeatedly returned to the topic with the same verbosity, adding new details to the
picture:

> Awful, awful. It was something horrendous, people grabbed on to anything, liter-
> ally anything. Everything, all the goods, all the food, I mean, I am talking to you
> now, and in my eyes I have this vision of Children's World. When we would run up
> and down every floor, holding places in lines, trading: you stand in this line, and I'll
> stand in that one, and then you'll come to me, and I'll come take your place in yours.
> And I had two children, I had to make sure to get everything in two copies, and to
> have money for both . . . It was scary. I wouldn't want our children to see this.

The centrality that the imagery of consumption seemed to hold in the
people's memories of the 1980s can be partly explained by the fact that, during
the years of late socialism and in the early 1990s, obtaining goods and products for the household was a major undertaking which, in terms of the amount

of time and efforts it required, could be effectively compared to a second job (Nikolaev 2000). Yet the consistent pattern of evocation and the pleasure many clearly derived from contrasting their own behavior during shortages with their later shopping experiences appeared to have a deeper root. Recollecting the absurd and comical elements of the shopping experience of the late 1980s–early 1990s (such as the boots bought ten years ahead of time, or soap and shampoo purchased in bulk and still lingering in some dusty drawer in the house) enabled people to narratively put the experiences they were retelling past themselves, into the safe category of "closed chapters" in their lives, thus emphasizing a sense of personal progression and transcendence of the past. This sensibility became especially apparent precisely when the social and economic circumstances seemed to challenge it. For example, when the economic breakdown of August 1998 triggered price growth and pushed many Russians to relive the impetus toward stockpiling and hoarding, many lamented it as an unfortunate return to the past:

> We all thought that we had left at least that particular aspect in our past. Life started to more or less get going, people could go about their business and buy things little by little, as the need arose. There was no paranoia that I have to run, grab, buy whatever just for the sake of buying. But, as it turns out, in our country you can't relax like this, because everything can come back in a matter of days ... (Sasha, male, 30)

Yet, common as it was, the tendency to posit the "new" pattern of more available but less affordable goods as superior to the "old" system of distributive economy was not universal. Other people evoked a similar juxtaposition but were more ambivalent, or sometimes outright critical, in their evaluations of the new consumption regime:

> Indeed, we were attracted by it, yes, democracy and such, some power, and foreign goods as well, we were lured by all this. So before, we used to stand in lines for shoes, boots, and such, there were lists and you had to sign up for things, and now—it's help yourself, you can go ahead and buy anything. But where's the money for it? (Maria, female, 37)

Regardless of the tone of the comments, however, the entanglement of the political and the economic, even their indistinguishability, was apparent throughout. The advent of democracy was entwined in Maria's eyes with the arrival of abundant foreign goods, just as the rise of Yeltsin's government was inseparable for Kseniia Anatolievna from the introduction of ration cards. Following this logic of equating politics and consumption, political statements in Russian narratives often oscillated between political terminology and purely practical consumer judgments. Here is the response that a question about the most important periods of the 1990s evoked in Andrei, a thirty-eight-year-old insurance manager and a proud father of three:

> I guess, when cooperatives started to multiply, when Uncle Misha [Mikhail Gorbachev] and Raisa [Gorbacheva] started hacking the window through to Europe,

with all of the consequences that followed,[18] with the indulgence of commerce, among all other things . . . When our eyes finally opened: Holy Moly, these nasty capitalists are not so nasty after all. This, of course, came little by little. When the goods and the groceries suddenly poured in, the foreign ones, just purely on the everyday level (*na bytovom urovne*).

AUTHOR: What do you mean, the everyday level?

ANDREI: I mean, it is one thing to grasp something in your mind, and quite another to see its realization in practice with your very own eyes. In kiosks, on the markets, on TV . . . It's a particular market style, when everything before was so gray, gray, gray . . . And suddenly it all became so interesting!

Yet, even if the introduction of the market involved an upsurge in goods and a general move toward a "more interesting" market, it did not ensure everyone her piece of the postsocialist pie. As Andrei himself readily admitted, making ends meet was still a project that required planning and discipline, especially in the period immediately following the economic crisis, which triggered a rise of prices for practically all categories of products:

> All of these state coups, defaults, and crises, they impact me only in terms of direct effects. Me, my wife who has to scrimp and save, because my salary has lost its value five-fold [*sic*]. So if before we used to buy expensive sausage, yogurts, Snickers, all that stuff, now—that's it. I mean, we've had enough of that stuff to grow sick of it by now, but there was no problem in buying it. And now my team eats sausage, let's say [pause] sometimes, there can be a situation when there is no sausage for three–four days. Other times there's no cheese. Overall, my homemakers (*khoziaiki*) stint themselves, and I leave myself less money for my personal use as well.

There were thus two contradictory aspects to consumption. On the one hand, it became associated with abundance, in contrast to the scarcity which Muscovites remembered from the times of late socialism. On the other hand, despite the wide array of products and services available in a market economy, the choice among them was still limited. Partly this reflected the material circumstances of particular individuals and their households, which forced them to limit their purchases to a small range of basic necessities, to consume primarily cheaper, Russian-made goods, or resort to differential consumption, in the course of which the needs of some members of the household (usually children or the sick) were prioritized over the needs of others. Even these conditions, however, did not bring consumers out of a market economy context, because the choice between Russian and foreign or cheaper and more expensive brands and products was only possible when all varieties were abundantly represented. In addition, hardly anyone relied exclusively on a set repertoire of the plain and the cheap. Temporary bouts of good financial fortune or mere paydays were seen as sufficient excuses to indulge oneself in one way or another, even if only by purchasing previously unaffordable ice cream.

Other, non-material factors contributed to the limitations on involvement with the consumer economy of postsocialism and shaped each consumer's outlook. Among these were deficits that were not material but "symbolic," such as the absence of skills and cognitive categories necessary to find one's place in the newly available consumer paradise (Oushakine 2000b). In addition, people's attitudes toward the morality of market and trade themselves were ambivalent in more than just one way.[19] For many, especially those who themselves had little personal contact with the sphere of retail and with those working there, the business of trading fell into the shady area of not completely wrong, and yet not fully legitimate. The main problem here seems to be rooted in the idea of nonproductive labor, which clashed with the ideals and perceptions actively cultivated during the years of socialism. Oftentimes, this distinction found expression in the juxtaposition of traders who produced their own goods and those who brought them in wholesale. And since it is the latter who tend to be outsiders in the community, disapproval of trading easily took on nationalist or racist overtones:

> VERA VLADIMIROVNA: These Chinese, in the midst of all our mess, when no one is watching, they just keep on coming [into Russia]. I'm not a nationalist or anything, all people are good for me. But what's been going on in our markets—this is just some kind of mockery of us Muscovites. I feel humiliated. When I go to the market to buy apples or potatoes, let's say, and I feel that I am being cheated, deceived, that scales are wrong, that they are just openly mocking me. Or I go to the market to buy shoes for my son, and I know that they don't cost what I'm charged, that I'm being deceived. But I can't resist, because I do need to buy something. Or take Luzhkov, people say he sold the Moscow markets for how many years?[20]
> AUTHOR: Luzhkov sold markets?
> VV: He did, to these, to the Azerbaijani diaspora or whoever they are. For I don't know how long, I think fifty years or so.
> AUTHOR: This is quite amazing. Where did you read this?
> VV: I don't remember, but it's widely known that he did . . . And again, supposedly it was for our benefit. But how can we benefit if they don't produce anything, they just trade the things they did not produce. And at the same time, I can see how the old ladies are being chased away by the police, those who are selling the produce that they themselves, perhaps, have grown. And to compare it with the way the police treat these [Azeri] traders. (Vera Vladimirovna, female, 43)

Vera Vladimirovna's narrative, fairly common for Muscovite discourse on markets,[21] exemplifies two more themes distinguished by social scientists in their research into early post-Soviet attitudes toward trade and consumption: suspicion toward "trading minorities" and a persistent sense of being cheated or deceived (Humphrey 1995; Lemon 2000). Roots of these attitudes can be traced back to socialism: ethnic tensions were closely connected to consumption as "locals" and "outsiders" competed for scarce resources (Verdery 1993; Nikolaev 2000), while the motive of deceit was related to the divergence between the propaganda images of a socialist consumer paradise and the far less attractive reality (Humphrey 1995). Their postsocialist forms, however, were exacerbated by the breakdown of state infrastructure and the corresponding growth of regionalism, which had reached its peak in the late 1990s, as well as the somewhat suspicious attitude to "abroad," both East and West, along with everything that came from there (Humphrey 1999). The diminishing faith in the efficiency and integrity of the agents responsible for organizing and controlling the field of consumption (as was demonstrated in Vera Vladimirovna's comments regarding police and the mayor) compounded these doubts even further.

Consumption Safari

An ethnographic analysis of the ways in which the post-Soviet consumers talked about and interacted with their purchases in the late 1990s speaks volumes about the lack of public faith in the effectiveness of regulating mechanisms in the sphere of consumption. In this crisis-induced vacuum of authority, individuals implemented complex arrangements in order to safeguard their consumer behavior from the multiple dangers associated with the postsocialist marketplace. Perplexed and somewhat disoriented by the new consumer abundance, they wanted to keep on their guard so as not to end up with an inferior product. They resorted to multiple strategies in order to achieve this goal, from meticulously inspecting the packaging, looking for smeared paint, uneven lines, and other indicators of a phony product, to grilling the salesperson regarding the location of all sites involved in manufacturing the product, from design to assembly to packaging. With home electronics and appliances, an elaborate producer hierarchy evolved that aimed to determine their value. The ranking had to do with the site of assembly and was remarkably uniformly accepted across consumers and salespeople. A home appliance salesman summarized it for me: "The highest ranking is the 'white' assembly (Europe or America), the second is 'yellow' assembly (Asia), and the lowest is our own Russian one. As for Japan," he added with some bitterness, "it's the highest of all, but we've known for a long time that things assembled there do not get here."[22]

Manufacturers and salespeople were not excluded from this social context of negotiating authenticity; on the contrary, they were heavily invested in it as a way of enhancing product appeal. Thus I witnessed a shop assistant recommending a Moulinex food processor to her customer not on the grounds of its superior quality, but because it was assembled in Poland, while an almost identical Braun product next door was allegedly assembled in Indonesia and only packaged in Eastern Europe. Similarly, producers of Borzhomi mineral water and Dovgan vodka advertised by emphasizing the uniqueness of the product and its multiple layers of fraud protection (a custom-shaped bottle in the former case and a holographic and, supposedly, uncounterfeitable seal of quality in the latter). Others were more blatant; take, for example, the producers of the No Deceit (*Bez obmana*) brand of dumplings, who advertised in the winter of 1999 on the Moscow subway. The poster featured a pack of dumplings with their ingredients displayed in front. The slogan proclaimed, "We guarantee the meat," addressing a deep-seated conviction among many consumers that manufacturers routinely replaced minced meat in dumplings and sausages with bread or, in more cynical versions, toilet paper (ironically, and probably by an artist's oversight, it was exactly meat that was absent on the colorful ingredient display up front).

The caution that went into making consumer choices applied not only to the product quality, but also to the place of purchase. When buying a large appliance, several or all family members discussed the potential sources for several weeks, drawing into discussion friends and acquaintances and weighing out comparative advantages of smaller shops, large shopping centers, specialized electronic stores, and open-air consumer markets. In this process, stories and personal experiences triggered one another, so that by the end of the discussion one was well informed not only about all instances of similar purchases made by the conversation's participants, but also about the experiences of their colleagues, neighbors, friends, and relatives. Stories about fraudulent items or faulty service encountered by the storyteller or (more frequently) by someone from his network of acquaintances typically enjoyed a far wider currency than the more boring cases of successful purchases. While the former were seen as reflecting a wider condition of the retail system, the latter were not.

Apart from the advice from the network of one's acquaintances, it was common to draw on print media from the mushrooming genre of consumer advice. Sometimes distributed free of charge, other times sold on an equal footing with other magazines and journals, these publications provided comparative information on brands and services and informed readers about the new trends on the market. But they did more than that. As a rule, such editions (*Spros, Klient, Tovary i Tseny,* or the daily TV program *Vprok*) also discussed instances of deceit and fraud, and provided the public with examples of an appropriate response.[23] Picked up from the media or from personal exchanges, these tales of deceit carried warnings about the potential risks of the purchase, and at the same time made the entire process look like something of a safari, with the same sense of achievement, adventure, and pride in outsmarting rivals and obtaining the trophy. Needless to say, the risk was perceived to be proportional to the amount of money spent, as was the emotional reward of a successful purchase.

Depending upon the venue selected for the purchase, the transportation of the household durable frequently turned into yet another adventure. While specialized stores usually included the transportation and installation of the appliance as a part of the deal, the open-air markets, which were favored by many because of their lower prices, usually did not offer such options.[24] It was for this reason that the anthropologist Melissa Caldwell labeled Sundays in Moscow "Take Your Favorite Large Appliance for a Ride on the Metro Day."[25] Sizeable containers with washing machines, dishwashers, microwaves, and even refrigerators could often be seen on the subway, to the great annoyance of the other passengers, especially on the metro lines hosting the major markets, such as

Gorbushka, Luzhniki, and VDNKh.[26] Occasionally, the arguments that erupted among the fellow-travelers as a result of the inconvenience of traveling among boxes with goods grew rather heated, underscoring the risky and adventuresome character of the enterprise and constructing the consumer as the active agent confronting and mastering an unfavorable circumstance.

After the sought-for object was delivered and installed, the entire family would gather around to adore its workings. For a while, the new appliance was actively discussed and demonstrated to guests, and, at least for the first several weeks, the fact of purchase officially fell under the category of "news." It was among the first things mentioned as a response to the general inquiries about the well-being of the family, and during visits it would become one of the centerpieces in the excursion around the apartment. Oftentimes it was the guest who paid attention to the novelty first, and her question would spur a detailed purchase narrative on the part of the owners. The attention of the guest was warranted, since these pieces of modern equipment tended to dramatically stand out in the otherwise fairly modest layout of the apartment. The "standing out" was not only aesthetic, but also physical. In many apartments the kitchens were too small to house two refrigerators, and it was not uncommon for an ultra-modern fridge or, alternatively, its predecessor, to stand in the corridor or in a living room, decorating the interior and being among the first objects seen by a visitor.

When used, the newly purchased commodity received reverence and care that the other household items did not enjoy. It was washed and cleaned more systematically and diligently than the rest and was spared in all possible ways. However, while it was clearly the new appliance that truly ruled the house, the old household item it replaced was not at all immediately forsaken. On the contrary, the relatively high occurrence of ownership of multiple durable goods of the same category in Russia was to a great extent explained by the reluctance of the owners, especially those belonging to the generation of Nikolai's parents, to part with durables that have served their term.[27] Just as they were usually at a loss when asked to explain their decision to purchase a new expensive gadget, my interlocutors had trouble explaining their decision to preserve old possessions. Typically, a new gadget was purchased not because the needs of the household had changed or because the old model became unsatisfactory, but merely because the household had accumulated a sufficient disposable sum of money. Similarly, the usefulness of the old model was defended in very vague terms. While the hypothetical "case of fire emergency" was cited frequently, the exact nature of this possible threat was not only unclear but also irrelevant to the speakers, who tended to answer further inquiries with an evasive "who knows what [may happen]" (*malo li chto*). In the meantime, since in most cases the actual needs of the household were not intensive enough to fully utilize several refrigerators, the old devices were often exiled onto the balcony, handed down to relatives, or sent to the dacha (summer cabin) where they might or might not get a second life. When kept in the apartment, they could be moved out of the kitchen or be used as a storage space, a cupboard, a shelf, or a TV or microwave stand, in which case they were often draped so that their function would not be immediately obvious; the most unorthodox storage strategy I encountered was mounting an old fridge on top of a large maplewood wardrobe in the bedroom.

Durables Old and New

Klara, a forty-five-year-old woman who works as a clerk in a municipal health clinic, lived with her ailing mother in a two-room apartment in northeast Moscow. Klara's household was one of the seventeen in my sample that, without considering themselves particularly affluent, owned multiple items of large household equipment, such as refrigerators, TV sets, or washing machines. Klara's fifty-square-foot kitchen offered a perfect example of the same attachment to both the old and the new that was exemplified by Nikolai's parents. The kitchen accommodated one tall modern fridge equipped with a no-frost system, and an older and somewhat smaller model. The latter had become obsolete a year and a half prior, when its replacement was purchased, but it was still kept in the apartment to be used in the hypothetical "case of fire emergency." At the time of the interview the old fridge stood unplugged and half-opened.

> KLARA: . . . [about the old refrigerator] And we even fixed this old one, spent so much money on it! So it works fine. And it runs like a beast, like a tractor, you hear it from anywhere in the apartment [laughs]. When it turns off, everything on it jumps, that's how strong its engine is. But we decided not to sell it. I mean, it's a good one, it's not bad. I use it as a kitchen cabinet [opens the fridge to demonstrate]. My pots and pans are in there. Pots, glass jars, all these things. Plus, I can turn it on at any moment. For instance, I may turn this one off [points to the new one], and turn the other one on. I haven't had to, but I could, because it's completely functional. And this one [the new one] could just stay around, so I could clean it. Cleaning is good, so I guess on the First of May . . . I decided to clean it for the May holidays . . .

While the old refrigerator had accompanied Klara for more than a decade, the purchase story of the new one reflects the contingencies of the more recent period. It was acquired due to what Klara characterized as "enforced savings"— two years worth of pension arrears, paid to her and her mother in one installment in 1997. Yet, while in this respect the new fridge symbolized the "disorder" of the 1990s, it also stood for the period's accomplishments. Further, Klara recurrently emphasized the surprising ease with which she bought it: "Still, it's pleasant (*vse-taki priiatno*). In the old times it would take months, and here—I just made a phone call, and they delivered and installed it the same day."

The juxtaposition of the "old" and the "new" consumer experiences, widely characteristic of postsocialist narratives of consumption, resurfaces here to serve a double purpose. On the one hand, the noticeable pleasure with which people remembered their stressful consumer experiences, together with the feel-ings of powerlessness and deprivation associated with the shortage economy, indicated an effort to articulate a sense of distinction and personal progression. A new consumer object can be interpreted in this context as further evidence that, if not their country, at least the speakers themselves were achieving some proximity to the living standards enjoyed in the developed capitalist countries.[28] In this respect, the object was constructed as a marker of personal advancement: it allowed individuals to think of themselves as belonging to a category of people who successfully took advantage of the changing economic and consumer climate in the country. Liudmila Romanovna, a forty-nine-year-old accountant, built her purchase narrative precisely on this theme:

> . . . Our old fridge was all right, but you know these old fridges—they need defrosting, and I just felt I was tired of that. I figured, I work, Gennadii [her husband] works, it's time we started living, you know what I mean? See, ever since our daughters were born, we've been slaving away making ends meet, and we've spent most of our lives doing that. It's time to start spending money on ourselves already. I figure—I deserve a high-quality thing, don't I?

New and expensive consumer goods served as embodiments of labor and achievement under the new regime regardless of whether they coexisted with their predecessors, but the frequency with which these two categories of objects were juxtaposed can reveal a great deal about narrative construction of postsocialist identities. It may be instructive at this point to remember the conflation between consumption and political regimes and to reflect upon its significance. In her work on the aesthetics of a Soviet apartment, Svetlana Boym quotes Mandelstam's autobiographical novella *The Egyptian Stamp*, written in 1928, to argue that in the times of rapid social change, "the fate of the things is parallel to the fate of persons" (Boym 1994, 159). In saying this, Boym suggests that memories of the past are intertwined with memories of consumer objects obtained during that period, and it is not uncommon for the latter to function as metonymic representation of the distant and long-gone experiences. With the benefit of hindsight, it appears that the capacity of objects to represent stages of one's life is only enhanced when the said stages are perceived to be as irretrievably gone and as exotic by today's standard as the period of late socialism:

> You know, the way we lived before, went to work, stood in lines . . . Of course there were less problems in many ways, but then again, it was impossible to buy anything. For anything you needed, you had to queue forever, and then get on the roster, and then sign in daily, or have a grandfather who was disabled in action in World War II . . . The old TV set we have [points in its direction]—I could only get it through my grandfather, same with the fridge, I could only obtain it through him. And even then, we had to wait about a year for the postcard to come in the mail telling us that our turn had come. So consider it our luck—if I didn't have a grandfather like this, what would we do? Now even the thought of this seems ridiculous. You can just go and buy any fridge, any car you like—cheaper, more expensive, whatever your soul desires. You do have to save for a while, but then you're free to get whatever you want. (Lena, female, 37)

It would be a mistake to think that, in remembering the strained conditions under which particular objects had been obtained under socialism, the sole desire of the post-Soviet consumers was to disavow their past experiences and to leave them behind. To the contrary, Boym's observations on Mandelstam suggest that remembrance of past possessions is inevitably imbued with nostalgic value insofar as these possessions are identified as representative of their owner's life stages. Moreover, one would be warranted to move beyond nostalgia and to see the old objects as instruments through which an individual's past may be reinterpreted and imbued with value. When people refused to dispose of their old possessions and insisted on their usefulness (which was particularly characteristic of those over forty), this preservation of the fragments of the "old order," along with the acquisition of new consumer items, appeared to be a means of symbolically breaching the gap between the socialist past and the postsocialist present on the level of everyday practice. In what was commonly considered to be the time of crisis, not least an "identity crisis,"[29] when a common complaint of entire generations was that they had been "thrown into the dustbin of history," this demonstrative attachment to the objects that were people's inanimate companions through the trials and tribulations of socialism acquired almost moral overtones.

By stating their attachment to old household appliances acquired in a laborious and time-consuming manner under the socialist distributive economy, people did not necessarily justify this economic system *in toto*. Rather, they preserved the signs of their own private accomplishments under this economy and endowed them with value and meaning. Liudmila Romanovna's narrative continued:

> ... I will never forget how I bought beds for my two daughters, what an epic it was! I ordered them in a workshop on Polezhaevskaia, and they didn't keep manufactured items on their premises at those times. And the day they called us to pick them up, Gennadii was at work, I still remember it. So, I rushed there, they brought out these beds, I hailed some truck and talked the driver into helping me to unload these beds in front of the house. He even helped me carry one mattress up, in the course of which I was overcome with fear that someone could be filching the other mattress we left in the yard. And then I threw myself on some man who was passing by, begging him to help me with the rest, and I was running in front of him, holding doors. [Laughs] *And how could you suppose I can ever part with these beds now?* After the girls moved out, I put the frames together, and made myself a queen bed out of them ... [Italics added]

Hence, the preservation of an old item or, as Russians sometimes refer to it, "its transfer to retirement" (*staryi ushel na pensiiu*) gained a meaning of preservation of one's past, indicating a reluctance to acknowledge it as useless and outdated. This emphatic unwillingness to part with old household possessions was reflected in rhetoric, for these items were often referred to as "veterans" or "old friends" not only in daily conversations, but even on the pages of consumer magazines.[30] Thus, when combined with the interest in acquiring new items, this consumer orientation filled consumer goods with a surplus meaning that transcended the ones examined by Baudrillard (1996) or Bourdieu (1984). Apart from functioning merely as a means of mapping oneself onto the contemporary economic and cultural field, it provided a way of articulating one's position vis-à-vis the succession of political regimes, inscribing one's past and present into a coherent narrative and thus creating a meaningful story of one's life.

What makes this strategy interesting is that, in the course of manipulating old and new possessions (both physically and narratively), the consumers used them at the same time to voice their discontent (as when they bemoaned the constraints and difficulties of being a consumer in both the "new" and the "old" Russian economy) and to manage their predicament by turning the old and new consumer objects into tools of their own kind of identity play. In other words, articulations of crisis functioned simultaneously as instruments through which this crisis was managed and navigated.

Consumption and Self-Protection, or a Crash Course in Being Ready for Everything

The dual character of the Muscovites' actions—as a way of both articulating and managing their predicament—becomes even more evident when one looks beyond affirmations of identity into other politicized forms of everyday practice. To speak of the politicization of everyday life may seem unwarranted for a period when the majority of the population professed to have little or no interest in politics.[31] Yet no matter how little or how much people would admit to caring about politics (which, incidentally, can be interpreted as a political statement either way), their narratives testified that they considered the processes impacting their everyday lives to be fundamentally political, in that they were seen as driven by political actors and serving political interests. But "political" has to be taken in a very narrow sense here. Price changes, escalating inflation, changes in the labor market, growing social differentiation, the instability of the national currency—all these and many other factors were typically interpreted and talked about not as products of complex multidimensional processes, but as results of the subversive and self-interested actions of political elites:

> This whole situation [the currency devaluation of August 1998] has ruined our financial base somewhat, but we're already used to that. It happened before—one, two years ago, when the dollar rate suddenly spiked. It's the same thing . . . They won't allow people to develop sustainably. As soon as people feel they've accumulated something, they are debased. That's our state policy . . . They are turning people into automatons, automatons fixated on survival. (Alexei Ivanovich, male, 46)

In the opposition between *us* and *them,* each side was ascribed its own motives, interests, and strategies of action. While those in power (*vlasti*) were commonly depicted as exclusively interested in pillaging the country of its riches (including appropriating the citizens' savings), the people (*narod*), with whom the speakers invariably identified, could respond by resorting to tax evasion, double-dealing, and other forms of behavior characterized by Scott (1985) as the "weapons of the weak." Consumption and daily life were perceived as deeply embedded in this kind of struggle:

> LENA: So many times they tried to bring us to our knees, and we got up. We have to get up again. Even now, these prices, they keep rising. For as long as I can remember, prices always rose around the holidays; I guess they think that it's a good chance to squeeze the last drop out of the people (*vytashchit' poslednee iz naroda*). Elsewhere holidays mean sales, but not here. Ah! Is this normal: eggs used to cost six rubles, and now they're eighteen!? What happened, I wonder, did the Soviet [*sic*] hens start laying their eggs in hard currency?! [Laughs.]
> AUTHOR: So why would you say this is happening?
> LENA: Well, it's someone up there, I guess. One store manager couldn't come up with that, not on the scale of the entire country, or all of Moscow. No, it's someone higher up. Using any means to pump money out of people (*vykachat' liubymi putiami iz liudei den'gi*). Take my word—everything will start getting more expensive . . . (Lena, female, 37)

Such personalized perceptions of the confrontation between the state and the people gave Muscovites a sense that they needed to be permanently prepared to ward off the state's encroachments. This quest for securing oneself had both a practical and a moral aspect. On the practical side, it offered people a glimmer of hope that they might achieve permanence and stability in their personal circumstances despite the erratic environment. Alexei Ivanovich's comment above hinted at the moral significance of this effort. Since the state was accused not only of impoverishing its subjects but also of dehumanizing them through this impoverishment, the moral economy of the subjects' response implied that, in resisting the systemic pressures, they preserved not only their material well-being, but also their human dignity:

> All these price hikes, if you look into it, you understand that it's completely artificial, and it shouldn't be growing the way it is . . . But my friends and I, we all have a kind of mutual warning system: "You know, there and there, around the corner, you can find things ten–fifteen percent cheaper." And so the people (narod) go there. And it's not thriftiness; rather it's some wireless telegraph of the people (*besprovolochnyi narodnyi telegraf*). I've experienced it many times. And not even just friends—some people I don't even know would say this. And you'd think, these people, they could keep this venue they found all for themselves, but they don't . . . And it's a purely Russian mentality, the mentality that I like endlessly, fundamentally. (Andrei, male, 38)

There is nothing new in acknowledging the sharp and dramatically conveyed binary distinction between the people and the powers (narod and vlast') in the Russian (and broadly, East European) rhetorical tradition. What interests us here is not the mere fact of the opposition, but rather the way it played out and the consequences it had for the sphere of everyday life. While it is fairly common to interpret indigenous tactics in the face of the power as a manifestation of resistance, I would suggest that, at least in the case of postsocialist Russia, the opposition between *us* and *them* bore a somewhat different character. It was not so much resistance (which is by definition an act aimed outward, in the direction of the opponent) as it was an effort of self-protection, achieved through cultivation of autonomy. Acts of self-protection differ from resistance in that they are interested less in restoring the balance of power through some form of retaliation (often symbolic) than in minimizing the vulnerability of the individual's immediate lifeworld to acts of disruption, sometimes before the danger even arises:

> I am investing all my money right now, so that at least ten or fifteen years ahead I may live more or less decently. We renovated the kitchen, the bathroom, we bought a washing machine, new faucets, a new refrigerator. You see? Perhaps we may not need all this right now, but I will keep investing all I have into these things. Because I know that when I'm retired, I will not be able to afford them. (Alla Alekseevna, female, 53)

> This past winter, they were talking about some economic reform once again, and my wife and I decided to buy another fridge. You know, before it strikes, just in case. (Roman, male, 44)

The distinction between resistance and self-protection is important, since it entails a shift of optics: instead of interpreting every action as a response reaction to an immediate threat on the part of the state, we may regard this action as a part of a larger project of building a kind of protective cocoon intended to shelter the household from all possible mishaps, including ones that are only anticipated or imagined. If resistance is a strategy, self-protection could be more adequately thought of as a loose behavioral orientation, since it did not respond to any particular threat, but rather cultivated a cautious attitude of enhancing one's multiple defenses against whatever threats may come up. Many of the strategies on which the Russian households drew in doing so, such as *blat* (connections) and informal relations, were familiar from the years of socialism, when infrastructural deficiencies were patterned and systematic.[32] Imported into the new context, these practices now served a more universal purpose, as they were employed to protect the household not merely from a dysfunctional system of production and supply of goods, but from the much more varied and unpredictable risks of the crisis.

There were several ways in which consumer durables were implicated in this project of creating a zone of autonomy around the individual vis-à-vis the state. For one, the purchase of a fridge or a washing machine secured the household's savings by turning them into something that could not be subject to inflation and fluctuation of currency. It firmly fixed in place what consumers knew they earned, and what they saw as being under constant threat of disappearance. It was for that reason that the most oft-cited motive for buying household appliances had little to do with household needs, and far more with accumulation of a certain amount of disposable savings:

MARIA: . . . It was all my mother-in-law, she said, "Listen, some money has piled up from my pension, go, get something . . ." She gets pension transfers, and they accumulate in her account.

AUTHOR: So, was it her idea to get a fridge?

MARIA: It was. She was like, "Let's replace the fridge while I am alive." She kept saying this. "While I'm alive, let's replace it, while there is still enough money." She thinks we can never have savings without her guidance. (Maria, female, 37)

By purchasing a durable household item as soon as there was the financial opportunity, consumers saw themselves as avoiding two dangers. The first was the danger of their current savings losing their value through inflation. The second, somewhat more remote, was the danger that household members might become incapable of earning in the future because of the volatilities of the job market and would not be able to afford the same item when such a need truly arose. This concern, which seemed especially pressing for the older-generation households, compelled them to run ahead of their current needs, as it were, in order to resolve the problem before it even occurred.

What effectively happened in both of these cases was that people's accomplishments, in anticipation of the coming crises, were converted into a medium that was not subject to the vicissitudes associated with postsocialism. In using objects as safeguards of one's own and one's family's achievements, Muscovites avoided the volatility of the economic system and protected themselves from the fluidity of the ruble, which over the course of the first postsocialist decade had been reformed and transformed so many times that it hardly represented a stable referent. In a world where prices in stores could change three times a day, and where "5,000 rubles" could designate the price of an ice cream or the price of a refrigerator, depending on the year, objects came to rescue the failing currency as a means of establishing value. What ensued was a peculiar state of symbolic barter, in which objects were routinely used as a measure of comparison between monetary sums, not otherwise. Indeed, the most common currency Russians used when talking about the savings they managed to make during the socialist era was neither rubles nor dollars, but the number of Volga cars these savings were worth. Needless to say, more often than not these savings were talked about in the past tense, since the bulk of them evaporated during the inflation and monetary reforms of the 1990s. But this only made it more sensible to continue the project of converting money into objects, not only in conversation but also in practice.

While the above applies to most purchases and investment strategies of the first postsocialist decade, household goods had a few additional advantages in this regard. First, because household appliances and furniture occupy an intermediate position between truly expensive commodities, such as cars, and everyday routine purchases, consumers were able to turn their savings over fast enough for them to be relatively unaffected by inflation, and at the same time to achieve a sense of accomplishment in this turnover. Second, as I have argued at length earlier in this chapter, the task of navigating the murky waters of the contemporary Russian economy was necessarily a collective task. The goal of achieving stability and financial security at the same time called for the involvement of all family members, but in different fashions: while one individual brought home the bulk of the family income, this income was enhanced by the fact that another family member had the time to track down bargains (a task that often could involve trips across city, directly to the producers of the goods in question), while another could provide security from modest but stable earnings at a state enterprise (which, furthermore, could be a source of cheaper products or discounted vacation tours). This fundamental complementarity of the employment strategies within a household turned it into an autonomous unit and made it impossible to understand the logic of employment choices out of this collective context. It was only logical that objects resulting from this collective navigation provided such efforts with an appropriately collective-minded reward. There were hardly better candidates for this task than household goods, since they served all family members without prioritizing one person's contribution and needs over another's.

Refrigerators took on an additional importance as compared with other appliances and furnishings. Apart from securing the household's savings and hence playing the role of the family's own peculiar investment bank, they served as food banks as well. In this respect, we may speak of shortage anxiety moving one degree deeper: while in earlier years there was a strongly felt need to stock food for security, in the late 1990s the security demand was satisfied by hoarding appliances in which food could be stocked in case of need:

> AUTHOR: So what did you do with your old fridges?
> VICTOR VLADIMIROVICH: One we moved to dacha, and the other one is right
> there, in Roma's [Victor's son's] room.
> AUTHOR: Do you use them both?
> VICTOR: Well, the one in Roma's room, that was basically our wedding gift,
> it's pretty old . . . It's turned off right now, but if you want to turn it back on, no
> problem—it will work. We haven't had the occasion to, but if, for instance, we are in
> a situation when we have to stock up for some reason—we'll have to turn it back on
> and put it to work. (Victor Vladimirovich, male, 56)

A parallel with the stockpiling strategy typical for the socialist shortage economy seems to suggest itself here, but it is crucial to keep in mind that, in contrast to the times of late socialism, when the main danger to be avoided was the possible disappearance of goods, the risks of the postsocialist context were seen as much more pervasive and ubiquitous, emanating from everywhere, beginning with the potential breakdown of worn out heating pipes and ending with the effects of larger political and economic restructuring. In a situation when, as I often heard, "one has to be ready for everything," the central effort was directed toward anticipating and forestalling the blows that come "from this direction and from that direction, from all over the place." This vague and unpredictable character of risks justified an equally vague rationalization of one's choices and preferences, insofar as they bolstered the general sense of self-protection. The frequent formula of "in case of fire emergency," which designated a generic unanticipated need, was indeed most fitting here, because in a context seen as pregnant with risk on practically all levels, everything gains value if it can be used as an insurance against everything else. In these terms, the new and old items of household equipment were not only strategic tools against inflation, impoverishment, and food shortages, but also each other's keepers: while the new could replace the old in the case of its final disintegration, the old tried and tested equipment could help out if the newly acquired consumer dream suddenly turned out to be faulty (which, as Humphrey [1995] points out, was a common suspicion among consumers). In all these ways, these appliances gave their owners a subjective feeling of protection, fostering a sense of autonomy and hence ontological security in the otherwise risk-laden environment.

The expressive aspect of consumption is important here. As Miller (1998, 35) argues in his work on shopping, apart from being an "expression of individual subjectivity and identity," shopping, and more broadly consumption, are expressions of "kinship and other relationships." While the former function of consumption found its illustration in the ways consumers manipulated their old and new possessions, consumption's capacity to express kinship was central to the discussion of the multifaceted self-protection by means of objects. In creating a zone of autonomy around the household, individuals drew a boundary between the safety and order maintained inside their homes and the disorderly environment outside, constructing the household as the last island of certainty in the postsocialist context.[33]

6   Building Autonomy in Everyday Life

Metal Doors, Steel Garages

Household appliances were not the only means enlisted in the project of constructing a cocoon of security around the household. A variety of practices from realms as disparate as consumption, health behaviors, informal exchanges, and everyday rituals all provided venues through which the uncertainty of the postsocialist condition could be resisted and domesticated. This domestication occurred in the context of a sharply experienced retreat of the state from fulfilling the many protective functions it had taken upon itself during the period of late socialism. Confronting and compensating for this retreat, everyday practices operated as universal buffers that served to exclude and neutralize the failures of state-run structures and institutions.[1] And even in cases where such neutralization was not needed, the knowledge that all necessary precautions were in place enhanced the individual's overall sense of readiness and ability to competently handle the contingencies of daily life in postsocialism.

Perhaps the most straightforward example of self-protection was the installation of fortified doors, intimately familiar to anyone who visited Muscovite homes during 1990s. Made out of solid wood or iron and furnished with at least two locks, these doors typically did not replace but supplemented the standard apartment doors, creating for the visitor the sensation of entering something of a fortress. The irony, as Muscovites frequently pointed out themselves, was of course that the apartments these multiple doors guarded rarely contained anything of a value that would justify such precautions. Many would agree with Andrei, who laughingly told me, "I believe our door is our most expensive possession." Yet, the need for such a purchase was rarely questioned and was typically rationalized in terms of ease with which the standard door (or doors, in the many cases where several apartments were separated from the staircase by an additional door) could be broken through.

The peace of mind Muscovites received from the knowledge that their apartment was duly fortified against attack rested on two assumptions. One was that, in the world in which they lived, an attack on their apartment and property was highly likely; the other was that alternative forms of protection from attack, such as vigilant neighbors or alert police, were not available. "Although police are needed, one is afraid of the police these days," said Sergei Mikhailovich, whose apartment had a fortified entrance. "The Ministry of Internal Affairs are the worst criminals themselves, it's better to avoid them by all means possible." The installation of fortified doors in this context transferred the functions traditionally associated with the institutions of law enforcement to one's own household, allowing people to run this household in a way that assured maximum protection from a threatening impact from the outside.[2]

Admittedly, one could question the accuracy of such a skeptical assessment of the "outside." After all, the number of registered cases of theft and breaking and entering in Russia was still lower than in many developed countries of the West—for instance, one third of those in Germany, despite the difference in size and population (82 million in Germany vs. 146 million in Russia).[3] While these numbers are not absolute and refer only to reported cases, the general dynamic they suggest indicates that the installation of a fortified door could be as much a symbolic act as a practical response to an actual danger. This act very visibly affirmed several things at the same time: distrust and skepticism toward those officially charged with the responsibility of protecting citizens, a fundamental conviction of a universal moral decline (in terms of both the proliferation of potential burglars and the apathy and disengagement of the neighbors), and an eagerness and capability of the household in question to resolve the issues of self-protection by its own means.

A similar function of self-protection was performed by *rakushki* ("shells"; singular *rakushka*)—easily assembled car shelters built out of several sheets of steel, which could be seen along practically every street and in every yard in Moscow and other Russian cities (see figure 6.1). The number of these make-shift constructions grew rapidly during the late 1990s, at a rate exceeding the increase in the number of registered cars, and in 1999 the city of Moscow estimated that about 200,000 predominantly unlicensed rakushki existed on its territory.[4] Rakushki were made for all car sizes and were relatively inexpensive in comparison with traditional garages ($550–700 vs. $5,700–7,000). Their ambiguous status as moveable property (unlike stationary garages, they were not affixed to the ground and had no floor, which was replaced by two parallel laths connecting the walls) allowed their owners to avoid the bureaucratic hassle of obtaining the permit for the use of municipal land. Up until the end of the 1990s, it was all but impossible to register rakushki with the authorities. Official permissions were granted only to those with physical disabilities, although, according to several owners, stories circulated of such permissions obtained by non-disabled Muscovites for a bribe. An overwhelming majority, however, put the garages up at their own risk (in the northwest administrative region of Moscow, for example, 14,346 of the 16,680 rakushki were unregistered in April 1999).[5] In fact, the rakushka responded to not one, but an intersection of multiple perceived risks. On the one hand, as in the case of the metal apartment doors, there was the risk of robbery or vandalism, as well as the risk that the individual's savings would evaporate due to inflation before being converted into material objects. On the other hand, because of the dubious legal status of the rakushki (not forbidden by federal regulations, they were the object of continuously shifting prohibitions and regulations on the municipal level), their owners found themselves in the precarious position of never being sure they would

Figure 6.1. A Moscow yard with *rakushki*.

not be ordered by police to remove their rakushka in a matter of hours, thus losing both their money *and* their security. While the common understanding was that cases like that could be settled by bribing the policeman at hand or pacifying the objecting neighbors, the uncertainty that this possibility generated replaced the uncertainty associated with leaving the car unsheltered, and essentially put one in a "damned if you do and damned if you don't" position. Yet the manner in which rakushki were promoted on the market emphasized precisely the aspect of security that this object provided and, moreover, explicitly equated it with another institutionalized but distrusted sphere, claiming that "A rakushka [is] your best insurance."

The tasks that Muscovites resolved through resorting to strategic purchases of durables, doors, and makeshift car shelters, as well as through "prophylactic" renovations of apartments or accumulation of unnecessary objects in "case of fire emergency," appeared to be quite mundane; and yet they were fundamental. These were the tasks traditionally delegated to various official structures and institutions, from banks (investment and protection of savings) to the social security sector (provisions for retirement), and from insurance (protection against accidents) to law enforcement (defense against criminals). Taking these tasks over, people observed with indignation that the protection of citizens and their savings was something they expected an effective state to do. But the postsocialist Russian state fell short of these expectations:

> We don't have here what people call "the state." It simply does not exist. The state, it's the apparatus which, although it exploits and this and that, yes, still the most

important thing [is] it somehow cares for its citizens. And in our case, absolutely no one cares for us . . . (Sasha, male, 30)

In taking charge of their own well-being, then, people at the same time ensured the continuity of their everyday life despite political and economic upheavals, and symbolically indicted the state for its failure to protect its own citizens, turning the purchase of a second door into a form of crisis discourse. In other words, the project of becoming autonomous had a performative and a practical aspect at the same time: it was a moralistic indictment of the times, and an effort to cope with them. As a performance, it emphasized the troublesome aspects of postsocialism and situated its subjects as the active and moral agents in a dangerous and risk-laden context. Practically, the attainment of autonomy fostered a feeling of independence from larger economic and political upheavals by placing control over the household's well-being into the hands of its members. Dubravka Ugrešić, who spent the past fifteen years in exile from her native Croatia, has written that "exile is changing voltages and kilohertz," comparing it to "life with an adapter, so we don't burn ourselves" while passing through cities, countries, and cultures (1999, 113). Extending this metaphor to the ground rules of post-Soviet life, one could characterize these strivings for autonomy as life with a surge protector, which shielded its owners from the fluctuations and breaks in the currents of supply. Softening, mediating, and/or substituting for the real or expected institutional failures to serve the citizens, this metaphorical surge protector ensured that, whatever they may be, the risks and problems of postsocialism did not have their full impact on the household, and thus it restored the ontological security otherwise endangered by what was seen as the collapse of all things public.[6]

The drive for autonomy contained no more ready-made prescriptions for action than did the metaphor of crisis that inspired it. It could be evoked in multiple contexts and in justification of diverse and sometimes contradictory choices and behaviors. In this respect it was not a blueprint: it did not dictate or determine particular individual responses to a situation. Quite the contrary; the goal of autonomy could be stretched to justify a variety of behaviors, as was the case with people's immediate responses to the consumer panic that ensued after the sharp rise in prices following the currency crisis of August 1998. While some promptly took to the shops, hurriedly buying products that had not yet been subject to repricing, others preferred to sit back and wait for the first wave of the panic to pass. But in both cases, people explained and rationalized their responses by linking them to the previous experiences of crisis:

MIKHAIL ALEKSANDROVICH: This [laughs] third time, I swear, we didn't buy a thing, not an extra matchbox. When the very first crisis hit—then yes, that was really scary.
AUTHOR: Which was the first one?
MA: I can't even say anymore . . .
AUTHOR: Not the Pavlov one? . . .
MA: No, not the Pavlov, the Gaidar one . . . When every single shop shelf was emp-

tied, when the inflation became ten thousand percent. [. . .] Back then, we did stock up. Like during wartime—and you haven't lived during wartime. Salt, matches, and sugar. I knew those who dried bread, one man told me, "I'm not afraid of anything, I dried three sacks of bread, and don't give a darn about any of them [i.e., the authorities]." Yeah, and he was a leading specialist in the Ministry of Mechanization [laughs]. That impressed me a lot, because we didn't go as far as drying bread . . .
AUTHOR: What about the second crisis, when was that? You said that this one was the third. . .
MA: The Pavlov one, that was just plain robbery.[7] And on the seventeenth [of August, 1998], the people also rushed [to the stores] (*narod tozhe rvanul*), they did . . . But the agitation wasn't nearly what it was eight years ago.
AUTHOR: Why not?
MA: I'll tell you. First, people were used to it. Second, everything was widely available, no shortages. Three—there was no money. And those who had money kept it in dollars, so they didn't care . . . After all, we all have already been taught by all past experiences, so many keep their savings in dollars, and change them day by day, as they need it . . . All this has softened the blow. That's why there wasn't as much of an uproar.

Mikhail Aleksandrovich's assessment of the situation was strikingly different from that of Lina, a retired chemical engineer who, feeling less financially secure than Mikhail Aleksandrovich and his family, made sure she got ahead of the rising prices. Yet, with all the disparities in actual circumstances and behavior, she also linked her response to the experiences of the former crises:

I even borrowed some money from a friend of mine, and we went to the market and made an effort to buy everything that was still available at the "old" prices. We couldn't buy much, of course, and, as you understand, this couldn't save us for long. You can't stock up for your entire future life. But it did help us out a bit. We bought some grains, and tea, and coffee. . . . I never had this attitude, that one should always have everything stocked up. To compare with the old times, it [the period of the past few years] was so good. Before, you had to stand in line for everything: for meat, for bananas, whatever. And this life, it forced us to stock up, because you knew, if you came across something, that this opportunity might not come by again for another six months. And during the past few years it was really good, you could just go and buy anything. I got used to not stocking up. And now it turns out that I was wrong, that in our country you always have to be ready for emergencies. Our country is unpredictable that way.

These examples demonstrate that the use of crisis imagery did not predetermine the individual's tactical responses to every challenge and dilemma. Although both speakers framed their actions in terms of a successive chain of crises, their understanding of the appropriate modes of reaction differed. What remained invariable, however, was that no matter what tactical arrangements were chosen, the overall thrust of their efforts was directed toward protecting their immediate environs from the ruinous impact of the instability, both psychologically (by highlighting its precedents) and practically (by exchanging money or stocking up on supplies).

Not only did the applications of the total crisis framework vary, but so did the social positions of the speakers. Indeed, what was perhaps most striking to me was the reproduction of crisis rhetoric by Muscovites across different age and income categories, from a young kindergarten teacher to an older distinguished researcher. Enacted by people occupying dramatically different social positions, this discourse revealed itself as a cultural form that transcended individual circumstances and functioned as a kind of social currency bridging generational, income, and educational groups.[8]

It is nothing short of a commonplace to consider the postsocialist milieu a society of atomized individuals.[9] But in fact, attainment of autonomy did not presuppose atomization, and often was even opposite to it. The task of minimizing interaction with the state in all of its incarnations, from banks to law enforcement agents, and substituting in its place parallel structures implied, more often than not, vibrant social networking and intensification of already existing informal ties (Rose, Mishler, and Haerpfer 1997; Ledeneva 1998). While post-Soviet individuals repeatedly evoked a widely shared assumption that "you just can't trust anyone these days" as part and parcel of the total crisis talk, the actual actions they undertook in order to navigate this untrustworthy world tended to rely heavily on cooperation with others. Activity that ensued after a series of explosions in residential buildings in several regions of Russia in the fall of 1999 is a case in point. The immediate response to the blasts, two of which occurred in Moscow, was not to rally for greater security citywide, but for each apartment building to organize a neighborhood watch that monitored the immediate vicinity of the building. Responses also called for the institution of a concierge position or the installation of a fortified building door, at the expense of the building inhabitants and without the involvement of municipal or federal forces.[10] Clearly, all of these tasks required careful self-organization of the community. Hence, in many ways the lack of trust in the efficiency of official channels and institutions called for, rather than inhibited, local loyalties and connections. This tendency, visible in the collective methods for making consumption and employment decisions, was equally apparent from the way in which Muscovites managed their and their families' health.

"Heal Yourself"

Some of the state's functions are admittedly harder to replicate (or at least supplement) on a household level than others. As one older Muscovite put it, commenting on the deficiencies in the medical and educational infrastructures, "Maybe, in the case of education, in an intelligent family both parents and grandparents can make up for school and educate the child, but with your health, your family can't step in to help you." Much like banking and law enforcement, the system of healthcare enjoyed little respect among its occasional clients. Vivid stories of corrupt or incompetent medical workers were just as common as the narratives of fraud and deceit in the consumer sphere, and much like the latter, they were recited not merely in their own right, but as yet another form of evidence of the profound disorder taking place in the country.[11] Take the narrative of forty-three-year-old engineer Gennadii, whose story of his father-in-law's health problems did not even allow for the possibility that a similar situation could occur in a better-run system of healthcare:

> Our impoverished so-called official medical system, a lot of times it can't help at all . . . We often remember how my father-in-law was suffering. It was back in perestroika times, before everything completely perished, I mean this official medical system. And imagine, for, well, not a year, but half a year at least, they couldn't even decide on his diagnosis. I mean, this poor soul had to move from one hospital to another, from one doctor to another, they shuffled him around (*futbolili tuda-siuda*) until finally they gave him this diagnosis. But everything he had to go through, and we're thinking, you know, finally they found out what was wrong, why couldn't they just send him there in the first place? . . . And granted, it was a rare illness, but it was a genetic one, he must have had someone in his family who had it, they should have asked . . . So, oftentimes, you don't even know where to turn—to the official medical system, or to the sorcerers.

In light of the profound skepticism regarding the state of the healthcare system, Gennadii's conclusion was more than just a rhetorical question. As statistical data suggest (Palosuo et al. 1998), Muscovites opted for unconventional alternatives to official medicine, and turned to healers, bioactive food supplements or folk medicine far more often than some of their Finnish counterparts. Russian chains selling "natural medicine" (*Lavka Zhizni*, [Life Shop], *Zelenaia Apteka* [Green Pharmacy], and many others) multiplied exponentially, with the market doubling yearly over 1994–2000 (Promptova 2000). They were as visible in the public space as were regular drugstores, with at least one booth with "natural" products represented in the immediate vicinity of every one of the 161 stations of the Moscow metro (figure 6.2).

A peculiar feature of the alternative medical trends in 1990s Russia, as Galina Lindquist (2001) has pointed out, was that in their self-legitimation they did not shy away from the authority of scientific biomedical knowledge. Quite the contrary; healers often drew upon the results of medical experiments and licensing in justifying their claim to truth, and expressed an overall eagerness to cooperate with the established medical institutions. From the patients' point of view, however, "official medicine" still represented the more desirable option, partly because it was free, and they typically turned to healers after the more conventional resources failed. As could be seen from Gennadii's comments above, such failure was often taken as evidence of a decline in the official medical sphere, and so the turn to alternative medicine was rationalized not as an expression of mistrust of biomedical knowledge *per se,* but rather of the ways it was practiced in what Gennadii called "our impoverished so-called official medical system." The relationship between the conventional and the alternative branches of medicine therefore tended to be of a peculiar kind. On the one hand, medical degrees, professional affiliations, and other types of association with the medical and research establishment were treated as symbolic capital that enhanced the credibility of the alternative methods of healthcare (research

Figure 6.2. Contents of a natural medicine booth at a metro station.

achievements of the "Soviet time," as well as those produced in the course of military or space research, were deemed to be particularly legitimate). On the other hand, these methods were positioned against the backdrop of the crumbling infrastructure and were expected to make up for its inefficiencies, both in terms of providing alternative medical care and in alleviating other problems, such as the state of the environment ("*nasha ekologiia*" [our ecology]), chemically polluted imported foodstuffs, and everyday stress.[12] Bioactive food supplements, less conventional than regular biomedical drugs but more scientific than most alternative remedies, offer a good insight into the complex relationship between the two spheres. A narrative of Elena Fedorovna, a neuropathologist in her sixties whom I met during my fieldwork in Moscow and who was actively involved in the marketing and distribution of bioactive food supplements, illustrates the interconnections between the themes of knowledge, morality, trust, and crisis in medicine:

> One danger with biosupplements is that the market is swamped with counterfeits, and the way they do it, an uninformed person will never see a difference, except there will be no effect, or even an adverse effect at times. Take *Iantavit* [she reached into a drawer and took out a bright box of pills], it's an excellent product, on the basis of succinic acid, excellent if you want to boost your immunity to illness and to protect the body from different adverse effects of the environment. A recent discovery, and until not long ago it was classified and restricted to those professions that work under extreme conditions (*zasekrechena i dostupna tol'ko tem, kto rabotaet v ekstremal'nykh usloviiakh*). I know it already has several counterfeit analogues. I receive my supplies directly from the research institute and distribute them around, so there is no danger here, but in drugstore booths one is not guaranteed anything, and [the researchers] themselves can't do anything about this counterfeit market, who can control it? They can't even sell some of the things they invented through drugstores because it takes so many procedures and tests [required for official approval for distribution], only through the doctors who know and understand [the usefulness of these products], like myself for instance . . . It's a real pleasure to help people, in this brothel of ours talented people have such a hard time, no one is interested in anything, and so I do all I can . . .

Elena Fedorovna's narrative left me a bit skeptical because of the obvious conflict of interest involved in her actions. She was both a doctor recommending the supplement, and a distributor whose ID number was written on the prescription slip and who had therefore something to gain from the transaction. But her intentions, pure or not, are less interesting than the ways in which she drew on the crisis narrative, intertwining the issues of biomedical authority with the imagery of disorder and the postsocialist "brothel." In Elena Fedorovna's interpretation, the prestige of new food supplements (succinic acid was soon followed by placenta extract and selenium) was only supported by the authority of medical research and the high secrecy in which these products were reportedly developed. At the same time, their potential was eroded by what the doctor saw as the inherent plagues of postsocialism—carelessness and lack of encouragement, combined with bureaucratization and ineffectiveness. The morality of this transfer of medical knowledge was thus enhanced by the fact that the doctor not only helped patients with their ailments and supplied them with authentic products, but also aided talented researchers in evading the pitfalls of postsocialist economy and administration.

Alternative medicine thus stood at the same time inside the medical system (insofar as it drew on the expertise of the latter for legitimation), and outside it (insofar as it was critical of the medical infrastructure and endowed its users with ways to circumvent it). Its project of self-legitimation was predicated on the affirmation of an all-embracing crisis, particularly the crisis of trust in state institutions and in generalized others more broadly. This mechanism of generating trust through affirmations of universalized *dis*trust was visible, to take another example, in how Alexei Makoveev, the president of one of the leading "natural medicine" chains, Lavka Zhizni, couched his business mission.

I met Makoveev in his headquarters store in the center of Moscow. It was the middle of a working day, but the store was teeming with customers, most of them middle-aged and older women. Despite the fact that the store was located a far walk from the subway station, it drew customers by its relatively lower prices, in comparison with those in the company booths in subway station entrances. Makoveev's past business ventures included, he intimated, many diverse projects, but the creation of a natural medicine chain was by far his most successful and favorite project to date. He spoke of the decision to concentrate on natural medicine in mystical terms, as a "mission [he] received from Up Above," but more significant for our purposes was the clear juxtaposition he built between his business project and the rest of Moscow's medical enterprises. Unlike all other businesses, Mr. Makoveev claimed, Lavka Zhizni functioned in the interests of the people. For his company, profit-making always came as a secondary concern after fulfilling its social mission and "purifying the country's aura from within." The company's pricing policy was geared toward the poor and the elderly. Pensioners were entitled to a 10 percent discount, and periodically the company distributed "free gifts" to its clients. While all of the above were not unique to Makoveev's business and could be interpreted as rationally calculated promotional strategies, he was eager to emphasize precisely the opposite—that the company stood alone in the post-Soviet business arena in terms of its social responsibility, and that it advanced these policies on purely moral grounds.

The company's selflessness was "inexplicably" rewarded during the economic crisis of 1998 which, as Makoveev pointed out, ruined many of his aggressive biomedical and pharmaceutical competitors, but spared Lavka Zhizni. However, the other drug companies were not the only adversaries the company had to face. Equally socially irresponsible were the medical authorities, exemplified by the Russian Ministry of Health, and the Moscow municipal authorities, headed by Moscow's Mayor Yuri Luzhkov. While the untrustworthy practices of Makoveev's competitors explained the successes of his own company, the actions of medical and municipal authorities justified the infringements he had to make against the interests of his clients. Thus, when in my presence one customer reproached him for the escalation of prices in some of his central stores, Makoveev's response was quick: "Luzhkov's property tax is strangling us," he said, "it all fully depends on the government."

It is possible that Makoveev's rhetoric was exaggerated in order to produce a dramatic effect. But what is more interesting is that this rhetoric fed on the themes of crisis and distrust in order to achieve something directly opposite—trust and a sense of solidarity with his project. By contrast to the rent-seeking bureaucrats and businessmen (later joined by equally corrupt advertisers and medical experts who were "eager to drown us, out of envy"), Makoveev's company came across as fundamentally moral and trustworthy. Its morality was rooted in a sense of social responsibility and buttressed by the fact that the company's products offered its clients a chance to develop their own independence from the same predatory powers that were conspiring against Lavka Zhizni. By making the "authentic folk remedies" (together with the inevitable "findings of rocket science research") available to the public, Makoveev was proud to help them lessen their dependence on "our entire Russian medicine [which] has found itself at a dead end."

The Moscow subway, which housed most of Makoveev's booths, contained other sites that aimed to make medical knowledge available outside the context of medical institutions. Such were the mobile ultrasound stations located in small rooms right in the underground corridors of the Moscow metro (see figures 6.3a and b). For a fee, these stations provided ultrasound diagnostics for any of the client's ailments and were open to all comers willing to take their health into their own hands. The clients of such stations included, according to a nurse who interrupted her routine tasks to answer my query, "those from out of town" (and hence not covered by the socialized medical insurance available to all Muscovites), "those who don't like their doctor," and simply "people in a hurry."

Diagnostics of vision and the purchase of eyeglasses were also available on the spot, in the same corridors, as were advertising boards for electronic blood pressure monitors and inhalers enabling "a continuous independent control of your health." Television further added to the repertoire of independent self-protection measures with a large number of programs providing information (and, necessarily, advertising) on various aspects of decision-making regarding health. Within one week of spring 2000, the following programs were featured on the six main channels available to an average Muscovite: *Zdorov'e* (Health), *Bez retsepta* (Without a Prescription), *Stomatologiia dlia vsekh* (Dentistry for Everyone), *Bud'te zdorovy* (Be Healthy), *Istoriia bolezni* (Case History), *Klub Zdorovaia sem'ia* (Healthy Family Club), *Ekstrennyi vyzov* (Emergency Call), *Konsilium* (Consilium), *Formula zdorov'ia* (Formula of Health), *Bez strakhovki* (Without Insurance), *Gomeopatiia i zdorov'e* (Homeopathy and Health), *Esli khochesh' byt' zdorov* (If You Want to Be Healthy), in addition to the above-mentioned daily program *Vprok* (For Future Use), which was dedicated more broadly to helping viewers navigate the world of goods and services (including medicine) without being cheated by multiple shams and impostors.

Figures 6.3a and 6.3b. Mobile ultrasound station in an underground crossing. The poster prompts, "Start with an ultrasound."

Equipped with this knowledge, Muscovites took a certain pride in the fact that the inefficiencies of the healthcare system could not catch them off guard:

NINA ALEKSEEVNA: I don't trust doctors today. And also, this attitude of theirs . . . At our institute clinic, they've recruited novices, young girls . . . I mean, I don't know how young they are, but younger than me, about thirty-five. I came to this one [doctor] one day at 3:00 PM because I had a headache, and she told me it was the wrong time, because she finished working at 2:00, and it wasn't an emergency . . . She goes, "Why didn't you come earlier?" So I said, "Sorry, but this headache only happened to start at three," and I almost left, but then she said that with this, I should go to the neurologist. I said, "Wherever, as long as it helps . . ." So I went to the neurologist, and she gave me shots of magnesium, it used to help me before, but that time it didn't. So I went back to my desk, and I felt that nothing was helping, the headache was still there, so I took two Citramon pills.[13]
AUTHOR: Was it your own medicine?
NA: Yes. I always carry pills with me. Don't ever leave the house without them. So I took these pills, and by the time I came home my headache was gone. (Nina Alekseevna, female, 51)

Nina Alekseevna's story is significant, first of all, because it was recounted in response to my general question about the sites she usually turns to for medical help. Yet, while the inadequacy of Russian medicine seemed to be Nina Alekseevna's very first spontaneous association on the topic, her story also showed that existence of alternative strategies (in her case, the pills she had in her bag all along) did not actually decrease the number of visits to traditional clinics and hospitals.[14] Despite expressions of distrust, Muscovites regularly drew on the system of official medicine, not least because "natural" and home remedies often failed to produce the desired effect. In this respect, non-traditional remedies should not be seen as total replacements of official medicine; rather they were symbolic expressions of doubts in its powers, and at the same time, efforts to protect oneself with all available means in a patchwork fashion.[15] The measure of uncertainty these unorthodox methods of (self-) treatment provided were just as great as those associated with official medicine. This was all too well known to Lina, whose four-year-old granddaughter had chronic eczema:

Myself, I always say, "Who can you trust?" My son, he told me about one leaflet for a medicine . . . not a medicine, but bio—how do you call them? Food supplements or something, made in Russia, there are lots of them out there. So I said, "Let's get them," and he goes, "Mom, it's not hard to promise whatever." And I answered him, "And who should I trust then, if you can't trust anyone? You can't trust doctors, and you can't trust what these ones write." But if you think about it, it's true, they really can write whatever in this leaflet, that this powder is great and all. And no one will know if they tested it as they should have for the required time period.
AUTHOR: So do you actually trust leaflets?
LINA: Well, I have to. I have to treat the kid. So oftentimes I have to draw on some of my own knowledge, on intuition. As in our medicine: doctors come, but they don't tell you anything definitive. They only say, Don't practice self-treatment (*ne zanimaites' samolecheniem*). But at the same time, they don't treat you. So what

should you do? You simply have to practice self-treatment. You can't run away from it.

The deficit of trust toward all branches of medicine certainly created enough confusion and doubts. They were further exacerbated by the sheer number of newly opened clinics and medical offices. The existence of multiple competing healthcare providers suggested, according to the logic of the market, that there were wide discrepancies in service and quality. This was a perplexing idea for individuals used to the standardized and socialized medicine that was supposed to uphold the same standard for all. While, clearly, an opportunity to choose one's treatment held the promise of finding a higher quality service, it also posited the danger that one would be forced to pay for a mediocre treatment that was available for free elsewhere (such as one's district clinic). While the general ambivalence of Russian customers toward the task of choosing between competing brands seemed to have waned in comparison with the early 1990s when it was described by Humphrey (1995), it was in the sphere of health that it seemed to linger the longest, perhaps because the stakes were higher:

> These days, you don't even know where to run if something happens. Let's say, dental work, you can do it free of charge in the district polyclinic, but their fillings are such that there are no guarantees, and they don't even anesthetize properly. As for private clinics, here, too, there are so many of them, you just can't figure them out . . . (Gennadii, male, 43)

It was this desire to make up for the inefficiencies of state-run medical institutions, combined with ambivalence toward the wide array of available options, that made the interpersonal exchange of information and advice even more crucial than they were during the Soviet era.[16] Much as in the case of durable consumption, informal connections were drawn upon as an antidote to the multiple risks and insecurities associated with state institutions. These connections took various forms—mutual recommendations of efficient medicines, both "natural" and traditional, or warnings regarding particular brands or venues. It could take the form of a "wireless telegraph of the people," in Andrei's formulation (or, as one woman referred to it, "*sarafan radio*," sarafan being a traditional summer outfit worn by country women)—an informal system circulating information about low prices or alternative channels of obtaining medicine.[17] Alternatively, it could involve recommendations of trustworthy healers or physicians, as well as, importantly, a referral of patients *to* particular healers and physicians, which was commonly seen as a measure for ensuring full consideration on their part. Finally, and most frequently, it could be a combination of all the above, held together by the logic of a mutual exchange of favors, in which an opportunity to obtain medicine cheaply might be rewarded by the recommendation of an outstanding specialist which, in its turn, would ensure further exchanges.

Informality and network exchanges were thus central to the successful attainment of autonomy, and the moral economy that evolved around it. In drawing on interpersonal advice and connections, Muscovites did not simply achieve a convenient shortcut to a better and otherwise unavailable service. They also articulated a certain vision of their surroundings as spaces riddled with gaps and contradictions, and of themselves as actors capable of expertly navigating these surroundings through alternative means, which were perceived as both more reliable and more moral than those associated with the official "system."

Autonomy from "The System": Variations on a Theme

The notion of autonomy from "the system" is problematic on several counts. I have already mentioned that the notion of "the system" involved a great deal of misrecognition, both of the subject's own participation in the state infrastructure, and of the benefits that this infrastructure continued to provide. But more importantly, while the impetus for developing one's autonomy was shared across various population groups, resources for making this autonomy possible were not. Some families were simply better than others at this task, due to differences in income, social status, network connections, and the like.

Sites of employment played an important role in providing their employees with tools for cultivating autonomy apart from state institutions, and in this respect were an essential source of inequality not only in terms of income, but also in terms of a subjective sense of personal protection from recurrent risks and infrastructural breakdowns. Thus, while low-ranking employees of state-funded research institutes or contract workers had to exchange their savings into hard currency or invest them in household objects in order to retain their value, those employed in successful private-sector companies often received the bulk of their salary already in a dollar equivalent, and hence had less fear that their income would be eaten away by perpetual inflation. Similarly, doubts regarding the efficiency of the crumbling medical infrastructure were assuaged at the more successful companies by company-wide health insurance policies providing the employees, in addition to the free medical treatment available to all Russian citizens, with access to the exclusive and much better staffed and equipped medical centers. This differentiated system of limited-access institutions intertwined with the remnants of the Soviet system of privileges that used to be reserved for specific population categories (party cadres, academic elites, and so on). So, for example, a successful manager's private health insurance could entitle her to partake in the system of clinics originally reserved for the party bureaucrats, while an impoverished retired chemist could still draw on the *akademicheskaia poliklinika* (health clinic affiliated with the Academy of Sciences), which presumably provided better care than his local one. Insofar as people could achieve it, then, they withdrew from the public infrastructure in search of a parallel system of institutions. Many business opportunities, such as private kindergartens, schools, security firms and health clinics, were founded precisely on this drive for withdrawal, which thus formed the fledgling capitalist fabric of the Russian society. What made it peculiar, uniting it with the practices of the less privileged majority described earlier in this chapter, was its comprehensively defensive character: the sense of well-being was based on ensuring a possibly broad and all-encompassing separation from the "system." To quote Anton,

> Comfort—it's when a thunderstorm outside makes you feel even more cozy and comfortable at home. I would not say that I have some idyll in my home, but we have a normal family relationship. I do my best to provide protection for my family . . . That's the very crux of it: I have fully resolved this issue. I have fully shielded my family from this crisis. I have found sufficient resources, energy, and willpower to shield, to make sure my family is not affected. It's a different issue that outside [things are not as good]. When my mother goes for her class reunion and sees people she hasn't seen for forty years, she comes back almost in tears: "Dear God, she used to be this and that, a secretary of the Regional Party Committee, and how she lives now! They haven't seen meat for four months!" Or something like this. She does not experience this in her own life. But she does bring this cold in from the outside. Yet at my house, it is warm, dry, and comfortable.

Hiding behind Anton's pride in his ability to "shield [his] family from this crisis" was the diligent labor of creating as complete a separation from the postsocialist context as possible. This work stretched from setting up, through help from some friends, a savings account in a German bank, to the complete re-modeling of his apartment, to the point that even the water his family used for cooking and drinking was supplied in an office-sized water cooler by a Western company. The art of interior design is inseparable here from the drive to purge all signs of the postsocialist system from one's living environment. Testifying to this is the name by which complete apartment renovations were known in Russia at the time: *evroremont* (euro-repairs). The "euro-" component of the repair referred to the completeness with which interiors were redone in order to reflect "Western" residential conventions, from painted rather than wall-papered walls to plastic rather than wooden window frames and sills. While evroremont was rather expensive as compared to standard apartment remodeling, it was a prized source of distinction and was widely deemed worthy of a significant investment. While no other family in my sample could afford a evroremont as complete as the one Anton had, many families invested in separate components of the evroremont, most notably (and noticeably) plastic windows. While some nostalgics (including me) could argue that the wooden frames were in fact more attractive, the proponents of remodeling countered that "European windows" were not only more practical but also more beautiful and modern. Regardless of one's aesthetic take on the subject, the windows clearly achieved two goals. They provided their owners with the sense of a more civilized, European environment separated from the decrepit condition of the postsocialist "outside,"[18] and they separated these owners from their less fortunate neighbors (figure 6.4).

The installation of "European" windows, and evroremont in general, helped Muscovites achieve a sense of physical separation from the disorderly and crisis-ridden postsocialist system. But this practical activity went hand in hand with a similarly laborious task of constructing a sense of mental and psycho-

Figure 6.4. Stratification in action: Although architecturally on top, the unreformed balcony on the highest floor suggests that its owners have more modest resources than their neighbors.

logical separation. Similar metal doors and European windows, if you will, had to be installed in one's mind to ward off potentially distressing information. Much as with the project of insulating one's physical environment, the success of one's mental separation from the system depended on one's position in the social structure of Russian society. Understandably, those with access to social and financial resources found this task less problematic. Zhenia, who held a job with an oil company, stated with a degree of pride, "I have no fears. I am an optimist. You know why? Because I am not well-informed. I have no interest in getting informed. Those who have information, they may be scared of what's to come, but I make a point of avoiding it."[19]

The factual accuracy of Zhenia's claims could be debated. If nothing else, the demands of her job hardly allowed her to be fully disconnected from the larger political and economic processes. Moreover, on numerous occasions Zhenia, as well as other self-proclaimed news-avoiders, briefed me on the intricacies of political alliances and macroeconomic developments in such detail that their professed ignorance became questionable at best. It is hardly doubtful, however, that even if a lifestyle disconnected from the manifestations of crisis was not always fully achievable, it held a wide appeal and was considered highly desirable.

Those whose financial circumstances were less secure that those of Zhenia and Anton strove toward the same ideal of mentally switching off from the unpleasant developments in the larger world. On numerous occasions in conversation, my contacts spontaneously brought up the efforts they undertook to separate themselves from the depressing context:

> I try to know as little as I can: the less you know the better you sleep, you see . . . Whenever you open a newspaper, it starts immediately: there they are not paid for six months, here there is a war, here it's bad and there it's bad, and I just can't take all this. You know, I am being paid regularly, more or less, I am more or less fine, but whenever I get exposed to all this information, I immediately get the feeling that the same will happen to me. I start asking myself how they live without salary for half a year, if a husband and a wife work in the same enterprise and the enterprise stops working. How do they live? What do they eat? . . . So I just don't read newspapers, don't listen to the radio, so that I don't have to listen to all this. (Nina Alekseevna, female, 51)

> I don't look closely into the news and don't read newspapers. It's calmer this way. Just sometimes, I may hear a thing or two in conversation, or see a headline somewhere, nothing more. (Konstantin, male, 53)

Nina Alekseevna and Kostantin, much like Zhenia, showed themselves in the course of the interviews to be more knowledgeable about the news than they portrayed themselves to be. They did read newspapers and they did watch the news. Just as it was impossible for them to avoid leaving their fortified apartments, it was not viable to maintain the kind of mental hygiene they described during the turbulent 1990s. Expressed in these statements were not their actual adaptive behaviors but their conceptions of ideal autonomy, perturbed neither by actual disasters nor by the informational echo of disasters happening elsewhere. It was this total practical and psychological autonomy that characterized a savvy postsocialist subject. The next chapter will examine the social consequences such an understanding of autonomy inevitably entailed, but before addressing these, let us look at how the drive for autonomy structured Muscovites' time at home.

Routine: Sacralizing the Profane

In addition to the purely practical consequences of the drive for autonomy for the task of daily household management, it was a significant factor in how time off of work was defined and spent. If I am reluctant to call this time "free" or "leisure" time, this is because few Russians I met referred to their evenings, weekends, and vacations this way. Rather, people asserted that they had hardly any free time whatsoever because their routine duties took their lives over so thoroughly and completely. Their "free" time, therefore, lacked one fundamental characteristic often assumed by sociologists of leisure: an element of difference and contrast with the routine, the holiday's ability to introduce a break in the profane symbolic order and to temporarily liberate individuals from the constraints of the monotonous daily grind.[20] This "free" time was mainly spent at home doing small chores around the house, watching TV, or in fact not doing anything at all. Only a few of my contacts reported having a hobby or making a point of breaking their routine and leaving the Moscow region during family vacations. The rest tended to let their holidays slip by almost unnoticeably. Thus, although sociological time budget studies showed an increase in the absolute values of individuals' free time after the fall of socialism[21] (a development that Muscovites noticed as well and that they connected, first and foremost, with spending less time on queuing for foodstuffs), the manner in which this time was utilized belied the distinction between leisure and routine altogether.

This non-festive take on festivities was confirmed by quantitative studies finding that over the course of the late 1990s the collective significance of holidays sharply decreased (Dubin 2003). The waning of significance was particularly striking in cases of old Soviet holidays, such as Labor Day (May 1) or the so-called International Women's Day (March 8), but could be observed even with some of the less politicized festivities, such as people's own birthdays. And while the fading of the "ideological" holidays was rightly explained in terms of the general lack of legitimacy of Yeltsin's regime,[22] this wider apathy regarding holidays and celebrations suggested that the unenthusiastic response to post-Soviet national festivals could be a particularly striking instance of a more general phenomenon.

Overall, the effect was described by Boris Dubin as the "graying out of life," the "consistent domestication of leisure which is increasingly dominated by collective TV-viewing" (Dubin 2003, 57). Muscovites themselves recognized the shift in their attitude to festivities and celebrations, reporting less time and energy spent than before on holiday celebrations, trips, and getaways. The moments of leisure were interpreted in the late 1990s not as occasions for doing something special, but rather as a chance to reproduce the domestic routine, by going with a husband/wife to a wholesale market, assembling for a long domestic meal, or gathering in front of the TV:

> We hardly do anything on our weekends, hardly anything. Before, we used to go to the springs,[23] or downtown. Now, we mostly just sit at home or go to the market. One patient stopped by recently, she said, "I gave myself a treat and went to the History Museum with my husband." It was a holiday, the eighth of March, you know. So I came home, said to my husband, "Listen, Boris, let's go there sometime too." He said, "Sure, we should." But we never did [she laughs] . . . And that's it. I don't even know why, somehow, it just doesn't sound so attractive anymore, I'd rather stay home, watch TV, lie around . . . Everything goes as if by a template, nothing outstanding, just monotonous. And I don't need any particular stresses either . . . (Maria, female, 37)

In many families, the sacrifice of a more active style of leisure was merely a response to their changing financial conditions. Many of the more adventurous pastimes, such as mountain skiing or traveling, became unaffordable, and even the cost of roundtrip transportation across town for a family of three could become an argument for spending more time at home. This, however, was only part of the story, since many of the less cost-intensive pastimes, such as camping, exploring a new section of the city, or simply celebrating birthdays or seasonal holidays seemed to have waned in popularity. "New Year's is just not fun anymore"[24] was a standard complaint, and even those who tried to keep up with their active social schedule, such as Igor or Zhenia, commented on the difficulty they had in assembling their friends for a social event. The increased appreciation of household routine was emphasized even by those who did not forgo active leisure altogether, suggesting that the issue at hand was not only the pattern of the actual leisure, but also the very hierarchy of what made a worth-while and valuable activity. The narrative of Mikhail Aleksandrovich, one of the better traveled members of my sample, is instructive in this respect pre-cisely as a negative case. The substantial side income his family received from an apartment they were renting out, as well as the private lessons offered by his wife and help from their grown-up daughter, allowed the two of them to take a number of bus tours and trips to Europe and around Russia, sometimes accom-panied by their granddaughter. Comparing his current lifestyle with the one he had known previously, however, Mikhail Aleksandrovich emphasized precisely the opposite—his attachment to the home, and the monotonous recurrence of his everyday routine:

MIKHAIL ALEKSANDROVICH: For today, our living standard hasn't become lower, it is just more restless. One has to hustle around, shop, cook. We dedicated much less time to that before.
AUTHOR: Why?
MA: Well, maybe we used to buy processed food before. And these days I try more to ... [pause] I guess we save a little, because it's more cost-effective to cook from scratch than from prepared food. But this also takes more time ... Before, we used to buy sausage, or some burgers, meat cuts, so on. And now, instead of buying beef stroganoff cuts, I buy just a kilo of beef. This means preparing it, cutting it. Also, if you buy frozen potato fries, they are pan-ready. And if you buy regular potatoes, you have to peel them, cut them ...
AUTHOR: So does it perhaps mean that your standard of living did get a little lower, if now you feel you have to economize?
MA: It's not that we have to ... [thinks for a moment] It's because there is another aspect: we have more free time right now. Before, we used to have different interests, more of a desire to go out, to a concert, to a theater, to visit friends, and now we get out substantially less. So we have more time. And with time on my hands, at home, I will always cook better from scratch than if I have to deal with processed foods.
AUTHOR: Why would you say your attitude toward free time changed like that?
MA: [After a pause] I don't know, somehow, our interests are completely different, maybe to an extent it's because this green entity (points to the TV and VCR) allows you to bring everything home. So you don't have to go out to the movies, you can just watch a video at home. There are good programs on TV. And also, after a day at work, where would you go? The museum—that's only for the weekend, but on the weekends, we go to the market, we go shopping, we shop for the week ahead because we don't just feed ourselves, As'ka [their granddaughter] eats here often as well ...

The conversation revolved around the same topic for a while longer, follow-ing the same pattern, with Mikhail Aleksandrovich coming up with possible rational explanations for his and his wife's homebody attitudes and then dismissing these explanations as inadequate. Coming from an individual with an extensive and continuing travel record, these attitudes suggested that the increased emphasis on domesticity and attachment to the family routine were not necessarily dictated by economic necessity. If they could coexist with and enjoy the same if not greater legitimacy than the more active types of leisure, it was because, in the cultural logic of the late 1990s, the motives of predictability, succession, and repetitiveness acquired positive connotations. For one, they fit well with the high value placed on family domesticity more generally, if one interprets domesticity in the mode Muscovites envisioned it, as a safe haven in the otherwise risk-laden environment.[25] Secondly, the monotonous succession of undifferentiated days fit well with the postsocialist sense of temporality. Devoid of meaningful distinctions and periodizations, the time of postsocialism seemed to flow uninterrupted and yet stay unchanged, and the succession of domestic routines fed on, and at the same time reinforced, this sense of monotony. More importantly, the undifferentiated flow of time, forged through systematic adherence to routine, allowed individuals to achieve the very sense of disconnection from the larger crisis to which they aspired through the practices of fostering autonomy. While collective celebrations and events imply a breakdown of the established order, a sense of collective effervescence, and the inversion of everyday norms, the rituals to which people seemed to gravitate were of an opposite kind. They emphasized the repetitiveness, ordinariness, and predictability of daily existence. Long leisurely meals, collective trips to the market on weekends, and occasional cleaning and domestic repairs may be far from what is traditionally considered leisure, yet their predictability was opposed to the chaos of the crisis, and thus they reinstalled a sense of order and firmly anchored a feeling of normalcy in the individual's personal life. These *anchoring rituals* let people know that, despite the crisis, their own families were still carrying on.

One example of such anchoring rituals that combined elements of leisure with a deliberate reproduction of routine was the activity of working on crossword puzzles, a pastime that mushroomed in popularity in Russia following the triumphant path charted a few years earlier by "glossy" magazines, tabloid newspapers, and entertainment quiz shows.[26] All of these genres were argued to have made their contributions to the increasing "privatization" of postsocialist daily life, and to the withdrawal of individuals from the public sphere.[27] But the astounding popularity of serial puzzle publications, which spilled over into the 2000s when a particularly successful puzzle weekly, *Tri Semerki* (777), became the second most widely sold periodical in the entire country,[28] begs a closer look. While the late 1990s witnessed only the dawn of this phenomenon (the notorious *Tri Semerki* appeared in April 1999 with a modest circulation of 50,000, which by the end of the year grew 7.5 times to 385,000), puzzles were already becoming visible in public spaces. An average newsstand in 2000 carried about twenty such serial titles, typically published in magazine or tabloid format with about ten to twenty puzzles per issue. Puzzles themselves were surrounded by jokes, quotations, bits and pieces of trivia information, letters from readers, and photo illustrations (more often than not, photos of scantily dressed young women bearing no relation to the topic of the puzzle, nor to the readership of the publication).[29] The quality of design varied from the cheapest black-and-white eight-pagers to glossy colorful monthlies.

I first became aware of the role puzzle publications played in everyday Russian life due to a passing comment by Konstantin. He pointed out that he took up both making and solving puzzles after he lost his engineering job and landed, after a string of unsuccessful enterprises, as a salesman on one of Moscow's open-air markets. At the market, crosswords became a way of ensuring that "[his] mind doesn't go numb." My subsequent trips to the market revealed that Konstantin was not alone. Puzzle publications abounded, apart from market stalls, at security posts in office building lobbies, in shops, ticket offices and museum information desks, and most visibly of all, on the subway. One of my journal entries from the time reads,

> The frequency with which one comes across people doing puzzles in the metro is uncanny. I took the metro five times today, and on all five occasions I could spot one or two people in my car working on a collection of puzzles. One young man was standing up, periodically losing his balance and groping for the hand-holds when the train was departing or approaching the station, but not letting go of his pencil and booklet.

Why crossword puzzles? After reading through more than sixty crossword "newspapers" and "journals" (as they are called in Russian) from the late 1990s, interviewing several puzzle editors, carrying out systematic spying operations on puzzlers who solved their crosswords in public places, as well as doing a fair share myself, I would argue that the appeal of serial puzzle publications hinged on their successful incorporation of three resonant messages: the unfulfilled intellectual potential of their readers, puzzles as salvation from the dangerous and depressing environment, and familial sociality as an alternative to the anemic state of the public sphere. All three messages were rooted in the imagery of total crisis.

Nowhere is the connection more evident than in the issue of individuals' intellectual potential and cultural capital. The lack of fit between individuals' skills and cultural knowledge and the new reality to which these skills were to be applied was, as we know, one of the most aggravating aspects of the early postsocialist years. Thus, it is hardly surprising that themes of intellectual frustration, of one's inability to convert one's qualifications into recognition and worthy compensation, struck a sensitive chord. Granted, social dislocations were in many ways inevitable, since the system of higher education in the Soviet Union was geared toward heavy industry and produced enormous numbers of engineers and other technical personnel who could hardly be absorbed without pain into the postsocialist economy. But this did not make the shock of one's sudden professional irrelevance any easier to accept. In this context, the puzzle publishers' marketing strategy, which emphasized the intellectual challenge of the puzzle-solving task both in editorial messages and in the collections' titles and slogans (*Brainstorm, Erudite, Quiet Hour—the Paper of Intellectual Leisure, Krot—the Paper for the Smart and the Venturesome*) came as a welcome antidote. Taking up a crossword collection, an individual could feel (and show others) that his knowledge and cultural capital, although not appreciated by "the system," still deserved respect and recognition.

The sticking point in this logic, however, was that the types of puzzles available in most serial publications were a far cry from the intellectually challenging tasks that the publications' titles promised to deliver. In this they contrasted sharply with both the brain-teasers the English-speaking public comes across in the *Times Literary Supplement* or the *New York Times,* and with the more simple-minded but still erudition-dependent crosswords that the Russian audience remembered from Soviet newspapers and journals. In fact, despite the continuing use of the term "crossword," what most publications offered were not crosswords at all, but a variation on the theme known as *scanvordy*[30]—word puzzles with far more intersections between words, and far shorter clues geared toward stirring an association, as in "hockey" serving as a prompt for "game," or "ketchup" as a prompt for "tomato." In other words, the types of word games that dominated the market in late 1990s Moscow were precisely the ones that are marketed in the United States by emphasizing their do-ability and easiness. Available in newspaper stands in train and bus stations across America, albeit in much lesser numbers, these publications flaunt such titles as *Easy, Fast'n'Fun,* and *Super Easy-To-Do.*

This appeal to easiness was entirely alien to the self-presentation of the post-Soviet puzzle periodicals, whose titles, as well as the readers' letters chosen for publication on their pages, continued to represent this pastime through the lens of its former intellectual prestige.[31] Furthermore, these letters testified not only to the intellectual aura of the puzzles, but also to the fact that this aura was rooted in the assumption of total crisis. The connection between the two was often implicit. For example, a retiree from Vladivostok wrote to the puzzle periodical *Tri Semerki,* "Solving [your] puzzles . . . I experience true satisfaction: you don't allow our brains to go dry. Thank you!"[32] While this writer did not explain why he expected his brain to "go dry" without puzzles, another correspondent stated the same point a bit more explicitly, suggesting that in "our country" most people's intellectual potential was unused:

> We wish you great health and prosperity, and success in your work. It is truly noble [work], for you essentially make us exercise our stagnating brain curves. And the fact that a great number of our compatriots succeed at this proves that smart people have not vanished in our country.[33]

The same connection between the (waning) intellectual capital in the country and the social context of the total crisis was stated even more dramatically in another letter:

It's good that the newspaper *Russkii Krossvord* has recognized that there are still some not completely degraded individuals among crossword fans. Thank you for not testing us on our knowledge of criminal jargon. As for using the word "sucker" (*lokh*) in your puzzles, I forgive you, since the bulk of our compatriots have proven themselves to be precisely that.[34]

In other words, it was not just that readers interpreted the successful completion of the puzzles as evidence of their intellectual potential, but this confirmation of intellectual viability had a special significance for them in the context of the "complete degradation" of the country. The increased accessibility of the puzzles in the 1990s meant, essentially, that a greater fraction of Russians could comfortably make this claim through partaking in the puzzle phenomenon.

If puzzle-solving meant, in the eyes of the readership, their successful resistance to the intellectually corrupting effects of the prolonged postsocialist crisis, it had an even more immediate autonomy-fostering mission for the younger generations. Again and again, I heard the belief that the puzzles contributed to the intellectual development of Russian children, development that was threatened by two elements of the total crisis: the flow of low-quality popular culture in the media,[35] and the notorious weakness of the educational system. This belief was expressed even by those whose children's education provided no grounds for such worries:

> For Olezhka, I'd say, I am not as worried, because I think we have been exceptionally lucky with our school. But if you take some provincial school where there is one teacher for all subjects, and even he is absent half the time . . . I personally don't know what one is to do in this situation. I guess self-education, by whatever means possible . . . Encyclopedias, crosswords, just making them read . . . There's not that much that parents can do, especially if both are working. (Gennadii, male, 43)

Crosswords were thus placed alongside the other ways through which an autonomous family unit could take charge of a child's cultural upbringing, as the solvers' letters to the publications amply demonstrated:

> The adults in our family participate in solving crosswords no matter what they do. But especially it is beneficial for my grandchildren: let them encounter the world. I wish you good health and well-being.[36]

While the crossword puzzles did offer symbolic compensation for the unfulfilled intellectual potential and cultural capital of their readership, they also provided select readers with a very tangible kind of compensation as well. Most puzzle collections carried a prize fund, but their professed rationale for the administration of rewards was strikingly different from that of quiz shows, whose popularity rested on the incommensurability of their prize fund to the level of the game's challenge. Rewards given out by the puzzle publications, by contrast, were modest, ranging from the equivalent of ten to fifty dollars, and their distribution was often framed in the language of social justice, as in the following comments by a puzzle editor I interviewed in Moscow:

I know that German publications, for example, they have huge prizes, 500 DM, or $500 or something. This is a different psychology. There you have some cashier in a supermarket, she sits there and dreams of finding herself in the Canary Islands one day. I am against this. I think we have to send poor people some modest aid, you know, 700 or 1,000 rubles, that's what we need. But to more people. Instead of giving one person some silly dream like this. Let it be less money [in our case], but it will be a tangible sum to a tangible number of people.[37]

Another editor expressed similar ideas on the pages of a puzzle periodical. Talking about the mission of her publication, she emphasized the role that the edition's prizes play in redistributing resources in the interests of the "little people" slighted by the postsocialist system:

We frequently receive letters from people who have, to put it mildly, modest incomes. Alas, in our country such people constitute the majority. With our work, we try to distract our readers from depressing thoughts and give them a chance to earn something."[38]

The autonomy that puzzles provided was therefore wider than merely the autonomy necessary for cultivating one's intellectual potential. Rather, crossword publications claimed to offer a more general "compensatory space" in which their readers could redress a variety of injustices: economic, moral, political, and so on. This message was reiterated both in the editorial messages and in the readers' letters published on the pages of the puzzle periodicals. The very first issue of *Russkii Krossvord,* one of the earliest crossword publications (and virtually the only one delivering actual crossword puzzles, rather than the easier *scanvordy*) made it explicit in its editorial message, which drew, somewhat counterintuitively, on the "heal yourself" theme discussed earlier in this chapter:

So many factors have appeared these days that negatively affect our health! The tap water is to be avoided since it has some additives in it, breathing is said to be safest in a gas mask, since the air is polluted beyond all limits. Food represents a problem as well, you're never really sure what you're getting . . . But does everything really have to be so depressing? Isn't there anything out there that could improve our well-being? Thank God, there is a reliable solution.[39]

The text went on to claim that, according to the latest (unspecified) scientific research, the completion of one crossword added an average of fifty-four minutes to one's life, reduced stress, normalized blood pressure, and crosswords could therefore be used as an antidote to all of the negative factors mentioned above. This medicalized self-legitimation is telling in that it combined many elements of the total crisis discourse, such as the conviction of the hostility of one's environment, the construction of the body as the last island of purity, and the emphasis on self-protection, interpreted as minimizing damage from the "outside." But interviews and readers' letters provided abundant examples of other injustices redressed, in the speakers' eyes, through recourse to puzzles:

Your puzzles—all of them!—we have been doing together, me, my husband, our daughter (a student), and our son, who is still in school. All problems and tribulations in our lives have been subdued due to *Tri Semerki*. Today, Dagestan is going through a difficult period because of the insurgents (incidentally, our region borders on Chechnya). Your newspaper is not only leisure, but also a healer. An incredible stress-reducer! (K. Akhmanbetova from Terekli-Mekteb, Republic of Dagestan)[40]

Thank you for bringing us small joys in our difficult times. When I solve *Russkii Krossvord,* all my troubles, anxieties, and illnesses fade away. I am not so rich—my pension is only 388 rubles, but I buy [your publications] every time. Your newspapers affect me like some kind of potion, like an elixir. (T. Temereva from Tyumen)[41]

While one would be justified to question the direct medical effects of crossword puzzles, it appears plausible that this hobby did contribute to its fans' positive self-image by providing a small sense of accomplishment, of a task that was manageable, straightforward, and at the same time sufficiently complex. Russian puzzles were not much different from their back-page equivalents elsewhere in this respect. What did appear exceptional was the degree of the readers' enthusiasm regarding such an opportunity of self-affirmation, as well as the explicitly political context into which this self-affirmation was placed. Interpreted along the lines of the total crisis framework, crossword puzzles were seen as an opportunity to separate oneself from the hostile environment, to redress (or at least to suppress) postsocialist injustices, and to give order and logic to a world that was being experienced as chaotic and disorderly.

The positively marked party standing in opposition to "the system" was interpreted in kinship terms, which will not come as a surprise to the reader familiar with the preceding discussion of the family's importance in fostering an autonomous postsocialist existence. The prominence of the family, and the extent to which it embodied all things opposite to the alienation and injustices of "the system," are apparent in the frequency with which family-related themes arose in the letters from readers. Correspondence to crossword publications was often signed as if authored by the family unit and not a specific person, as exemplified in the letters from the Storzhuk family as well as the correspondence from Tregupova cited on the pages above. In other letters, activities and attitudes of the correspondent's kin were listed in detail. It was as if only a unanimous enthusiasm of the family unit as a whole could testify to the beneficial effects of the puzzles.

As a result, crossword puzzles emerged as a fundamentally collective hobby whose locus, as with other autonomy-enhancing practices, centered on the family unit. While in some readers' letters this family focus functioned as a background assumption,[42] feedback from others placed family solidarity at the very center of the crosswords' effect. For example, a letter from a reader named Krasnov, published in the monthly puzzle collection *Teshchin Iazyk,* thanked the publication for helping him reinstate peaceful relations with his mother-in-law by means of joint work on crossword puzzles.[43] Another reader reported that the prize she was hoping to receive from *Tri Semerki* would be used for purchasing a toy for her two-year old son Levka.[44] In a different issue of *Tri*

Semerki, a reader from Kaluga disclosed that work on crossword puzzles helped her stay awake by the bedside of her elderly parents, closing her letter with "Without you, I don't even know what I would have done."[45] Most strikingly, a letter from Valentina, Inna, and other members of the Zelentsov family thanked the publication *Russkii Krossvord* for nothing less than helping them to "keep going, getting over" the pain when "our father Valera died" that past fall.[46] In this particular example, the very intimacy of the tragedy that the family was sharing with the paper pointed to the fact that the publication itself was construed as a relative or a close friend who offered a helping hand in times of trouble.[47] In keeping with the same theme, another correspondent called the same paper "my best friend," asserting that prizes carried no significance for her because "friendship cannot be measured in money."[48]

The kinship theme was reflected in the titles of some publications, such as *Teshchin Iazyk* (which can be translated as *Mother-in-Law's Tongue* or *Mother-in-Law's Language*) and *Ziatek* (*Dear Son-in-Law*), as well as in subtitles, such as *AiF Umnik: Crossword Journal for the Entire Family,* and in editorial practices, which adhered to confessional tones and in some cases dedicated entire sections to publishing lists of readers whom they congratulated on their birthdays and wedding anniversaries.[49] A number of publications explicitly invited and published family photos and family narratives of their prize-winners in every issue, and one journal, *AiF-Davai,* went as far as to solicit photos of readers with their pets.

With the help of these editorial practices, puzzle periodicals offered their readership an image of an organic, supportive community juxtaposed to the alienated postsocialist condition. Within this community, loyalty and solidarity reigned; it was a space where, to quote a reader's verse published in *Ogo!-Scanvord,* "Mutual help abounds and flows, / Each contributes what he knows."[50] In the context of recurrent references to "our difficult times," expressions of readers' solidarity read as affirmations of an alternative sociality to "the system." The logic of this sociality, however, remained kin-based. Each correspondent emphasized his or her own narrow circle of close associates, but the pages of puzzle publications bore no evidence that a wider puzzle fan network might be emerging. Despite sharing a hobby and an intimate link with their favorite publication, the readers, dispersed all across Russia, showed little awareness of sharing anything in common among themselves, or at least did not seem to act on that awareness.

Geography of Crisis and Autonomy

While crisis does have its own temporality, it also has its own geography, "the way in which the crisis is inscribed in the everyday urban landscape" (Mbembe and Roitman 1995, 327). Much of what has been discussed above points at this spatial dimension of crisis, at its physical presence in the postsocialist urban environment. Metal doors and makeshift rakushka garages, as well as iron bars on the windows of apartments and ubiquitous security guards in the lobbies of office buildings and shops, participated in the shaping of this geography; but there was, perhaps, no better site for exploring it than the Moscow metro, a place where millions of Russians found themselves daily as they traveled across the city toward their various destinations. The metro was reported to be on the brink of collapse (allegedly, the system had not been substantially repaired since its construction in the 1930s), but the appearance of the stations and trains did not suggest this. The most visible marks that the postsocialist decade had left on the metro were not in the stations, which were still tiled with marble and bronze and cleaned continuously, but in the underground crossings and station entrances. As one walked down the stairs underground, one strolled past the multiple rather uniform-looking kiosks with candy, crossword puzzles, medical self-help literature, newspapers, socks, and souvenirs, booths with alternative medicine and food supplements, as well as regular medical kiosks. Dispersed among them and surrounding the metro entrance outside were numerous small peddlers—elderly women selling ciga-rettes, more newspaper salesmen, sellers of flowers, sometimes women selling cheap (usually Chinese-made) T-shirts or blouses right out of the box. On the steps, two or three ladies from the "former republics" would usually be selling fruit out of sacks propped right on the stairs. Everyone was cautious of the arrival of police, and all had mastered the art of recognizing their approach from afar, signaling it to the fellow-peddlers and dispersing in a matter of sec-onds. Police tended to know "their" peddlers well, and doubtlessly entered into arrangements with them, but the outcomes of the interaction with the police were always unpredictable. "One day they want money from you, another day they'll even say hello, and on the third they need to fulfill the plan in arrests so they won't let you go," a flower saleswoman told me when I was buying some tu-lips from her. The status of the peddlers was uneven—some had a permit to sell and were working for a boss, exhibiting their permit on the stall, while others were there fending entirely for themselves and feeling much more vulnerable. They were the ones who were most afraid of the police, and one could recognize them by the way they looked around (see figures 6.5 and 6.6).

The same variety of activity and goods awaited one in the long underground corridors as one was transferring lines; the gamut of goods I saw offered there included newspapers, crossword puzzles, wall hangings and calendars, student travel passes, foot scrubs, hair rollers, dresses and blouses, tubes of toothpaste, hairbrushes, eyeglasses, theater and transportation tickets, church icons and crosses, mirrors, bandages and razors, photo frames, pashmina shawls, femi-nine hygiene pads, books on history, astrology, and alternative healing, potted plants and fresh flowers, wallets, scarves, makeup, postcards, beads, first aid kits, fake university diplomas, umbrellas, T-shirts, wooden dolls, notebooks, and underwear. Between this and the peddlers and booths surrounding the stations, one could conceivably go about life without entering regular shops for weeks, and, taking into account the presence of quick ultrasound diagnos-tic rooms and ATM machines in the same corridors, one could hypothetically make do without banks or hospitals as well. And although this would hardly oc-

Figure 6.5. Peddlers near a subway entrance.

cur to anyone realistically, the very organization of this bustling underground universe, as well as the space on the ground, suggested this as a possibility.

One winter evening I was returning from an interview with Alena, who lived a couple of subway stops away from me. It was the second interview that day, and I was a little tired. Alena's building stood rather far from the metro, and the bus was not coming, so I took a *marshrutka* (plural *marshutki*)—one of the many small vans that operated on bus lines known for their lax adherence to schedule. Following the same logic as the producers of metal doors and rakushki, the entrepreneurs who launched the marshrutki were among the first to go into the business of compensating for the inefficiencies of the municipal infrastructure. Slightly more expensive than buses, the vans followed the same route and were far more frequent. They were much used by Muscovites, except for pensioners; their right of unlimited free travel did not extend to marshrutki and, being richer in time than in money, they often opted to keep waiting for the bus.

Having climbed out of the van upon its arrival at the metro station, I walked underground, and as I passed by the already closed kiosk with alternative medical literature, I saw a book that Alena proudly showed me toward the end of the interview. The book was written by a healer whose lectures she had attended and from whom she had learned a technique of caring for periodontal disease, her major healthcare expense. "The trick," she said, "is to vividly imagine a very hot ball, a ball of fire, and to physically feel it as it moves inside your body around your jaw, where the problem is. It takes a while," she added, "and I'm still learning. I do it during rides on the subway, or when I knit or do something me-

Figure 6.6. Peddlers near a subway entrance.

chanical." This recollection triggered another one, of the conversation I'd had earlier the same day, in the course of which my host complained about the motion sickness he started feeling on the subway. "I've tried everything," he said, "homeopathy, traveling on an empty stomach, everything. I don't know why it is, maybe there's not enough air down there or something. And a funny thing I read recently in the paper—that if you are motion-sick, what you should try to do is to sing with your mouth closed, not even humming, just sing in your mind, and it helps a little." And as I was riding toward home, looking at the faces of my fellow-passengers, some reading, some dozing off, some filling in the ubiquitous puzzle magazines, others just sitting quietly, deep in their thoughts, I imagined that I was hearing a kind of choir—a very strange choir, granted, since each voice was singing to its own tune, but a choir nevertheless, of the many autonomous individuals trying the best they could to take care of their own lives.

7   What Changes When Life Stands Still

I was coming back [from a research trip abroad] with doubts: What if during the past six months, history had advanced so far ahead that I would return to a completely different country? But once I had looked around: No, things have changed just within the limits of predictability. "Is that so?"—said V. Sm.—"I think history has advanced rather far, but across a very uniform landscape."

—Mikhail Gasparov, *Zapisi i Vypiski*

When one talks of coping or adapting, the assumption is that needs and infrastructural deficiencies precede the actual adaptive responses and define the form that they take. But there is every reason to look at what is usually classified as adaptation in a less teleological fashion. While many postsocialist behaviors, indeed, were spoken of and thought about in Russia as a direct response to the practical dilemmas of the 1990s, they also had a deeper performative dimension. By analyzing the ways in which consumption, health behavior, patterns of daily leisure, and political talk contributed to the formation of symbolic and practical autonomy from the much-criticized state, we can trace the emergence of new symbolic axes that allowed people to articulate their identity without relying on the categories of identification that lost their power.

Perhaps paradoxically, then, the notion of crisis had a number of enabling aspects. It allowed individuals to construct themselves as competent postsocialist subjects through displays of autonomy, skepticism, and the ability to debunk appearances, and thus gave them a sense of agency and moral worth. But the repeated use of crisis imagery also had a number of unintended consequences, brought on most notably by facilitating particular kinds of collective identities and, by extension, making certain other, political possibilities less conceivable. My general argument is that practices centered around the attainment of autonomy from the postsocialist Russian state impeded collective action in two ways: (1) by circumscribing the repertoire of acceptable political responses to emerging problems, and (2) by minimizing the recognition of the role that state structures continued to play for the welfare of many Russian citizens (and thus reducing the likelihood of protests against further retrenchment of state welfare). When competence got equated with practical and psychological autonomy from the state, the options of engaging or challenging state authority through contention became less appealing.

"If There Is Famine—Let There Be Famine": Reverse Political Socialization

The problematic aspects of widespread reliance on crisis rhetoric in the 1990s were, in many ways, extensions of its immediate functions. On the psychological level, deflated expectations of the future could be instrumental for accepting one's immediate reality, but they also had the effect of normalizing the conditions that might have been questioned and continuously widening the scope of "acceptable" aggravations. Through the repeated activation of crisis imagery, people could continue to incorporate new developments and trends into the same picture of the world without getting the sense that anything had qualitatively changed. Quite the contrary: when skeptical predictions proved to be true, speakers interpreted that as yet another confirmation of their worldview, often misrecognizing the fact that they had a markedly more narrow definition of what the "crisis" was back when they were making the prediction. In other words, the continuous supply of new, discouraging information was interpreted as a progressing elaboration of the same state of the crisis that merely revealed its new, previously latent manifestations, rather than as a successive unfolding of events in a direction that could be reversed, altered or at least questioned.

What evolved as a result of the (successful) efforts to normalize the crisis was a simultaneous conviction that anything was possible and that, at the same time, nothing was "too" bad. On the one hand, as the picture of the crisis broadened to include new aspects and dimensions, the scope of conceivable possibilities widened correspondingly. On the other, with the entire decade behind them, people had the sense that almost nothing could catch them off guard. Competent demonstration of a combination of these attitudes became a part of the art of self-presentation; it characterized one as an individual who had been "wised up" by the transformation. Thus, when fifty-seven-year-old Nelly Romanovna, who, due to her active career as a private tutor, enjoyed relative prosperity, calmly described her prospects for the future as "if there is famine—let there be famine" (*golod—znachit golod*), this was hardly a fatalistic statement. Rather, the sensibility she was communicating was that of a person who is sufficiently in control to handle all turns and twists of fate. The same image was communicated by Alla Alekseevna, a fifty-three-year-old office manager, when, sharing her vision of prospects for the future, she said, "Well, dictatorship—this is ridiculous, it's completely impossible now," and then, after only a brief pause, "although nothing will surprise me."

Alla Alekseevna's reversal of her initial reaction turned her comment—originally concerned narrowly with the likelihood of a particular political development—into an implicit statement about Alla Alekseevna's own personality. What matters here is not merely her political disenfranchisement or emotional distance from the vicissitudes of the political process. By virtually dismissing the possibility of a dictatorial regime and then immediately suspending her disbelief, Alla Alekseevna reminded herself and the listener that the depth of the downfall could not be determined in advance and presented herself as someone who does not lose her grip on reality even when the circumstances may look deceptively benign. Her actions and consumption patterns (consistent investments into the apartment in which she and her husband lived, refusal to use banks, active reliance on networks, and many other tactics described in the previous chapter) only worked to reinforce and give substance to this claim.

Nelly Romanovna's and Alla Alekseevna's comments illustrate what happens when an individual's practical competence is equated with emotional distance from politics. Both of these older women, whose actual autonomy and control were fundamentally jeopardized in the course of the 1990s, were able to construct themselves as competent agents insofar as they remained unshaken by political cataclysms and stayed prepared for the ones yet to come. The actual degree of danger was not as relevant here as the moral stance of the speaker who emphasized her demonstrative emotional disengagement, thus rhetorically separating herself both from the instigators of the political havoc and from those who were unable to competently handle its aftershocks.

This emotional disengagement stood in sharp contrast not only to the much more dramatic orgies of lament that Ries (1997) had observed in Moscow during the late years of perestroika, but also (albeit to a lesser extent) to the rather expressive criticisms I heard in the summer of 1998, prior to the default. Far from being the evidence of an unfolding civic order, however, this shift of sentiment represented precisely the opposite: a widening acceptance of crisis as the only conceivable reality—moreover, the only reality that individuals had the cultural and social tools to address. In light of this acceptance, emotional distance from all things political was considered a measure of successful adaptation—a form of post-Soviet cultural capital—whereas attempts to dedicate oneself to reforming the discredited "system" were seen as naïve and self-defeating, as in this example:

> How can you take our politics seriously at all? For me it's just a collection of idiots and swindlers, and if I ever look at them, it's the same way I look at animals in the zoo. (Zhenia, female, 34)

Also illustrative is a conversation I had with Andrei:

> ANDREI: Roughly speaking, there are two groups of people who take politics seriously. One is professionals, those who know it inside and out, and two is . . . we can provisionally call them idealists, those who don't know much, but believe whatever the politicians tell them. There are idealists who protest, and idealists who support, the whole gamut. But overall, just these two groups. Professionals have their own interest, their own goals. They are the diplomats, those who climb into coalmines earning political capital, and then use it in their own interests and those of their family . . . And then there are the realists, the rest of us.
> AUTHOR: Well, who's in the majority?
> ANDREI: In the majority? Well, there aren't so many professionals out there, for

understandable reasons. As for the rest, it depends on where you look. If you take Moscow and the [surrounding] villages, as far as I understand, the majority are realists, those who have no interest in politics. [Pause] The majority have no interest in politics because it's constantly demonstrating how dirty it is. There are many more people who realize that than there are idealists who take an interest, who try to prove some point while frothing at the mouth, or try to make sense of who said what. These are all these Communist babushkas and other frustrated characters . . . (Andrei, male, 38)

Andrei's association of the antiquated pattern of political activity with the older generation is understandable, not necessarily because, as he implied, its members were less attuned to the demands of post-Soviet life, but rather because it was markedly more difficult for them to achieve full autonomy due to their dependence on state subsidies and pensions. Yet even among this generation, as Nelly Romanovna's and Alla Alekseevna's comments testify, practical competence was measured by the person's capacity to develop an emotional distance, as well as practical safeguards against the effects of the crisis. In this context, political emancipation was understood as emancipation *from* politics first and foremost, a realization that only retreat into personal life could give one shelter from the uncertainties of the postsocialist era:

When this euphoria was with the White House, in 1992–93, when Gaidar invited everyone to defend democracy, and people came out . . . My husband's colleague from the university went, and they only found him several months later, killed. Can you imagine? There was such euphoria, people went to defend the White House, Yeltsin,[1] but when they saw everything that followed—that's it, no one will go anymore. People are tired . . . To an extent, it is the end of trust. But the important part is that people understood that they were defending Yeltsin, defending Khazbulatov, and so what? . . . Nothing changed because of the change in government. And now it's not millions that go to these demonstrations, but handfuls, and it's all because people understand the worth of this activity. They understand that politics isn't worth anything. Everyone should take care of their own business. If you chose the politicians, fine, they should think about the people, but they don't do it, they only look after their own interests. And now people have understood that, and they don't even go to vote.[2] Instead everyone has started taking care of their own lives. They understand that if they don't take care of their lives, no one will. And since the situation in Moscow is somewhat better than in the country in general, you can find ways of arranging your life these days. Life is not so bad in Moscow, especially in municipal enterprises. New museums are being opened, new companies all the time, life is going on . . . (Karina, female, 63)

This sharp rhetorical distinction between the personal and the political conforms to the traditional assumptions concerning the mutual alienation between the populace and the powers in Russia[3] or, on a broader plane, to the distinction proposed by Linz and Stepan (1996) between "ethical civil society" and "normal political society," in which the former serves as a moral precondition of opposition to an oppressive authority but is unable, without the latter, to reconcile conflicting interests and to negotiate the formation of normative political institutions. Yet to construe this trend as merely an expression of historical continuity would not only be to commit the logical error of collapsing the distinction between similarities and continuities. It would also mean ignoring the central function that these (anti-)political sentiments served. Indeed, post-Soviet citizens did not consider their political sensibilities simply mechanically inherited from the past. On the contrary, the new sophistication (read: disenfranchisement) was widely perceived as the outcome of encounters with the unfolding crisis in its various manifestations, from political (as in Karina's statement above) to economic and cultural, and as a *reversal* of many prior beliefs and attitudes. The images of preceding crises, particularly of the 1991 coup and the constitutional crisis of 1993 with its aftermath, played a central role in depicting the new political "emancipation" as a direct product of postsocialist experiences.[4] In this respect, if the developments of the late 1980s–early 1990s, with their "spectacle of moving and flying monuments" (Boym 1994, 230), their boom of newspaper readership, and the mushrooming of civic associations (Urban 1997) could be interpreted by an optimistic observer as evidence of democratic political socialization, at the end of the decade Muscovites cited the same experiences primarily as examples of their initial political innocence, or, to use the language of one publication, as evidence of "how naïve we have been."[5] The true political socialization they saw themselves undergo over the past ten years was the reverse: an increasing skepticism regarding the fruitfulness of political involvement, and a reorientation toward narrowly personal concerns and agendas.

Thus, while it is fairly common to dismiss the political culture of postsocialism as inert and plagued by legacies of socialism (Sztompka 1991, 1993; Levada 2000), this outright dismissal fails to recognize the ways in which the more recent postsocialist experiences contributed their own logic to the persistence and even intensification of familiar attitudes. Indeed, the contrast between the current political skepticism and the "idealism" of the perestroika period served a double purpose. It supplied evidence for claims concerning the universal decline and the widening scope of possibilities for further deterioration. But this increasingly private stance could also be interpreted as a wise response to prior events—an interpretation that offered individuals a sense of personal progression, and thus constructed them as competent players on the post-Soviet field. However, this response also inhibited further action. In a sense, it objectified and naturalized the unwelcome political developments and created a situation in which the socially sanctioned course of action involved a successful mastery of life during crisis rather than the mastery of the crisis itself. Macro-societal developments were likened to an act of nature, both implicitly and explicitly. As stated nine years later by Georgii, a car mechanic in his forties who, in his own formulation, "made the mistake" of participating in the defense of the White House during the August putsch of 1991, "You can only be mad at things that depend on you personally. How can you be mad at a thunderstorm, at a tornado, at the eruption of a volcano? And what is done by the state is equally not subject to our influence."

(De)Constructing the Crisis, or
Gullibility as the Main Postsocialist Sin

Perception of crisis as the ultimate reality had another important implication. Because the crisis was assumed to be all-embracing, and the capacity to foresee and anticipate unfavorable future developments acquired such high symbolic value, people spent much time demonstrating to others their ability to see through seemingly innocent events and to discern in them carefully concealed schemes and omens for the future.

The motif of disparity between engineered appearances and the underlying reality, between word and action, pretexts and true intentions was not new to people who had spent a significant part of their lives in the atmosphere of late socialism, where the correspondence between ideological claims and lived reality was questionable at best. This is not to say that ideology was routinely contested by late Soviet subjects. On the contrary, as Alexei Yurchak writes, although "in Soviet late socialism people recognized much ideological falsity," they did not contest it because "it was apparent that no other public representation of reality within the official sphere could occur" (Yurchak 1997, 165–166).[6] Instead of either engaging in a direct contestation of ideology or offering it their whole-hearted support (which was considered to be the business of two equally marginal groups, dissidents and activists respectively), the majority of Soviet subjects chose merely to reproduce the ubiquitous official rhetoric without any emotional or cognitive investment in it, while simultaneously engaging in "parallel events"—activities that took place concurrently with the official ones but were perceived as more meaningful, such as reading a book during a Komsomol meeting, or drinking and socializing during a demonstration, all the while continuing to shout slogans and carry portraits of a Party leader (whose identity, as Yurchak points out, one frequently did not, and didn't care to, know).

In contrast to the Soviet era, people in the 1990s did not feel the need to reproduce the official rhetoric in the course of their everyday lives. The past rhetoric was no more. The unified body of ideology disintegrated with a speed that left many individuals with a sense of emptiness, not because the socialist slogans and rhetorical clichés were badly missed, but merely because the sudden evaporation of the grand narrative seemed to suggest to many that a new grand narrative had to be devised to replace it.[7] Yet ironically, in the absence of such a clear-cut body of doctrinal rhetoric, the task of being a competent political subject became more complicated. As it was frequently pointed out to me, "in socialist times we knew how to read between the lines, and these days you never know who is serving as a mouthpiece for whom." Implied in this statement was the belief that although in postsocialism, unlike the preceding period, the modes of representing reality could vary, the fact of its distortion in the course of representation remained invariable.

A preoccupation with debunking appearances and uncovering hidden motives was a logical consequence of this belief, and it was particularly apparent in discussions about the media. Perhaps unsurprisingly, this tendency coexisted with the proliferation of programs that were themselves dedicated to debunking both the larger political rhetoric and the biases of other programs.[8] Dedicated to overviews of political events of the week (*Zerkalo, Itogi*) or to economics (such as *Bol'shie den'gi*), these programs claimed to lay bare the foundations of politics by exposing the interests, alliances, and biases involved in seemingly transparent moves of political figures. The less sophisticated deconstructions consisted of publishing compromising information on many central figures in Russian politics, complete with titles like "Stately Pickpockets," or "Glide of Repugnant Butterflies."[9] Others were more complex and functioned as a kind of metalanguage. Providing diagrams, schemes, and charts that mapped out the field of politics and made every significant political actor a function of his/her political location and personal financial interest, these publications dismissed the ideological rhetoric and stated reasons as inconsequential; they cut straight into the embedded interests and inner political struggles as the primary motivators of all political developments. Since these critical messages resonated with people's own sense of crisis, such programs generally had a greater chance of being taken seriously and not dismissed as tools of political manipulation.[10] Terms drawn from these critical programs and publications, such as "the family" (*sem'ia,* referring to those surrounding Yeltsin during the final years of his presidency), "Luzhkov's people" (*liudi Luzhkova,* political and economic actors affiliated with the Moscow mayor Yuri Luzhkov during the parliamentary election campaign), "dirty technologies" (*griaznye tekhnologii,* strategic leaks of compromising information into the media and other manipulations of public opinion by the political spin doctors) received remarkably wide circulation. By the run-up to the presidential elections of 2000, there was hardly a political conversation in which the themes of manipulation and deceit did not feature prominently, overshadowing any other election-related themes or concerns.

However, it was not uncommon, especially toward the very end of the 1990s, for the critical tools to be turned against the very programs that made them widely available. In other words, the metalanguage of deconstruction and hidden interests, which was promoted by the programs and print media critical of the ruling establishment, itself became an element in a metalanguage of a higher order (a meta-meta-language, as it were), in which attempts to deconstruct the motives of a politician themselves started to be seen as a move in someone's political game. Media efforts to analyze political interests and actions lost their innocence and became inherently suspect:

> Television is completely fake. Every single channel pushes its own agenda. I just watch and ask myself: Whose? Whose? Gusinsky, Berezovsky, they all push their agenda very heavily on these channels. You just have to watch for a few minutes and it becomes perfectly clear who the channel belongs to. As for the newspapers, I hardly read them, because I have no money for them in the first place. Off and on I may read [*Moskovskii*] *Komsomolets,* as yellow journalism that seems to think it should poke its nose into every little thing, it may be funny sometimes. I read *Novaia Gazeta,* it's not so bad. Now it has gotten a lot more boring than before, but it used to be quite decent. I may read *Nezavisimaia* sometimes, but there I just skim

the political section and mostly go for the literary stuff. Other than that, you really can observe what's happening without any newspapers and draw your own conclusions. (Konstantin, male, 53)

As a result, while many continued to follow media stories and could still cite instances of the corruption and shady dealings they revealed, these accounts routinely ended with expressions of doubt about the credibility of the very source they were citing, and with acknowledgements of the fact that these were still "rumors" distributed by "someone's mouthpieces" and that "this could all be manufactured (*sfabrikovano*) from beginning to the end":

His [Yeltsin's] team, it's, how should I put it . . . Unpleasant, to say the least. And frankly, I don't know how much of what's behind the latest decisions came from him, and how much came from the team. But on the other hand, really, this very word, "team," "the family," these are all of the journalists' making, and they must have played their role, in terms of boosting negative attitudes toward him. And the politics of these journalists of ours, they are just purposefully aggravating things, using the fact that we cannot independently evaluate what this "family" did, all these bank accounts of this Tatiana [Diachenko, Yeltsin's daughter] and stuff. (Gennadii, male, 43)

Critical remarks about Yeltsin's circle naturally turn in Gennadii's narrative into critical remarks about the media's construction of this circle and the potential dangers such construction may have for the public order. It is this fundamental suspicion regarding the credibility and motives of the Russian media that Ellen Mickiewicz described as the "Russian viewer's extraordinary sophistication" and "impressive media literacy" (1999, 287). Russian viewers, she argued, had been taught by decades of media control and ideological indoctrination to "tease out what is important for them and to correct for methods that trouble them" (1999, 289). This conclusion, however, seems shattered by the outcome of the experiments that Mickiewicz reported a few pages later: when asked to spot the bias in a number of news clips, members of the focus groups, all of whom engaged in "critical media discourse," could not agree on the direction and intensity, and even the very existence, of the bias. What we are dealing with, then, seems to be not so much the command of a systematic and accurate critical tool-kit, but the general conviction of the necessarily falsified nature of all public representations, and the centrality of such a conviction for the individual's sense of personal identity. In other words, the viewers may not have had the tools of navigation in the boundless sea of questionably accurate information, but the very awareness of its deceptive nature made one feel a part of a skeptical and realistic moral majority:

These days, one journalist says something from his point of view, another one says something different, a third one says a third thing, and in the final analysis, they aren't talking for themselves anyways. These are some orders being fulfilled (*idut kakie-to zakazy*). Because every channel, it's designed for a particular party, a particular outlook, at least that's my opinion. ORT, and RTR, and NTV, they exist and they have their own agenda. And they broadcast according to their political agenda.

What Changes When Life Stands Still 151

It's another question whether we listen to it or not, but you can't help tuning in, and some things, they stick [in one's mind]. So I think a sort of cultivation is going on, maybe not full-blown hypnosis, but they do achieve a lot of what they want through TV, that's for sure. Take this same Berezovsky, they are showing him from a particular angle that they want us to adopt. Because I don't know him personally, so how can I judge him, discuss him, or understand? It's very complicated. So how on Earth? Or Yeltsin. They showed him in the light they wanted us to see ... They're trying to work us (*pytaiutsia nas obrabotat'*), because we can't check how accurate this is by ourselves. (Valentina, female, 31)

The implications of this constructionist view of the media are interesting. On the surface, the sensibility informing the critical media discourse in Russia was strikingly similar to the Western tradition of deconstructing media biases, which comes from critics on both sides of the political divide.[11] As such, this outlook could be expected to be potentially empowering, in that it could mobilize the informed public against manipulation and ensure critical reception of biased political coverage in a way that would make Noam Chomsky proud. The actual effects of media deconstructionism in Russia, however, turned out to be quite the opposite. Making sense of the news requires systematic reliance on alternative channels of information whose credibility has not been compromised, as well as a clear legal framework for tracking down abuses of journalistic ethics. In the absence of these resources, perpetual doubts regarding the objectivity of mass media can have a paralyzing effect. Not unlike the classic philosophical paradox dismissing all Cretans as liars, the postsocialist skeptical sensibility left people without options for action, since all potential alternatives and perspectives could be suspected of manipulation the very moment they were made public. This circular logic of generalized distrust was not confined to media attitudes, for politics in general was conceptualized in a similar fashion:

Politicians are politicians. My opinion is that it's all a dirty game. And on principle, there can be no fair play in politics. Any politics. Because everyone represents the interests of someone, someone is working through him. Someone is sponsoring him. And that's it. That's the game on the highest level. (Sasha, male, 30)

Too complex to be deduced from rhetoric and behavior, political interests and motives were thus assumed to be always unstated—a conviction that made the stated intentions automatically dismissible as deceptive by definition. The relevance of this view was in its implication for action (or inaction). Since the rules governing political interactions were unclear and purportedly immoral, the desire to participate in them characterized one either as an idealist (as in Andrei's quotation above) or as an immoral individual oneself. Either way, sincere support for such involvement seemed hard to find. This reluctance to extend full-blown support to any grassroots initiatives that held the promise of countering prevailing political trends could be seen in descriptions of political alternatives to the Yeltsin regime, such as the following:

If someone appears to organize people to step into the streets [to protest], my take would be, provided they are doing it with pure intentions . . . because I find it hard to believe that they will be doing it with pure intentions and that they will be taking people to the streets in order to improve their lives. Chances are, it's their own life that these people will be trying to improve. So that with their [the protesters'] help they would defend something, or grab some more of whatever it is that they want: power, or money, or banks, or something else. So this is a very difficult issue. (Nelly Romanovna, female, 57)

The very idea of a possible alternative to the status quo, initially contemplated as a positive development, was quick to turn here into a continuation of crisis talk, elaborating on the inherent corruption of all political motives. The very theme of collective self-organization thus became implicated in a Catch-22: one needs to organize in order to counter political corruption, but anyone willing to lead such a collective effort was sure to be labeled a self-interested political opportunist.[12] This general perception did not make voters uniformly prejudiced against all actors on the Russian political scene; some politicians were still believed to defy the stereotypes of political corruption. However, even expressions of support were weak and demonstratively cautious:

TATIANA: I was sad when he [Primakov] was forced to leave. He seemed like a caring person. But then . . . we didn't really try to figure it out. There were too many different things being said, and each [politician] was saying his own thing . . . I didn't take sides. Who knows what these people are up to.
AUTHOR: So you never considered protesting or, say, joining in on some meeting, or something like this?
TATIANA: With these fools, you mean? On city squares and such? I never was part of it, and I don't go now. And what I heard recently—Luzhkov spoke on TV today, did you hear it? He said, "Someone is collecting money, three thousand dollars, supposedly for [his] team." He said, "These people should be handed over to the police." That's what these folks are up to. (Tatiana, female, 68)

In opposition to "these folks," namely the charlatans who attempted to manipulate the public and the gullible people who fell for their promises, "normal" post-Soviet subjects prided themselves on being able to draw a clear line between the world of appearances (that is, politics) and the real world of their everyday lives. In fact, the most frequent opposition to the realm of politics I heard invoked in conversation was not cultural or spiritual matters, not even people's immediate economic concerns, but more broadly, the complexity of mundane but productive pursuits designated by the word *delo*. Delo, a noun of the same stem as the verb *delat'* (to do, to make), can have many translations: it's business, affairs, deeds (as "in word and deed"), and often bears overtones of down-to-earth but moral activity. Scheming, profiteering, double-dealing may formally be delo, and a *griaznoe delo* (dirty business) at that, but they will always simultaneously be evaluated as "*ne delo*" (no [worthy] business). Those were precisely the terms in which many political messages and activities were described. Conscious withdrawal from collective action was based on this contrast. It was assumed that, while the lazy and the gullible spend their time on the barricades, the more sensible and realistic segment of society was the one toiling away to make postsocialism work:

> Expressing one's vexations at all these rallies, strikes, demonstrations, all these collective things—I personally don't support such strategies. Yes, maybe it's great and all, to take to the streets, to vote for something, but still, that's no kind of business (*no opiat' zhe vse eto ne delo*). One needs to work (*Rabotat' nado*). That's what's needed now. To try to create some new workplaces. But protesting . . . that's not constructive. That will end with just another mess, and in the process someone will fill up his pockets again. (Sasha, male, 30)

> I don't like politicians. My opinion is, politics is useless. We have to work. I mean, politics is OK, but in combination with business acumen. If you have politics alone, everything will turn into chaos. If we don't work, things will never go right. I mean, what kind of politics can you talk about if the plants and factories stand still, while everyone is busy trading? Where would anything come from? . . . But they are all too busy with politics [to see it]. Passing laws that don't work . . . (Klara, female, 45)

The juxtaposition between conscientious work and politics, with the latter interpreted as a synonym for unproductive arguments at best and for methods of personal enrichment at worst, spoke volumes about the moral economy of the postsocialist period and about the deep interconnections between political attitudes and crisis talk. One's understanding of oneself as a worthy subject did not have to include political activity, but it depended heavily on drawing moral boundaries between the productive and realistic attitude of the collective "us" and the socially useless and detrimental rhetoric of the politicized "them."

If, in the realm of post-Soviet affairs of state, politics as usual was juxtaposed to delo, in everyday life it stood in opposition to the realm of personal relations. Within this moral and emotional logic, fragile webs of personal connections and trust could only be polluted by the interposition of the political:

> I was traveling recently to visit family, with all these different people in the compartment, and I was thinking, what keeps us from living in peace? Because here we are, we are all sitting here together. But then one starts with Zhirinovsky, another one with Zyuganov, a third one with someone else. Whenever we manage to forget who is who, we start talking with each other, remembering a film, telling jokes, we eat together, we turn into humans. But as soon as this social level comes up—all these bestial things start. (Vladimir, male, 40)

The degree to which political motives were distrusted and renounced was particularly visible in the reluctance with which Muscovites admitted to the political underpinnings of some of their own actions. The rationalizations of voting and other politically informed behaviors (such as participation in rallies or donation of signatures in support of particular politicians) was telling in this regard as, in the course of my fieldwork, the cycle of Russian political life advanced from the mid-term session of the parliament to the parliamentary and presidential elections. As the time of the elections approached, the theme of political participation was ceasing to be speculative and started to gain real and practical meaning. "Practical," however, did not necessarily mean political. One way to assert the moral superiority of delo over political arguments was exactly to frame one's actions pragmatically, as a down-to-earth practical response to the situation. In this spirit, one's voting decisions were represented not as political choices, but as efforts to minimize the disruptive effect of political struggle and to get out of the electoral period as quickly as possible. Victor Vladimirovich, a fifty-six-year-old lathe operator, rationalized his political preferences as follows:

> I haven't fully decided [whether to vote or not], but I think it is actually important to participate, so that extra money does not get spent on the second round. That is, it's better that the president is elected in one round. Because in any case, Putin will be the president.
> AUTHOR: Why are you so sure?
> VV: Because there is all this widespread campaigning. He is advertised all over and, indeed, they show that he is busy with all kinds of different affairs (*dela delaet vsiakie*). While the others are just promising so far. Just promising. No one is doing anything . . . So I'll be glad if it happens without the second round, because that will be just a waste of money. Our money. This money could be spent for the retired, for someone else, and here you'll be wasting it for the elections, for nothing. So my take is to vote right away for Putin, and get done with it.

The opposition between delo and empty rhetoric was involved in Victor Vladimirovich's narrative on two levels. On the one hand, it was the juxtaposition of the busy and practical Putin against his competitors who, although full of promises, were idle. On the other, it was the opposition of the efficient resolution of elections in one round to the costly (although, one could argue, crucial) public debates that could ensue if the elections were protracted.

Overall, the meaning of personal political participation and the place where it fell on the continuum between delo and fruitless political debate was changing as the elections approached. This is not to say that the legitimacy of elections was in any way reevaluated. However, denunciatory rhetoric and statements of distrust, which during my earlier interviewing waves were used to dismiss the appropriateness of democratic procedures altogether, during later interviews were employed by the same people in order to justify their intention to participate in the very procedures they used to dismiss. During an interview in December 1998, Igor, a thirty-one-year-old car mechanic, explained his disregard for voting as resulting from the fundamental corruption of this process:

> There is no point to voting whatsoever. If someone has money, they'll get elected either way, so I have no faith in this crap and don't even go to participate anymore. Last time I went I voted for Zhirinovsky. And what's the use? I could have voted for Yeltsin just the same. I could have not voted at all. What's the point? No point at all, absolutely none. It is all bought up wholesale in advance, and all the results are fixed.

In early spring of 2000 some fifteen months later, between the time of the parliamentary and the presidential elections, the topic moved from the realm of theory to the sphere of actual personal plans, and Igor's position notice-ably changed. He expressed his attitude toward the campaign for boycotting the elections rather indignantly (and, obviously, without recollecting the state-ments he made earlier):

> Well, this [boycotting idea] is just idiocy. Why? Because, if nothing else, someone can use your vote for whoever they have on their agenda. That's one thing. You don't care, so you don't show up. And they fix the results with your help, however they want it. Besides, a person has to have some ideas, it's not like it's all the same for you, right? [After a pause] Although it *is* all the same, in a way. But I will still go, just out of principle, so that someone else doesn't cast my ballot for me, I will go out of principle. Although I have no faith in this pile of crap. That we will have honest elections with observers from the OSCE[13] and what have you. I still think it's all baloney. But I will still go, because then even if they are corrupt, it won't be because I gave them a chance. Let's put it this way. At least I'll know that I went honestly and cast my vote myself.

What is interesting in the reversal of Igor's attitude is not so much the fact that he had changed his mind (after all, unpredictability of electoral behavior is one of the most widely known problems of pre-election opinion polls), but rather that, in order to express each of these two contradictory positions, he used practically the same arguments. In several instances even the phrasing was identical; both times, he evoked the same imagery of fixed results and proclaimed that he did not believe "this pile of crap." This and many other similar cases I encountered suggested that demonstrating one's distance from, and disbelief in, politics was a rhetorical convention that endured even as spe-cific behaviors or intentions changed. In other words, this rhetoric was *the* meta-message of the communicative exchange, the cultural and social constant that remained relevant in a variety of otherwise discrepant encounters.

This means that, conversational mainstay though it was, the crisis discourse was nevertheless non-deterministic. While it created space for common defi-nition of the situation among several speakers, it also allowed for considerable variability in the actual positions they chose to express. The only common de-nominator was the lasting need to distance oneself from politics even in those moments when one was engaging in it. In this sense, expressions of cynicism and self-distancing worked as face-saving techniques that helped the speaker to maintain an image of competence even while admitting to such supposedly naïve pursuits as civic activism. Such disclosures, which took place mostly dur-ing the last wave of the interviews (when the proximity of elections made the topic more relevant), sounded almost apologetic in the way more morally ques-tionable activities, such as bribery and tax evasion, did not. Zhenia, a thirty-four-year-old accounting manager who repeatedly emphasized her disinterest in politics, framed her actions as follows:

> Many years ago, I used to give my signature to nominate him [Yavlinsky[14]], it was back when you had people walking around knocking on doors with these lists. And

here recently, I was told that in the subway crossing at the Revolution Square station they were collecting signatures for Yavlinsky again. So I went and gave mine.

AUTHOR: So you are planning to go vote?

ZHENIA: I am an apolitical person. I told you, overall, I don't care . . .

AUTHOR: Well, but if you gave your signature, then maybe you're not all that apolitical.

ZHENIA: [Reluctantly] Well, yeah, I gave it, but mostly just because it was on my way, you see. Not because I, like, went there specifically for this purpose. Because I knew they were collecting them there, and I was downtown that day, so I went through this crossing to sign up. It's not a hard thing to do. But if I have some other business, if I go into the country for that day, I won't go vote for his sake. Although I don't think I'll go anywhere, because they're showing Formula One on the 26th [of March 2000, the day of the presidential elections], and so I'll stay in Moscow.

Zhenia's reluctance to take ownership of her political sympathies is apparent here through the multiple conditionals with which she surrounded her disclosures. By emphasizing the *accidental* nature of her support, she managed to combine two positions at the same time—that of an espouser of liberal values (Yavlinsky being the chosen candidate of the liberal intelligentsia) and that of a hardened and mature postsocialist subject who has parted with the illusions of the past and has no emotional investment in the deceptive drama of postsocialist politics. Several minutes later she returned to that image when she said,

I don't talk politics much, because . . . because in order to talk about politics, you have to be well-versed in the subject. I mean, it's a kind of a game,[15] you have to at least know the rules, because if you don't, it makes no sense to play it, right? Let's say you don't know how to play poker, you won't take your place at the table and play. And this is the same thing, same as a card game, or so it seems to me. Maybe it just looks that way because I don't know better, but I think they are simply playing.

AUTHOR: And what are the stakes?

ZHENIA: The stakes are well-known. Who will occupy a particular seat, who'll get more money.

Displays of considerable cynicism allowed Zhenia, while having political sympathies and beliefs, to still consider herself an apolitical and thus "normal" person. She supported her candidate almost reluctantly, all along continuing to insist that she had no illusions regarding the principles of political struggle in postsocialist Russia. Similar displays of role distance routinely accompanied political statements, regardless of the speakers' political persuasion. Vera Vladimirovna, a forty-three-year-old cleaning lady whose electoral sympathies were diametrically opposite to Zhenia's, expressed her voting plans in the following terms:

You know, Olia, take it or leave it, I don't like Zyuganov, but I am going to vote for him. And many will do the same, as a form of protest against what's going on. But this is all useless. It's all useless, I believe, because they will falsify the results anyway. Because all these new electoral technologies and stuff . . . It's not that simple. It will all be done to order (*Vse sdelaetsia kak polozheno*). Because I don't believe in ratings, because I have talked to many people and many do not like Putin. And they say his rating is fifty-nine, or fifty-five, or whatever? Our people are not that gullible.

The logic standing behind Vera Vladimirovna's comments is the same as we observed in Zhenia's narrative: an affirmative statement of political sympathy is immediately followed and undercut by a qualifying skeptical message concerning the credibility of the electoral procedures, the value of the candidate, or the intensity of the speaker's support. Significantly, these expressions of political dissatisfaction did not provide a basis for discussion of possible channels of inciting change, but instead served as tokens of the speakers' awareness of deceit and their ability to see through it, as testimony that, in Vera Vladimirovna's words, "our people are not that gullible." Because of this narratively constructed distance from politics, success or failure of a candidate could never result in "loss of face" for the speaker, since the identification with the candidate was never complete, and the acceptance of failure was built into the structure of popular support from the very beginning.

Electoral Technologies, Falsification of History, and the Triumph of the Observer

The vision of the political sphere I encountered in Moscow in the late 1990s had a dual nature. Seemingly, political developments were seen as obscure and incomprehensible, the "rules of the game," to use Zhenia's formulation, were unknown, and the possibility of full involvement was circumscribed exactly by the lack of clarity in the principles that structured political life. Yet at the same time, the basic mechanism fueling the political process was considered transparent and unambiguous, the "stakes," to continue the same metaphor, were apparent, and the ultimate interests of the main actors were painfully clear. The concept of the "new electoral technologies" mentioned by Vera Vladimirovna captured this tension very well: the strategic goal of their application was always the same (power, influence, money), while the tactical ends to which they were employed in each particular case continued to be perplexing and not obvious to an uninformed observer. The idea of "electoral technologies" gained a remarkable circulation during the late 1990s. It therefore seems appropriate to take it, along with such related notions as "dirty technologies" (*griaznye tekhnologii*), "black PR" (*chernyi piar*) or "image-making" (*imidzh-meikerstvo*), as guiding concepts for the exploration of the postsocialist political imagination.

The term "electoral technologies" was usually evoked in reference to such methods of propaganda as unequal framing of the candidates, fragmentation of the opponents' electoral base, dissemination of rumors and accusations, and other similar instances that abounded during the months of electoral campaigning of 1999–2000. The notion of electoral technologies foregrounded the gap that was assumed to exist between representation and reality and colored the entire electoral struggle with overtones of falsification and illegitimacy. This was admitted even by the self-proclaimed spin experts whose books and manuals flooded the post-Soviet book market in the late 1990s, both triggered by this deconstructionist political sensibility and contributing to its perpetuation. In the preface to the book *Exaggerate and Rule: Technologies of Contemporary "Soft" Propaganda,* its author, Arsenii Mironov, defined his target audience as "those independent journalists who aim to secretly manipulate the consciousness of their readers, to influence the range of topics raised in public discussions, to address the issues of political advertising and 'spinning' of images while necessarily preserving the illusion of quality of the conferred information, of political independence, and of a balanced attitude toward the events in question" (2001).

The most blatant and unseemly instances of manipulation of public opinion, such as the fabrication and release of false documents and compromising information, comprised the subgroup of "dirty technologies." Falsification of poll results, to which Vera Vladimirovna alluded in her comments, fully belonged in this repertoire. The "newness" of these "new electoral technologies" was questionable and had more to do with Vera Vladimirovna's recent exposure to the information about techniques for manipulation of public opinion.[16] If anything, the electoral campaigns of 1999 and 2000 were argued by many self-proclaimed spin experts to herald the *end* of the era of crude "dirty technologies," which were slowly coming to be replaced by the more "sophisticated and highly effective methods [which] have long been used by the specialists of so-called 'soft' propaganda in the West" (Mironov 2001, preface).

The significance of the late 1990s, then, was not that this period introduced a formerly unknown form of political struggle, but that in the course of these years this form of struggle achieved new visibility and, more importantly, defined much of the vocabulary in which public events and political developments were thought and talked about, both in everyday conversations and in the media. The latter were openly implicated in the propaganda war,[17] and thus served a double purpose: as providers of the terminology for political criticism and as sources of material for its application. Both of these functions are apparent in the conversation below, in which Dmitrii Kirillovich, a fifty-four-year-old medical doctor, discusses the explosions in Moscow apartment buildings that occurred in the fall of 1999, providing the Putin government with justification for launching the second war with Chechnya:

> There even was this despicable thing, some journalists claimed that these blasts were engineered by the FSB itself.[18]
> AUTHOR: And what was your take?
> DK: Oh, but this is all this black . . . it's called . . . black, black . . . Black PR. And these, electoral, what do they call them? [snaps his fingers looking for the word]
> AUTHOR: Technologies?
> DK: Technologies. All they want is to slander, to defame, and once you do it, let them try, try and prove that it wasn't them. Because it sounds despicable. But then again, who knows?

As Dmitrii Kirillovich's and Vera Vladimirovna's responses demonstrate, familiarity with the "professional" terms of political manipulation did not necessarily make the analysis of the goings-on any more insightful or powerful. If anything, they were arguably counterproductive, since they obfuscated important differences between routine campaign management practices and illicit and often criminal arrangements, such as political pressures on the judiciary or physical threats to independent candidates. According to this logic, any instances of pandering to the audience or long-term strategizing were functionally equivalent to character assassinations or large-scale double-dealing, and thus were equally compromised.

But the above criticism should not miss the point of the "electoral technologies" discourse. What made these terms resonate was not their analytical potency, but the semblance of clarity and logic as well as the sense of an insider's competence they provided. At the same time the terminology remained consistent with the tenets of the total crisis by presuming the misleading nature of appearances and the disjunction between the presented image and the underlying grim reality. The terminology of "electoral technologies" was thus used primarily metaphorically, as a way of indicating emotional distance from the practices under discussion. Only a few people were taken enough by the idea to explore it in depth. For an example of such exploration, consider the framing of politics delivered by Alexei Ivanovich, a forty-six-year-old military engineer, on the eve of the presidential election of 2000:

> The technology is developed to the state of the art. Putin's victory is predetermined by the entire logic of this electoral campaign . . . Creation of an image, that starts from afar. Incidentally, it's even taught in the universities today, under the title of public relations—my daughter's friend takes this course and I used to ask her, what are they studying, this has no substance! . . . But apparently, now every firm has a public relations office, or a press secretary or something. And I have not studied it professionally, but I believe that the work of an image-maker is the same thing, same public relations, except that here your image is thrust upon the public. It's a well-planned project that makes a person appealing. Not a day's work. Takes a few years, at the very least. And every step is planned out in advance. This plan can even include some economic breakdown. That's why these people earn this much, because one has to be shrewd, foresightful. That's why this profession is in high demand now. Because there are a lot of people who long for power. And how can you get power? By creating yourself an image. And how do you do that? You develop a long-term program for presenting yourself. That is, let's say I'm a director of some enterprise and I hire a team of image-makers, pay them a lot of dough, of course, and they start working. And so they come to me and say, Alexei Ivanovich, we have created a program for ten years for you. So I'm forty-six, and until I'm fifty-six we would be performing this program. In such and such a year we do so-and-so, issue this information, create negative advertising, then follow up with positive, it's all thought through and calculated, and at the end of this decade, look— now I'm a prime minister. [Pause] Same thing with Putin, it was all set in motion in advance, thought out and calculated: his jet flight to Chechnya, his interview in the coal mine.[19]

It was apparent from Alexei Ivanovich's long narrative that he was quite taken by the idea of the "electoral technologies" and the opportunities they offered for political advancement, and thoroughly enjoyed being able to competently explain the mechanisms of their workings to me. There was one aspect, however, that was missing in his account. It was the question of the substantive content of political life—the development of a sound political program, the establishment of an electoral base, the articulation of distinct interests of particular social groups. This glaring absence was telling: all these issues were assumed by Alexei Ivanovich to be the secondary by-products of the image-makers' work rather than primary considerations for which public relations are but an optimizing venue. In other words, a competent navigation of the political scene implied the capacity to unveil its hidden schemes and ploys, but not a critical examination of competing programs, which appeared from this standpoint as nothing but froth on the stream of political struggle.

This enchanted and at the same time dismissive view of politics combined faith in the power of the political machinery to create agendas and manipulate the electorate with an effort to assert one's independence (including analytical and moral independence) from these political projects. In contrast to the active involvement and loss of autonomy that would be entailed in substantive engagement in the form of rallies, civic initiatives, or political discussion groups, competent political performance in the late 1990s required the sensibility of a skeptical observer who was too well aware of the stakes and methods of politics to waste emotions and time on it.

The historical sensibility I often encountered in Moscow reflected the same desire to communicate aloofness and detachment. While historical parallels figured prominently in Muscovites' conviction that Russian history moved in circles,[20] their general take on history was far from credulous, and for many of the same reasons as those informing their mistrust of politics. Political falsification was expected to be reproduced and aggravated by historical falsification, with the same factors (material interests, alliances, and political struggles) shaping the nature of the distortion. In other words, history was seen as politics writ large, a product of corrupt ruling elites, and emphasis on historical distortions and falsifications was an important argument in favor of political wariness (and vice versa; the political scandals and struggles of interest served as an argument for the distrust of history). Initially unaware of that, I prompted many indignant responses by implicitly suggesting that history was an arbiter of today's disputes. For example, when I asked Konstantin about the label that he would expect the decade of the 1990s to receive in the history books of the future, he initially responded, "Well, I guess another Time of Troubles."[21] But then he quickly corrected himself:

I don't know how it will be remembered. Because to know this, you have to know history. And our history is entirely . . . We were all brought up on history that was written up for us by someone else. In reality, everything was different, and that's why it's impossible to foresee how it will be evaluated . . . All we have are recountings of someone else's accounts. And apparently, as they've started probing deeper into history right now, even the annals and chronicles are not trustworthy, because the chronicles were all rewritten for every ruler (*pod kazhdogo kniazya letopisi vse perepisyvalis'*). And if so, then what can you expect from Soviet times!

AUTHOR: I think I've heard something along these lines . . .

KONSTANTIN: There was a program recently on TV. And yes, that's exactly how it was. If you take all the chronicles and put them together, I just read a little about the chronicles, it's true, there are a lot of inconsistencies, things that don't fit together. What does that tell you? That it was simply amended for every new ruler.

The historical arguments Konstantin was referring to in this passage belong to Anatolii Fomenko, a mathematician and a prolific maverick historian whose revisionist history was so popular during the late 1990s that one of the central bookstores of the capital, Dom Knigi on New Arbat street, dedicated an entire subsection to his and his followers' works.[22] Fomenko's work and the popular reception of his ideas deserve exploration as symptomatic examples of the high premium put on such postsocialist virtues as skepticism, distrust of authority, and the ability to uncover, under benign appearances, the self-interested motives of power—in short, the qualities that made one a "normal" postsocialist subject.

Fomenko's arguments (which he continues to publish, primarily in coauthorship with Gleb Nosovskii) were rooted in a revisionist chronology according to which all ancient chronicles were fabricated during the thirteenth–seventeenth centuries on the basis of events that actually occurred during the tenth–thirteenth centuries. Building on this hypothesis, which Fomenko labeled "the chronological shift," he then proceeded to reconstruct the dating and geographical location of events as they "really" happened, in the course of which the birth of Christ, for instance, was dated to have taken place in 1053, the figure of Ivan the Terrible was argued to be a collective representation of four different rulers who reigned consecutively, and the Golden Horde was merely another name for pre-Romanov Russia, which was delegitimized and vilified by "the Romanov historians" as they carried out "a global revision and tendentious editing of the historical documents . . . in the light of the order imposed upon them by the new rulers" (Nosovskii and Fomenko 1997, 170).[23]

Fomenko's historical arguments did not generate any significant controversy within the Russian academic community because of the evident flaws in his methodology as well as his evasion of any dialogue with conventional historians.[24] His books were written for (and read by) lay readers, and hence the main effort of the academic historians was (and continues to be) to refute Fomenko's claims in the eyes of the public. The inventory of critical articles and papers put together by one such critic, historian Iurii Begunov, far exceeds even the seemingly endless list of Fomenko's own writings, amounting to 156 publications. Apart from purely professional criticisms of Fomenko's methodology and epistemology, the problematic assumptions and misleading parallels promoted in his works, critics frequently point out the dangerous social implications of Fomenko's general conception of history with its postulation of a two-century-long Russian (=Hordean) domination of Eurasia and virtual denial of the ethnic and historical specificity of Turks, Scythians, Goths, Khazars, Tatars, and Mongols, all of whom were declared by Fomenko merely misnomers for Slavs.[25] However, while ethnic megalomania is doubtlessly one of the defining features of Fomenko's project, the aspects of his theory that seemed to resonate with his readers the most were not the Russian ethnic superiority or the country's heroic past, but rather the vision of Russian history and politics as a conspiratorial project fabricated to someone's order and in someone's interest. The transitions between political denunciations and historical descriptions were made smooth precisely by the commonality of their presumed *modus operandi*. Fomenko's own, or similar-sounding, revisionist statements were spontaneously mentioned in this context by many as a way of adding historical depth to the argument, as in the example below:

> Our government . . . it's not independent . . . It wants to satisfy itself, but does not want to give space for growth to others, not to producers, not to you and me, not to anyone else. It is a mentality, it is formed through years and years . . . In other words, I don't know if I mentioned it before, but there is this Fomenko who made up a new chronology. He has a bunch of books on the new chronology of Russia, he's been doing this for a while, and he subjected all of our Russian history to some well-argued criticism. He was the one to say that Ivan the Terrible was actually four people, and that one person couldn't be so inconsistent. There was a lot of stuff there. And it was in his book that I read about the Romanov-Zakharyins who seized power; she was Ivan's first wife, and in the course of several generations the relatives of this wife started to rewrite the history of Russia and to implant in people's minds the perception of authenticity and traditionality of their clan. The same principle of trickery in Russia, the same for centuries on end. The chronicle *The Tale of Bygone Years*[26] was fabricated for Peter [the Great] in Königsberg, simply made up for him. I could talk and talk about it . . . And this trickery in Russia, it is remarkable and it continues to this day, nowadays in conditions of complete impunity. (Andrei, male, 38)

As telling as the responses to Fomenko's arguments may be, his were not the only examples stimulating the disenchanted vision of history and politics described above. In fact, if Fomenko's conspiratorial view of history held such a wide appeal for readers, it was because their own encounters with transformations and revisions of the historical canon had been firsthand. This topic was becoming increasingly salient during the later waves of my fieldwork, when the proximity of elections made the arbitrary and non-transparent nature of postsocialist politics especially frustrating. In the late summer of 1999, Nelly Romanovna cautiously responded to my question about the future historical label to be given to the decade of the 1990s with a phrase I heard often at that time. "It depends on who will be giving out the labels then," she said and, after a brief pause, continued:

> It depends on who will be labeling. Just the same way as we have been lied to for many years about what happened in Russia in 1917, in 1941. That's history for you. History founded on lies . . . Russia has had a sad history, starting from 1917.

AUTHOR: What about before?

NR: Well, before, I like Russian history before [1917]. Strange, but I do. Although there are a lot of things that I've missed; the more accurate books, those more reflective of Russian history, they appeared rather late, when I was already an adult. And this country's history is truly interesting. And after [1917] it is, of course, much less interesting . . . When I was young, I didn't have the chance to read books on Russian history, but having lived for a long time and being a witness to this history, I've had plenty of opportunities to see that history, the elucidation of what goes on in Russia, is perpetually intertwined with lies, all the time. All the time. One time Brezhnev writes a book, another time he heroically fights on Malaia Zemlia [laughs], or something else.[27] Whoever wants to make something up, does it. But these are all fabrications. And as an absolutely ordinary person . . . Maybe someone more competent, more well-versed could make sense of it. Personally, I like Radzinskii,[28] he reads and studies issues seriously, he is competent, but for me it all remains, you know, some kind of a disgusting concoction of lies. You read something somewhere, and it sounds more or less logical. Then elsewhere you read just the opposite, and so on and so forth. And in the end, after all these efforts, you realize that one just cannot figure out, even tentatively, what is and was going on.

Distortions and permutations of the historical narrative were thus considered to be the products of deliberate self-interested actions of the very same individuals who were deemed responsible for the corrupt nature of contemporary politics. While, as Nelly Romanovna pointed out, this attitude was built on an awareness of the historical revisionism of Soviet times, the consistency and spontaneity with which it was raised during the late waves of my fieldwork indicated its special relevance to the period of the late 1990s. In other words, these schemas of late socialism were found to be increasingly useful, and the new freedoms of the postsocialist period (such as, for example, the freedom from censorship enjoyed by Fomenko and his circle of followers) fed into, rather than contradicted, their renewed appeal.

The topic of relativity and the impossibility of definitive knowledge seems to suggest a peculiarly postmodern sensibility among postsocialist subjects, and indeed such arguments have been made.[29] But such a far-fetched conclusion is hardly warranted. Despite the frequent displays of skepticism regarding the authenticity of most narratives of power (whether historical or contemporary), this arbitrariness did not evoke a postmodernist delight. To the contrary, it was framed as a deviation from the norm (the norm, however, being highly speculative and unrealistic). This nostalgia for lost objectivity was evident, for example, in the way Victor Vladimirovich expressed his take on the credibility of historical narratives:

As soon as a new ruler walks in, you have a new history. And it should remain the same, one would think. Unchangeable—but instead, it is reissued and reedited, and you have these books that say "Second edition, revised and amended" [laughs]. However many rulers, that's how many histories. That's why I say ahead of time, "Whoever writes history, that's how it will be written" (*kto budet pisat'—tak i napishet*). That is, who exactly is it going to be written for? It will be written for the leadership (*napishetsia pod rukovodstvo*).

The ideal of an "unchangeable" and objective history (or, alternatively, straightforward and honest politics) resonated with many Muscovites and was, in fact, the very foundation on which their discontent and criticism rested. Their deconstructionist approach to the political realities at hand, hence, was seen not as a legitimate and desirable way of "doing politics," but rather as the only adequate response, which was necessitated by the sorry circumstances of the day, a way of making the best of the worst.

Collective Identities and Collective Action

The assumption that falsifications and distortions inevitably accompany public representations and forms of behavior cannot fail to have its consequences for the character and intensity of the bonds of trust that develop (or fail to develop) among individual citizens. The issue here is not merely the absence of institutional mechanisms by which trust can be reinforced through the enforcement of contracts, as Luhmann (1979) would have it.[30] More fundamentally, expressions of distrust developed a value of their own as they informed identities and solidarities and gave individuals a meaningful framework within which to think about the developments of the first postsocialist decade. Soviet legacies of suspicion are not irrelevant here, and my interlocutors often acknowledged the continuities between their past and their current wariness regarding all things political. But at the same time, they also asserted that their responses had a fundamentally contemporary logic and were developed on the basis of specific and disappointing encounters with postsocialism. This made distrust more than a mere habit, since it was conceptualized as the outcome of a learning curve, the lesson one was expected to draw from the experience of navigating postsocialism. In other words, far from being a symbol of succession, it was used as the evidence of progression, both psychological and practical. The imagery that accompanied this framing had developmental overtones, casting the progression from late socialism in terms of personal maturation. Speaking of the early 1990s, Alena said,

> I can't believe how naïve we were back then with these [privatization] vouchers, what a big deal we thought they were, the lines we stood in to invest, putting our names on lists, showing up for daily roster calls (*otmechalis' kazhdyi den'*) . . . Instead of just selling them right there, on the spot as some smart people did.

Andrei, now a reasonably well-paid office worker, depicted his first postsocialist decisions in the same spirit:

> When I left my job at the institute, I left counting on the income, because I was naïve. And when I started working, I realized that I was being blown off, that I shouldn't have left, but it was too late.

Similarly, recollections of the pyramid schemes ubiquitous between 1991 and 1994 were often accompanied by comments on the gullibility and naïveté (or as one man put it, "the pioneer diligence" [*pionerskaia ispolnitel'nost'*]) of the Russian people of the early 1990s who, still under the illusion of credibility of banks and other financial institutions, unsuspectingly entrusted their money to a bunch of "conmen."[31] The conviction that such incidents were "impossible in a normal Western country," as well as recurrent references to the Soviet mentality that supposedly explained these early postsocialist mistakes, all pointed to the historically specific nature of these blunders.

While Muscovites were perhaps overly hasty in assuming that vulnerability to pyramid schemes and investment scams was a characteristically Soviet or even post-Soviet feature,[32] this assumption allowed them both to express their discontent with the sudden rupture of the habitual social order and to construct the passing decade as the time of personal progression, in the course of which the "pioneer diligence" of the earlier period was slowly replaced with a more hardened and shrewd attitude. The objectification of this attitude took place, among other things, through the practices of consumption—manifestations of distrust, strategic investments in household goods and domestic repairs, and other expressions of one's autonomy from the postsocialist state. These practices therefore played an important role in the construction of post-Soviet personhood, which was juxtaposed on the moral plane to the indifferent and inefficient state, and on the temporal plane to the gullibility and lack of practical competence of the earlier period.

Expressions of distrust and autonomy from "the system" provided individuals with the language in which to talk and think about themselves as parts of a certain collective entity, the *narod* (the people), without at the same time suggesting the connotations of passivity and victimization that this concept frequently bears. Ries, who astutely characterized "narod" as the "key word" in the Russian discourse (1997, 27), described its most common usage as

> "the people" as distinct from those who have power or, as has been heard often in recent years, those with wealth—the new business classes. Narod always suggests by implication its opposite—all those who have power over, exploit, and do not take care of or appreciate "the people." Narod may mean "the heroic people" but it more commonly stands for "the victimized people." (Ries 1997, 28; italics in the original)

While the symbolic division of the Russian society into narod and "those who have power" was as salient in the late 1990s as it was years before, the practices and discourses centered around the attainment of autonomy seemed to provide a much-needed alternative to the dichotomy of "the heroic" and "the victimized" people by introducing a more prosaic vision of everyday activity founded on skepticism and aspired-to self-sufficiency. In postsocialism, this collective identity was juxtaposed against a somewhat different "them" than before; as Ries points out, images of economic prosperity and wealth were increasingly becoming a part of the imagined community that narod was opposed to. What this suggests is that the formation of collective identities, still undifferentiated and in flux, was taking shape along the lines not only of status but of class, and that the practices of autonomy-enhancement were among the early metaphors through which the emerging imagined communities came to envision themselves.

However, the very same mechanism of fostering autonomy that enabled the formation of such identities made certain practices of the wealthy and powerful "them" look conspicuously similar to those of rank-and-file autonomous citizens. Indeed, the erection of ubiquitous fences and checkpoints around "luxury apartment complexes" followed the same logic of privatizing public space and warding off outsiders as did the construction of self-assembled rakushka garages and installation of fortified apartment doors.[33] In a similar vein, the nepotism and corporatism of power networks made more than just a little sense to individuals who built an entire moral economy around the importance of mutual support and interpersonal loyalty. It is significant in this context that the accepted designation for the widely resented Yeltsin inner circle was *sem'ia* (family), as if parodying by moral inversion the central role that family and kin networks played in everyday discourse.

Muscovites were not unaware of this paradox. My interlocutors' narratives of the universal corruption of the powerful rarely ended on a conciliatory note, but the few instances in which that did occur came when I asked them to imagine themselves in a position of power. Consider the following fragment of my conversation with Nina Alekseevna:

> The richer people become, the greedier they become, and the more they are bothered by their neighbor who has more than them. In our country people have always lived poorly, and they're used to stealing. People were always stealing everything they could from work. Stealing, stealing. And if people have this mentality, they will never stop, especially if you give them political power. They will never stop stealing, the more they can take, the better. Because they are already hungry, they are used to this life. And no matter how much they have, they won't stop.
> AUTHOR: How do you explain it, is it just that corrupt people are the ones that get to power first, or is the power itself corrupting?
> NA: [Somewhat puzzled] I'm not sure . . . I don't know.
> AUTHOR: Well, would you be tempted to steal if you found yourself in the position of authority?
> NA: I wouldn't get into that position in a million years. I don't have the pushiness, this whole . . . walking on people's heads to get to the goal. [Pause] But once you find yourself in this position, who knows? . . . I mean, we all fend for our families. I know I would do anything for Alik [her son], whatever is in my power . . . So who knows . . .

Nina Alekseevna's rhetorical turnaround, of course, would be a poor guide were we to use it for predicting her actual behavior, particularly given the highly speculative nature of the situation into which she was projecting herself. However, two things appear significant. First, no matter how great a leap of imagination she took, Nina Alekseevna was unable to conceive of a situation in which her son would not be vulnerable, and hence not need her continuous protection. Second, it was some of her own deeply held convictions that made the practices she disapproved of, if not acceptable, then at least conceivable. Thus, considering the self-segregating and exclusionary aspects inherent in the drive for autonomy (the emphasis on physical boundaries, self-sufficiency, and informal networks), collective identities that rose on its basis remained problematic, since they contained within themselves the germs of the very realities that they opposed.

Furthermore, the notion of collective identities implicitly suggests the possibility of collective action, and this was precisely the aspect that the skeptical postsocialist sensibility seemed to inhibit. In late 1990s Moscow, competence was measured not by successful promotion of one's agenda through political engagement, but rather through contemptuous dismissal of the possibility of such engagement as naïve and unrealistic, and the cultivation of alternative solutions instead. In other words, this particular collective identity was contingent upon the *absence* of collective action in its traditional understanding of political contention.

This predication of collective identity on *dis*engagement from the framework of political activism points to a need to reexamine the association typically drawn by social scientists between the existence of vibrant open social networks and political participation. Indeed, the three essential elements of the public sphere as defined by Habermas (1989) are that it is a sphere of association of *private persons,* discussing issues of *public concern or common interest* on an *egalitarian basis* (i.e., in a forum potentially open to all those interested in participating). Creation of such a public sphere, it is argued, is crucial to the success of participatory democracy and the furthering of the common interest of its citizens. With all the recent criticisms of the concept (such as Fraser [1992], Poster [1997]), the basic premise underlying the study of the public sphere still remains the same: its essence is in helping ordinary citizens articulate through interaction "communities and interests and power," which become potent political forces in a democratic society (Eliasoph 1998, 18). Seemingly unproblematic, in practice this definition is built on one important assumption: that politically minded talk is necessarily an enabling and politically potent device. In other words, it is assumed that, wherever citizens gather together in order to discuss issues of public interest, whether social security or media policies, this talk by itself can gain political power and have an impact upon the larger political process. A similar line of reasoning is offered in Gibson, who draws not on Habermas but on Putnam (1993) and network theorists (Granovetter 1973; Meyer 1994) to argue that "the existence of expansive social networks may well be the most important precursor to the development of the effective and autonomous political organizations thought necessary to the successful consolidation of a democratic transition" (2001, 52). Applying this logic to Russia, Gibson contended that civil society had great potential there because "Russian social networks [were] politically charged, dense, and characterized by high levels of trust" (65), implying that the density of networks translated into increased democratic participation.

However, this book suggests that quite an opposite process was at work at the time of Gibson's writing: interpersonal cooperation and mutual identification were built on the shared premise that all larger political engagement was to be avoided. A group here was seen not as a miniature model of society at large (as is often the assumption in much of the sociological literature), but as an entity that was opposed to it, and that provided refuge from total disorder. Particularized trust was developed and valued in its opposition to universalized *dis*trust. It was this common definition of the situation that made it possible for individuals both to relate to one another and to view themselves as competent actors in the framework of postsocialist society and politics. And while the outcome of these collective efforts could indeed be, as Gibson suggested, "effective" and "autonomous," their political impact remained questionable, since the cultivation of mental and emotional autonomy from politics implied that political solutions were somehow unnecessary and that political arguments had, in the final analysis, no intrinsic value:

> NELLY ROMANOVNA: Sometimes, we have arguments [in the household], clashes of all sorts because of these ones [politicians] on TV.
> AUTHOR: For instance?
> NR: Well, let's say they are saying something, and I respond in one way, and Misha [Nelly Romanovna's husband] in another, and so we start to argue. And then you think, what is this, what is this monkey house (*obez'iannik*), let's turn it off. So we turn the monkey house off, and everything is all right again.

The most obvious problem with this antipolitical thesis is its stifling effect on the likelihood that the criticized order of things could ever be challenged or changed through contention. Indeed, such a challenge would explicitly contradict the very rules that structured postsocialist Russian political talk, and erode the framework through which many post-Soviet subjects had come to envision themselves. But perhaps the most troublesome aspect of the logic of autonomy for political action was not so much the antipolitical sentiment discussed above, but the kinds of political vision it *did* lend itself to. Given how heavily people were invested in seeing themselves as acting independently of state structures and owing their livelihood to their own ingenuity (and not to any structural arrangements), they were naturally predisposed to misrecognize the benefits they received from the state. But the common adage "The state owes me nothing and I owe nothing to the state" had its own problematic repercussion: it produced an illusion that individuals, indeed, *could* manage their business entirely on their own, and thus created fertile ground for precisely the kind of neoliberal policies that they detested. A comment made by Kseniia Anatolievna is illustrative in this regard. Political decisions, she suggested, have no bearing on everyday life:

> Let them do whatever they wish—even stand on their heads if they want, in this Duma. As long as they don't bother the regular people. Let the people work and have stuff in the shops, a chance to eat and to live till old age in tranquility.

A similar sentiment was expressed somewhat more emotionally by Nikolai, a thirty-one-year-old freight operator:

> The state, it doesn't help me with anything. What has the state done for me lately? Nothing. I am not counting Soviet times. And one thing I want to say [to the state], OK, you are not helping me, but at least get out of the way! But it does get in the way, it hampers my business with its tax policies, with its regulations. This is what I don't accept. At the very least—don't get in the way!

Although both Kseniia Anatolievna's and Nikolai's family members did benefit from a number of federal budget–supported institutions, from schools to clinics, their desiderata (employment, consumption, and tranquility in Kseniia Anatolievna's case and smooth business operations in Nikolai's) were envisioned as something that could develop parallel to, and without any interaction with, the state. This aspiration to the independence of one's own life from bureaucrats and politicians ("as long as they don't bother the regular people") was, of course, the very stuff of autonomy Russian-style. But the effectiveness of alternative arrangements was often overstated, and this overstatement, flattering as it was for the speakers' self-image, only narrowed the horizon of political possibilities, and if anything made it easier to rationalize and accept the waning of already meager state welfare provisions.

The practical and psychological import of crisis narratives lay in allowing speakers to develop a sense of commonality of perspectives, normalize the unfolding events, and exchange information and assistance. Yet at the same time, discourses and practices of fostering autonomy contributed to the ongoing acceptance of the criticized events and formed new criteria for practical competence and a new hierarchy of valued skills and talents. Among the cultural tools in the "tool-kit" of a savvy postsocialist subject were the ability to unmask deceptive political and media imagery, the capacity to foresee and forestall potential mishaps, awareness of the fundamentally constructed nature of historical and political narratives, distrust for all forms of civic participation, and the ability to insulate one's life from all of the above. In the cultural logic of postsocialism, these skills, developed or rediscovered during the postsocialist decade, designated one's competence and personal emancipation from earlier political illusions. By equating political emancipation with their emancipation *from* politics into the autonomous household, potential political actors inadvertently passed up the chance to change the conditions they bemoaned. On a practical level, after focusing on the implementation of multiple informal security arrangements, they began to see their households as disconnected from and to an extent unaffected by larger political processes, which diminished the incentives for political engagement. On the level of identity and symbolic boundaries, too, they identified their competence so closely with the ability to maintain emotional distance from politics that joining forces and actively rallying behind a candidate or an idea came to mean an eventual loss of face. In the final run, of course, no matter how savvy in insiders' terms (such as "electoral technologies" and "black PR") an individual may get, this knowledge alone cannot guarantee an intelligent choice of actions if one's own interests and agendas are not articulated through interaction with others. No one put it better than George Orwell, who wrote in a letter that "the more one is unaware of political bias, the more one can be independent of it, and the more one claims to be impartial, the more one is biased" (1968, 505). It was precisely this "impartiality bias" that made the professed distance from politics self-defeating. While it did give individuals the vocabulary and the occasion to articulate their collective identity and a sense of moral worth, it is also true that this very process allowed the criticized postsocialist order to continue reproducing itself.

8   Conclusion

> The tradition of the oppressed teaches us that the "state of emergency" in which we live is not the exception but the rule. We must attain to a conception of history that is in keeping with this insight.
>
> —Walter Benjamin, *Theses on the Philosophy of History*

This book is based on conversations that took place in the late 1990s, and now, ten years later, this period seems both near and distant. It is near because it has not been too long since my last interview was done; as I know from follow-up phone calls and occasional meetings with some of my contacts, most of them are in the same line of work, live in the same apartments, and report little change in their material circumstances. Yet it is distant because, at least in macro- and geopolitical terms, a major shift took place as the "era of Yeltsin" gave way to the "era of Putin." Petrodollars boosted the Russian economy, and global events and ethnic conflicts overshadowed, both in the media and in everyday conversation, the plight of "ordinary Russians." Partly due to the change in political leadership and partly because this change coincided with the turn of the decade, century, and millennium, the years of the 1990s are now seen as a bounded historical period, which is looked back on, discussed, and evaluated as a discrete chapter of history. Singling out the decade of the 1990s, books and periodicals address the peculiarities of this period, analyze its developmental trajectory and inner logic, and debate its historical significance, suggesting by the very statement of the problem that the period in question can be evaluated holistically and in retrospect.[1]

In light of this mindset, the discussion of the daily routines and conversations of the 1990s would have only a historical interest, as an indication of the "way things were" during the turbulent late Yeltsin years. But this is not exactly so, since social phenomena never mirror electoral cycles. Instead, they should be thought of processually, as perpetually unfolding as people negotiate between the old familiar practices and ways of doing things and the new realities with which they are confronted. Understanding the lived experience of the first post-socialist decade is thus important, and not only because, as Buckley put it in a different context (1993, 13),[2] "many views of problems and perceived obstacles to solving them persist." The cultural logic of the late 1990s matters because it informed the responses to the political, economic, and social changes that followed. Today, many of the ways of comprehending and navigating that decade continue to have a bearing on the present; they remain the prism through which many people assess today's opportunities and choose methods of pursuing them.

The processual approach to social change effectively means that any transformation is, among other things, a transformation of the *subjects*—those who, willingly or unwillingly, find themselves in the midst of fluctuating systems and institutions. This is even true in cases when the subjects themselves are less invested in taking advantage of the opportunities offered by this structural transformation than they are in ensuring their personal immunity from its threatening effects. The activity of preserving one's routine in a changing environment requires the cultivation of skills and attitudes one did not have before; in the midst of continuous social change, much as in Carroll's Wonderland, "it takes all the running you can do to keep in the same place."

It is this dialectical relationship between subjects and their environs that makes the vision of crisis as an external reality overly static. In a situation of continuous transformation, the binary opposition between the external circumstance and the adapting (successfully or unsuccessfully) social actors becomes blurred. This is not to say that adaptation is impossible, but rather that the actors emerge from the experience transformed. This transformation demands attention, since it contributes, often in unexpected ways, to the way in which the situation develops over time.

Muscovites participated in the mutually constitutive circle of social change in several ways. On the most fundamental level, by adopting the framework of total crisis as the overriding metaphor of postsocialism, they embraced a particular vision, one that emphasized the extremity, gravity, and extraordinariness of the situation, but at the same time, its continuity. This framing made it crucial that the arrangements they implemented in their everyday life to deal with the contingencies of social change corresponded to the pressures of a chronic crisis in that they were reliable, multidimensional, and permanent in their perspective. No matter how acute the situation could be considered at various points in time, the strategies implemented on a daily level were long-term. This naturalized the condition people bemoaned and made it more acceptable subjectively, since they often felt that they were prepared for it in advance. In essence, by adapting to the crisis, they prolonged it. They also made themselves vulnerable to political uses of the total crisis framework, and the first electoral success of Vladimir Putin testified to the fact that political operatives were not deaf to this possibility. Putin's first book of interviews, which instantly became a bestseller when it came out in 2000, made strategic use of the total crisis, closing with the following calculatedly offhand remark: "When I was appointed prime minister, it was interesting and it was an honor. I thought, 'Well, I'll work for a year, and that's fine. If I can help save Russia from collapse, then I'll have something to be proud of'. . . . And then I'll move onto the next thing" (Putin 2000, 204). The following eight years passed under the mantra of "stabilization," and there is no doubt that the implicit contrast to the preceding crisis helped to legitimize the many sacrifices that this stability entailed.

By the late 1990s, the popularity of deconstructionist rhetoric had already helped pave the way toward a gradual narrowing of political and media freedoms that occurred later on. Such were the unintended consequences of an outlook whose attractions lay elsewhere. The deficiencies of the postsocialist order, the loss of habitual reference points and guidelines, the lack of new categories through which one could conceptualize change, made crisis rhetoric seem a natural choice for postsocialist subjects. But it was not merely a forced choice, because the imagery of the total crisis gave them more than just a framework for articulating their grievances; it also provided a basis for forming alliances, building a sense of community, and maintaining moral boundaries.

Given the popularity of crisis rhetoric, it is hardly surprising that it played an important role in the construction of post-Soviet personhood. In the midst of the tectonic shifts in Russia's social structure, when social distinction, hierarchies, and grounds for belonging were in constant flux, the imagery of total crisis provided a common vocabulary and a set of moral categories on which individuals of varied social backgrounds could agree. The downside of such a wide consensus, of course, was that the community it constituted was so broad as to exclude virtually no one but the rhetorical chimera of "the system." Hence it failed in the inherent sociological purpose of "groupness"—that of maintaining relatively stable boundaries and hence creating grounds for social differentiation. However, while the crisis framework may not have been the best vehicle for constructing difference within postsocialist society, it offered its adherents a unique opportunity to articulate difference both *among* themselves, in the ways they dealt with the crisis and, more importantly, *within* themselves, as a measure of their personal progression on the journey through postsocialism.

During these years, family became a site in which the crisis could be tamed and domesticated and the continuity of everyday life preserved. The centrality of family and kinship networks is not precisely a typical feature expected to rise to prominence in the course of market liberalization. Yet in this particular context it was well warranted since, in contrast to constantly shifting economic and industrial relations, kinship networks could provide a measure of predictability and continuity. Given the degree of skepticism toward the productive potential of public infrastructure and institutions, the family became the locus of autonomy from the state, in the course of which it aimed to provide a possibly complete and versatile set of defenses, both moral and practical.

The idea of taming the crisis by buffering it with informal arrangements and multiple protections from potential emergencies lay at the heart of what many Muscovites saw as one measure of their competence. Since the perceived dangers emanating from the system were, in contrast to those of late socialist times, all-embracing and vague, so was the character of the defense. Far from being isolated responses to clearly perceived threats, individuals' actions were part of a broader orientation that valued autonomy and self-sufficiency for their own sake. In other words, one's capacity to disengage oneself from all things public became a value in itself, a value manifested not only in practical actions of economic self-provisioning, but also in the position postsocialist subjects took on a variety of issues, from media to voting to history. It was through stating this detachment that one could provide evidence of one's personal evolution by juxtaposing it to one's substantially more engaged and idealistic reactions a few years earlier. Thus, the crisis narrative furnished ample material for identity construction, and as with all markers of identity, the individuals were too invested in them to worry about their potential consequences.

Ann Swidler wrote, "Institutions set the problems actors solve, and culture organizes those solutions" (2002, 7).[3] Institutional absences, one may add, do something very similar: it was in the voids created by failing institutions and missing identity markers that Muscovites were formulating the discourse on autonomy and the identities connected to it. For an identity discourse built on the contrast between the present hardened sophistication and the cluelessness of the past, it was ironic that many of the practices through which it was articulated could be directly traced to the socialist or even presocialist period. And this added the sense that these attitudes were tested and proven optimal by history, giving them the overtone of superiority necessary to turn isolated cultural practices into cultural capital.

What Swidler's insight does not address, however, is that in the course of time, the cultural tissue that bridges institutional gaps becomes itself institutionalized, and this process of gradual institutionalization invites attention. Patterned responses to crises generate the supporting infrastructure which, for its part, is already invested in the condition that it amends; what are gaps to individual actors are market niches for the businesses built to serve them. This gives an aura of permanence even to behaviors that could initially have been seen as temporary and explains the inertia with which they resist change. The most obvious example here is the institutional infrastructure that emerged in Russia in the late 1990s in response to the popular preoccupation with the state's inability to contain fraud. The industry of consumer magazines, free instructional newspapers, and TV programs all dedicated to the art of spotting faulty products and forgeries gave institutional support to the practical activity of self-protection and developed a genre of cautionary advice, which reflected the assumptions of the total crisis framework. They also created the impression that the problem could be effectively dealt with at the level of the autonomous citizen, and hence that it was not worth the trouble of fighting for higher effectiveness or transparency of the administrative governing bodies officially responsible for quality control.

The built environment of today's Moscow, with its rapidly proliferating gated apartment complexes, offers another resonant example of the gradual institutionalization of the cultural patterns I have described. The Soviet-era utopias of privacy, legitimated and intensified in the course of the postsocialist transformation, blend here with the post-Soviet compulsion for self-protection and separation from the threatening "outside." In form and function, these gated residences for the wealthy have an obvious affinity to the neoliberal logic governing the "global cities" around the world. Yet in their spirit, they cater to specifically post-Soviet longings.[4]

Finally, cultural patterns matter not only for the forms of nascent institutional infrastructure, but also for spaces in which it fails to emerge easily. In the late 1990s, just when the institutions of marriage and family were carrying such a heavy weight of expectations, I was struck by how little discussion intra-family problems received. The issue here was not so much the lack of counseling centers and organizations, but rather the absence of a public discourse that could articulate the need for institutional support to the family and help to shape it. The reason for this "structured silence"[5] was not that there were no problems to talk about. On the contrary, expectations of complementarity in a family's navigation of the postsocialist economy, its role as a buffer and refuge from the disruptions associated with the crisis, the multiplicity of state functions it was expected to replicate, all exerted an enormous pressure on the family unit. Yet people's reluctance to discuss family problems even when they were visible was striking by contrast to the eagerness with which the other kinds of crises were discussed. This happened because the discursive logic of postsocialism ascribed crisis to the "outside world," and effectively denied the family the right to admit, or even to recognize, problems within the unit itself. In other words, by being constructed as a symbolic refuge from the uncertainties associated with the transformation, the family effactually lost its right to fail, not least in its own eyes.[6] So much support was expected from intergenerational and intra-household connections that inability to generate it amounted to a stigma. These unrealistically high expectations could hardly provide a foundation for the long-term stability of the institution of family, and the true toll that this took on society at large remains to be determined.

Tracing the institutionalized responses to the task of forging autonomy in everyday practice, one comes to see how much of the postsocialist order was defined by the notions of crisis and the drive for autonomy, and how these new social forms could be innovative (in terms of formulating ingenious solutions to postsocialist dilemmas) and socially reproductive (by enabling individuals to function amid these dilemmas instead of addressing them) at the same time. The postsocialist drive for autonomy could, and did, take many forms across the space of the former Soviet bloc. Some of these forms were explicitly adaptive and aimed no further than patching the holes in the postsocialist social and economic fabric. But the practical solutions that the drive for autonomy opened up contained in themselves, unintentionally, multiple possibilities for shaping the future. In a society where the market infrastructure had to evolve practically from naught, institutionalized responses to crisis gave rise to some of the first specifically post-Soviet structures. They shaped the very fabric of the emerging order. While many of these responses bore a primarily defensive character, others, such as private kindergartens or alternative health networks, did not. Motivated by doubt regarding the efficiency of the existing structures, these initiatives were among the earliest to explore possible alternatives to them, creating new business patterns and building the fabric of capitalism from below.

One turn that the drive for autonomy did not take in Russia, however, was the political one. Unlike other former Soviet states—Ukraine, Kyrgyzstan, Georgia—for which the twenty-first century brought not only political turmoil but also the formation of a viable political opposition—Russia did not see its own "colored" revolution. In fact, with the exception of several instances of protest against specific policy innovations, such as the mass protests against the monetization of privileges that took place across the country in January–February 2005, there has been so little oppositional political activity in the 2000s that the frantic efforts of Russia's political establishment to prevent a surge of popular resistance to President Putin seemed misplaced at best. But while a cultural ethnography such as the one at hand cannot arrive at a comparative model for explaining variation in political outcomes across the post-Soviet region, it does provide an antidote to the tendency to dismiss Russia's political culture as the product of a long-standing tradition of apathy and disengagement.[7] Indeed, it offers evidence that the thin veneer of professed disinterest in politics concealed in the 1990s many intensely political investments and frustrations, even if the discursive and symbolic economy that the pursuit of autonomy engendered precluded the resolution of these frustrations in a truly sustainable way.

This is not a revolutionary insight, but one that, with the benefit of hindsight, we are all too often prone to forget—unintended consequences are not the same as intentions, and intentions themselves are often tactical, not strategic in nature. Many of the post-Soviet social and political developments sprang from the efforts of individuals to arrest or neutralize the perpetual crisis in which their lives were locked for many tumultuous years. It is now clear that the emerging postsocialist order bears the imprint of these efforts, although perhaps not exactly in the ways these people would have foreseen, or intended.

In the final count, this is also a cause for hope. The first postsocialist decade may have made post-Soviet Russians mistrustful or even averse to change. But it has also shown that in many ways they cannot help but bring it about.

Appendix 1. Methodology

Site and Sample Selection

This book is based on the fieldwork I conducted in Moscow, the city where I spent the first twenty-three years of my life and where I had professional connections with the Institute of Sociology of the Russian Academy of Sciences and the Russian Center for Public Opinion Research (VTsIOM, now renamed Levada-Center). Obviously, the trade-off involved in selecting Moscow as a research site was that, while it minimized entry problems, it also confined the sample to a population not fully representative of the entire country. Social and economic differences, such as a wider and more complex structure of socioeconomic opportunities, better supported infrastructure, as well as a greater readiness of the population to support the economic reforms (Clem and Craumer 1995; Kolosov and Vendina 1996) made Moscow clearly distinct from other Russian regions.[1] This does not mean that Muscovites' lives were free from manifestations of social and economic instability. In fact, according to polls of the Russian Center for Public Opinion Research, Muscovites reported the same problems as their compatriots from across the country throughout the 1990s. It was the severity and rank ordering of these problems that differed somewhat. While the main problems plaguing the lives of Russians in general in the mid-1990s were, first and foremost, low income (72 percent of those surveyed), poor health (30 percent), and absence of prospects for the future (24 percent), Muscovites reported being troubled mostly by the same challenges, but at lower rates: low income (64 percent), poor health (25 percent), and fear of unemployment (24 percent) (VTsIOM 1997, 6). Other differences included Muscovites' greater vulnerability to housing shortages (20 percent vs. 10 percent), but a lesser susceptibility to the feeling of hopelessness and absence of perspectives for the future (12 percent vs. 24 percent).[2]

These differences make it impossible to argue that the findings of Moscow-based fieldwork fully represent the state of the Russian public opinion. But this book is far from making such claims. As with all ethnographic studies, this one does not aim to recreate a survey of how a particular set of behaviors or opinions is distributed in the Russian population. Rather, the goal is an in-depth understanding of certain discursive and practical patterns that could be traced through widely different segments of Russian society during the turbulent 1990s, with the intention of generating analytic categories that may enable one to better conceptualize the relationship between social crises and the everyday, the rupture and the routine, the shifting and the stability of social life. The unique quality of Moscow as a city of "all tongues," in terms of the variety of opportunities and behavioral scenarios it contained (Kolosov and Vendina 1996; Dubin 1997), was propitious in this regard.[3] A sample of Muscovites of different social backgrounds allowed me to investigate both the variability and the enduring features of the crisis framework, and to explore the extent to which its manifestations varied or cut across social and cultural boundaries.[4] In addition, by ensuring the variation of my sample by gender, age, and social group, I compensated for the structural advantages that are assumed to make Moscow an outlier among Russian cities.[5]

In order to maintain the diversity of my sample, I relied on a theoretically modified snowball sample. In other words, I drew on personal connections and referrals (with contacts made through friends, colleagues, relatives, and neighbors), but at the same time strove to include representatives of various social groups insofar as they had no professional knowledge of or involvement with the political and economic processes we were to discuss. Several considerations informed my choice of the snowball technique over random sampling. On the most practical level, the official phonebook listing, which is traditionally used as a database for random selection of an in-depth interview sample,[6] was not available for Moscow. Without such a legitimate source, obtaining relevant information would have been extremely difficult and time-consuming.[7] In addition, since many of the issues raised in the interviews could potentially be sensitive (such as instances of tax evasion or other semi- or illegal behaviors), it would be naïve to expect that they could be discussed in an interview setting without some basic degree of trust provided by a reference from an acquaintance or relative. In this respect, the sacrifices that random selection would have required in terms of rapport and openness seemed far greater than the dangers presented by the selection bias in snowball sampling.[8]

The ethnographic component of the fieldwork revolved around the in-depth interviews and followed upon themes and motifs suggested in their course. As the research unfolded, more and more ethnographic sites emerged as I was analyzing the already conducted interviews and using them as a lens through which to interpret episodes observed elsewhere—in the subway, in stores, on the streets and squares of Moscow. An occasional comment before the beginning of the interview session, a consumer awareness journal lying on the kitchen table, an interruption in the course of the discussion in order to swallow a "health pill" (the contents of which were completely unknown to my interlocutor)— all of these trivial incidents sent me out into the open-air markets, alternative drugstores, and newspaper kiosks, which, in their own turn, triggered further questions and interview themes.

At the same time, since interviews were conducted with each individual more than once over the span of two years, the interview setting itself grew increasingly central to the research as an ethnographic site, as I interacted with the members of the respondents' households, participated in their meals, and visited some of them outside of the interview schedules. The apartment tour that I often received after the first or the second interview contributed to a greater understanding of the everyday circumstances of their lives, and provided material for further conversations. Equally enlightening were the few interviews I conducted at my contacts' workplace, partly because they rarely ended when the tape recorder was turned off. Instead, I was invited to have some tea, oftentimes with a few of their colleagues, while on other occasions I might receive a tour of the building, or simply get a chance to sit in the corner and observe the daily operations of the office. Interestingly, the invitation to conduct an interview in the office came almost automatically if my initial contact was made through a referral from a colleague. At the same time, those referred to me by neighbors, relatives, friends, or any other "private sphere" contacts never suggested that I visit them at work. The surprise and bafflement I encountered when I first asked the "private sphere" respondents to meet me at their workplace, or the "public sphere" informants to see me in their homes, was only one of the many fieldwork experiences that sensitized me to the importance of the negotiated entry, of building up rapport, and of attending to the intricacies of the public-private divide.

The fundamentally ethnographic character of the interviews makes me feel compelled to propose that the true sample for this study is not limited to the thirty-three Muscovites with whom I carried out repeated interviews over the span of 1998–2000. It includes many of the members of their households, their colleagues, as well as the countless individuals I observed as I moved around Moscow in the course of my daily activities. However, it is these thirty-three individuals that constitute the sample's backbone. Among them there are two married couples, while the rest of the sample is completely unrelated.[9] The basis for this sample comes from the first wave of research, which was conducted in June–July 1998 and which was initially designed as a pilot study. Later on, in the light of the August 1998 financial crisis, the data gathered through this exploratory research acquired a new value, providing a baseline from which to trace the transformation of Muscovites' circumstances and perspectives by comparing their orientations before and after the breakdown. In the second wave, which took place in December–January 1998–1999, the sample incorporated the eight respondents who comprised the summer sample and was further broadened to the final number of thirty-three, sixteen male and seventeen female. Since I wanted to make sure that my contacts had conscious memories of the advent of postsocialism and experience of independent navigation in the new circumstances, I chose to recruit only those who were of working age during the late 1980s–early 1990s, thus setting the age threshold for the sample at twenty-nine. The sample was maintained consistently throughout my fieldwork, in the course of which I had three or four conversations with each of its members.

Data Collection and Analysis

Most studies dedicated to the ethnographic exploration of social change are based on a single stage of fieldwork and hence produce detailed but somewhat static descriptions. While such an approach has definite advantages—most notably, it allows for a larger sample size—there are issues that it inherently cannot address. A single-stage ethnography makes it difficult to assess just how much change there actually is on the level of people's everyday lives. It is hardly possible, without following up in-depth and over a period of time on a number of individual stories, to identify the ways in which the practical circumstances of individuals' lives have been altered by large-scale developments. In the absence of such an assessment one has to rely on self-reporting, and thus assume that there is perfect agreement between the lived reality of everyday life and the discourse about that life. I was not ready to make such an assumption, and in fact was most interested precisely in the discrepancies between the two.

Therefore, I designed this study as longitudinal, so that recurrent interaction would familiarize me with the dynamic of my contacts' everyday circumstances. Only such in-depth knowledge can create a certain fluency of comprehension necessary for ethnographic understanding, and at the same time permit the researcher to differentiate between the actual circumstances of the people's lives and the evaluation these circumstances may receive in their discourse.[10] In addition to allowing for a deeper immersion into my interlocutors' life-worlds, thus enhancing the traditional forte of qualitative methods, such a design had further advantages. For one, it was more attuned to change, both in the discursive modes of self-presentation and in actual social and economic circumstances. Moreover, longitudinal design logically accommodates the cyclical pattern of qualitative analysis, in which the process of asking questions and collecting and analyzing data brings forth new ethnographic questions to be explored in the next wave of the study (Spradley 1980). Finally, recurrent meetings allowed for developing a closer relationship between me and my interviewees, and thus were valuable for cultivating a high rapport and mutual trust.

The fieldwork was conducted in four waves over the span of two years, each wave encompassing ethnographic observation and informal in-depth interviews of a semi-structured format. I collected a total of 103 interviews. The first wave took place in June–July of 1998, prior to the August financial crisis, and was followed by the second wave in December 1998–February 1999, the third wave in June–July 1999, and the fourth wave in March–May of 2000. The combination of in-depth interviews and participant observation allowed me to get at both the discursive and the non-discursive aspects of everyday activity, while the sequence of waves was intended to capture the short- and long-term responses of my informants to the most recent instance of a drastic overturn in the economy.

The in-depth interviews lasted for approximately 1.5–2.5 hours and were tape-recorded. None of the respondents objected to being recorded, which was partly because they were assured of the confidentiality of the tapes. The very presence of a tape recorder, however, was not neglected, especially during the first fifteen minutes of the first interview. A number of comments (such as embarrassed disclaimers of "not having anything interesting to say"), as well as sideward glances at the tape recorder, made me painfully aware of the fact that at least by some respondents the interview was being interpreted as a public performance, with all the negative consequences that might have for the validity of provided information.[11] The decision to continue recording was, therefore, not easily made. I decided to continue with the recorder for several reasons. First of all, discussions of dilemmas and circumstances of everyday life often contained startling and fresh metaphors. While shorthand notes would have preserved the content value of these discussions, they would have irretrievably lost the bulk of the imaginative comparisons that animated them. This, of course, is an egoistic concern, and it would not have sufficed if there had been no others. More substantively, omission of a tape recorder also seemed to be merely a quick and careless fix for that fundamental dilemma of social science—intersubjectivity. Removing the tape recorder from the interview site would, of course, have made the setting seem less like an interview, but it would not have made the situation any more "natural" to the respondent, and me any less of a stranger. In this respect, attempting to eliminate all sources of distortion from the ethnographic locale could be an endless and a futile process, for it is impossible to define the moment when the subject finally becomes "herself"—when she is being interviewed, interrogated, or conversed with. In fact, it appears that even the formulation of the question in these terms is wrong, for the subject is probably being "herself" in all of these states, albeit projecting very different images. For this reason, I found it more appropriate to direct my efforts toward exercising a greater self-reflexivity in the interview settings, and to remaining aware of the particular modality in which my subjects were relating to me at each particular moment. In this spirit, instead of dismissing the tape recorder, I used it as a cue, a marker of switch in performance styles. I made a particular effort to note the changes in conversational styles that occurred in the interviews as the tape recorder was being turned on and off, and subsequently incorporated these observations into the interpretation given to the data.

The interview was loosely organized around a set of guiding themes. However, the discussion was flexible in structure, and I had no reservations about having my respondents participate in defining its direction and pace. It was common for new themes to emerge and be pursued at length in the course of the conversation; if such an exploration seemed worthwhile to me, I incorporated these themes into the subsequent interviews. Overall, I was working on the assumption that in discussing such a topic as the everyday, the respondents should be given maximum freedom in presenting their own agendas and concerns, for the selectivity and narrative organization of their everyday reasoning interested me more than making sure that all possible topics were covered in equal detail. In this respect, the guiding themes that I brought into the discussion served more for probing for the relevance of the corresponding subject areas than for ensuring against substantive omissions.

The first interview began with my self-introduction, in which I described the nature of my research as an effort to "get a realistic picture of how ordinary people really live," contrasting its dedication to "telling stories" with the commitment of survey research to "getting numbers." Sufficiently vague, this opening served as a good introduction to my first question, or rather request, that the respondents tell me about themselves and the major events that took place in their lives during the 1980s and 1990s. The interview proceeded through discussion of the themes I suggested (see the full list of questions in appendix 4), combined with elaboration on the topics raised by the respondents insofar as they pertained to the circumstances of their lives as well as the lives of their household members. Subsequent interviews returned to some of the initial interview themes, and included additional questions on consumption, health behaviors, political involvement, and media use. In addition, about half of the third wave of the interviews included discussion of the itemized family budget for the prior month, which the respondents were asked to prepare.[12]

The ethnographic component of the fieldwork contributed to in-depth interviews both in the interview settings (through observation at the respondents' homes and offices, interaction with the members of their household, participation in the family meals) and outside of it (when I went to facilities and places of public gathering, frequented shops, and used public transportation, as well as during the informal visits to friends and relatives). I functioned in the field in an active, and almost complete, membership role—a stance which, in contrast to the more detached observer-as-participant role, implies continuous involvement in the setting and sharing its typical activities, but without fully committing to the members' values and goals (Adler and Adler 1998). In this capacity, I kept a detailed ethnographic diary to record my observations about various aspects of everyday life in Moscow.

Finally, to test and explore the insights gained in the course of ethnographic observation and in-depth interviewing, I drew on a number of secondary sources, such as the yearly statistical handbooks and the surveys conducted by the Russian Center for Public Opinion Research, as well as on the images and themes from (tele)visual and print media. These sources, however, were auxiliary to the general conduct of the research. Data drawn from them were not used to produce working hypotheses so much as to confirm and elaborate on a pattern discovered in the course of the analysis of ethnographic evidence.

In my analysis of the fieldwork data collected in the course of interviewing, I searched both for the patterns and narrative conventions that consistently emerged across the interviews, and for individual variations and ruptures of the predominant rhetoric. I was interested in the patterns of reference and comparison, as well as the general context in which the notions of crisis and everyday competence were evoked. I noted the discursive forms and behaviors reminiscent of late socialism and concentrated on the context in which they were reactivated. I paid particular attention to the ways in which individuals used aspects of their previous experience in order to meaningfully frame the ongoing social change, as well as to the transformation their framing was undergoing over time. Furthermore, I looked for the rules according to which experiences were translated into narratives, and searched for silences, omissions, emphases, and selective interpretations. When analyzing the interviews, I juxtaposed the narratives with what I knew about the economic circumstances of my respondents' lives. In this juxtaposition, I explored the factual accuracy of their accounts in order to unveil the regularities and criteria according to which their discursive self-presentation was being constructed. In paying attention to the organizing principles of the respondents' accounts, to their construction of "otherness," as well as to the rules for omitting particular events from narration, I aimed at pinpointing the logics governing their presentations of self. Finally, I kept an eye out for notions that could elucidate individuals' working concepts of power and control, as well as the contexts in which these notions were evoked. I was interested both in their framing of political power, and in their sense of the "degree of freedom" that they possessed in dealing with everyday challenges and dilemmas.

My analysis of the ethnographic data proceeded along similar lines. I concentrated on the ways in which the cognitive categories and narrative plots I observed in the interviews presented themselves in the practical choices and arrangements people were making in the course of their daily lives. I looked for the symbolic vocabularies through which people expressed their practical competence in action. At the same time, I searched for contradictions and inconsistencies in the accepted ways of doing things, for newly emerging trends, as well as for the persistence of the old practices and modes of behavior. Finally, I looked for the ends that the practical actions were put to, and for the different uses and meanings that the same practice could receive in different contexts.

Dilemmas of Ethnography and the Researcher's Role

The appeal of ethnographic research lies in the immediacy of access it allows to the individuals' life-worlds, and in the richness and multi-dimensionality of the data that emerges from an ethnographic encounter, especially when it is compared with the inevitable reductionism involved in survey research. But ethnography also has its own challenges, which are closely connected with its appeals. One of them could be called the *dilemma of legitimation*. We know that social reality is always situational, always mediated through language and subjectivity. If this is so, then it is impossible to scientifically capture one unchangeable "true essence" of a person or a situation, and so the question arises, how can *any* representation be judged as sound? In the other words, if all ethnographic knowledge is, as Geertz (1973) has it, merely "fiction," what is one to learn from it or, indeed, how is one to tell a good ethnography from a bad one? Further, with the dawning realization of the embeddedness and subjectivity of one's own vision, how can one dare to claim that the discovered patterns and developments represent anything other than one's own preoccupations?

None of these questions are unfounded, and there is hardly a volume on ethnography that does not engage them in one way or another.[13] The danger of the textual metaphor is usually seen in the license it can provide for groundless speculation, but the recognition of the textual (i.e., "non-objective") character of the ethnographic account may have an opposite (but equally undesirable) paralyzing effect if it is interpreted as an invitation to treat ethnography as merely a reflection of the author's inner world. Such interpretation compels the writer to look inward, into the psychic depths, "in an infinite regress of cognitive dispositions" (Gergen and Gergen 1991, 79), in order to reveal the biases and complexes that have exerted their formative influence on the ethnographic text.

In my own view, the recognition of ethnographic "textuality" is useful when it prompts one to address the question of conventions and genres involved in the making of ethnography, in order to make this process more self-reflexive and to spark awareness of what White (1978, 47) called "the [discipline's] system of notation." In contrast to the introspective approach described above, such a quest is directed outward, into the realm of shared meanings and understandings that exist between researcher and subject, as well as within the researcher's discipline.

Insofar as the subjective character of the ethnographic research and interpretation are recognized and applied to further an awareness of one's own theoretical premises and subject position (as well as of their bearing on the research results), such recognition advances, rather than hinders, the investigation. This perspective is perfectly consistent with the hermeneutic texts that introduced the textual metaphor to social sciences. Indeed, for Paul Ricœur the concept of society as a text open to multiple interpretations does not exist separately from the idea of validation—a procedure of comparison between possible interpretations "in the light of what is known." Therefore, in Ricœur's words,

> if it is true that there is always more than one way of construing a text, *it is not true that all interpretations are equal* and may be assimilated to so-called "rules of thumb." The text is a *limited field of possible constructions.* The logic of validation allows us to move between the two limits of dogmatism and skepticism. It is always possible to argue for or against an interpretation, to confront interpretations, to arbitrate between them, and to seek for an agreement, even if this agreement remains beyond our reach. (Ricœur 1971, 550, italics added)

The impetus to legitimate a study's conclusions is what compels ethnographers to adhere to precision and accuracy in all records while in the field, to dwell on "negative cases" and discrepant details when fieldwork is over, and to write lengthy methodological appendices when the time comes to produce a written account of their findings. The function of these practices is precisely to maintain the soundness of ethnographic research in the spirit of Ricœur's notion of validation.[14]

The criterion of reliability is less central than validity to the assessment of an ethnographic study's legitimacy. This is due to the disagreement between the demands for reliability and the fundamentals of self-reflexive ethnographic research (Burawoy 1998). Focused on the context and deeply rooted in the intersubjective nature of inquiry, an ethnographic study is not interested in standardizing itself and eliminating all distortions that would preclude it from being replicated (nor, I should add, would it find such an enterprise feasible). Instead, ethnography examines the effects that actions, identities, and the circumstances of the encounter between researcher and actors inevitably have in the context of a research situation, elevating these "distortions" to the status of valuable research data.

This brings us to the second important dilemma of ethnography, the dilemma of *representation* and the effects of power. No matter how natural and life-like the ethnographer tries to make the research encounter with her subjects, the fundamental reality of this encounter is that one party in it (the researcher herself) is endowed with the power to frame, define, and interpret the meanings, acts, and intentions of the other party (the ethnographic subject). This power to define and speak for her subjects (and, by extension, to silence them) endows the researcher with a great responsibility and, at the same time, influences her perspective on more levels than one. Apart from creating a particular configuration of authority on the ethnographic site, it may also propel a social scientist to exoticize the subjects, as well as to objectify and normalize the social forces at work on the ethnographic locale, thus making any situation look natural. Even self-conscious awareness of this power on the part of the researcher does not preclude distortions, since it may impel an excessive advocacy for the subjects, unintentionally portraying them as helpless victims devoid of agency and will.

There are hardly any fast and definitive cures for the dilemma of representation. Authority and hierarchy are ubiquitous and permeate social relations both within and outside the research setting, and it would be naïve to expect that this fundamental aspect of the social world could be fully removed from the ethnographic encounter. However, although the effects of power can not be fully removed, they can be controlled and diminished. I tried to account for the dynamic of power on two levels—the level of actual fieldwork, and the level of the sociological interpretation.

In fieldwork, I tried to remain aware of how I was presenting my own role as researcher and interviewer, and how my informants were constructing it. While it is justly acknowledged that the status of a sociologist often bears connotations of class superiority and thus can be construed as intimidating,[15] I made an effort to emphasize those aspects of my identity which ran counter to this presumption. Following Eliasoph (1998) and Jorgenson (1991), I allowed my respondents sufficient information and freedom to construct my identity in an egalitarian and sometimes even patronizing way, by presenting myself as a young unmarried woman, a graduate student under the weight of academic requirements and expectations, and a person living with her parents, one who is hence naïve about the practical realities of everyday life in Russia. I explicitly conveyed my deference toward the respondents' expertise about the situation in Russia, both in terms of larger political developments and on the level of routine household management. My professed ignorance worked to the benefit of the interview by encouraging my respondents to go into some depth in their explanations of the political, economic, and social realities of the day, although at times it earned me a friendly scolding for "not keeping up to date." Another resource I found useful for alleviating the effects of power in the interview setting were the experiences and views of my parents and of my brother's family, all of whom live in Moscow and encounter in their daily routine many of the same dilemmas and predicaments as the members of my sample. Appealing to the parallels that existed between my family's experiences and the ones conveyed by my informants, I wanted to make sure that my questions did not carry a hint of judgment or disapproval. In addition, by rooting myself in circumstances familiar to the respondents, I mapped myself onto the plane of existence in which my own perspectives bore no superiority or primacy over my interlocutors'.

A special asset that my respondents possessed and that gave them a sense of leverage over me was the recurrent character of the interviews, all of which, as they knew, were needed in order to complete my study. In this respect the power balance was reversed; the respondents were aware of the centrality of their consent to the success of my project. This feeling of importance increased over the course of the project, and it was not uncommon for my contacts in the later stages to stress that, although they had to sacrifice some other activities in order to meet with me, they were eager to do it out of a desire to help me in my research. These comments, seemingly inconsequential, were significant in that they signaled the sense of control and importance that my respondents felt they possessed in our multiple meetings.[16]

Finally, it is impossible to overestimate the bearing that the recurrent character of the interviews had on the tonality and course of the conversation itself. While the first discussion could bear overtones of formality and intrusion by virtue of my respondents' unfamiliarity with the conventions of an in-depth semi-structured interview and with the interviewer herself, the later meetings could not help but partake of a more personal and unconstrained character. Since I quickly became aware of the richness of the ethnographic material such discussions may yield, I consciously contributed to fostering this informality by bringing along *chto-nibud' k chaiu* (something for tea, usually a cake or a pack of cookies) and not shying away from the respondents' questions about my own goings-on.[17] The discussion, then, would typically take place around tea in the kitchen or the living room and be far more spontaneous than it was during the initial meeting.

Effects of power remain a concern beyond the fieldwork setting as well, when it comes to the interpretation of the ethnographic material. No matter how inclusive and detailed an ethnographic account may be, it inevitably imposes some reduction on the data, and the decision to include or exclude certain perspectives and voices is one any researcher must face. There are also choices to be made about the interpretation that the selected voices receive. And, of course, the power to hold one interpretation as superior to the alternatives remains the privilege, and the responsibility, of the author. To compound all of these concerns, the fieldwork for this book involved not only a sociological but also a literary act of interpretation as I had to make choices between alternative ways of presenting the ideas and sentiments of my interlocutors in a language alien to them, with all the distortions that such a transition involves. Lastly, by virtue of education and socialization, any author is by nature an embodiment of discourses of power, which favor certain values, relationships, and practices over others and which can be read in the assessments that the activities and narratives collected in the field eventually receive.[18]

One of the ways to control these effects is to make one's informants "co-author[s] in narrative adventures" (Lincoln and Denzin 1998, 411). I tried to do that in this book by including extensive quotations, by consulting with my bi-lingual colleagues about the most accurate ways of rendering interview quota-tions in English, by providing the original Russian expressions when all transla-tion variants seemed wanting, and by placing these quotations into the context of the interviews from which they were taken. In doing so I treated the narra-tives of my respondents not only as expressions of their opinions and attitudes, but also as stories that they were telling about themselves, and that were later incorporated into my own narrative account. In addition, I followed the guid-ance of Morawska (1996) in treating many of my informants as experts who could provide feedback on some of the insights and working hypotheses that emerged in the course of the fieldwork. While no one source had the monopoly on the final interpretation, I did not automatically grant such primacy to my own perspectives either. Instead, I considered them in the light of the feedback and alternative interpretations they encountered.

As another counterbalance to the effects of authorial power, I tried to con-ceptualize my fieldwork not as an exploration of the life and perspectives of some hypothetical "Other," but as a chance to develop an understanding of some of my own deep-rooted behaviors. In saying this, I am far from under-estimating the distance between the experiences of my informants and my own position of a young Russian with an American degree, relative financial sta-bility, and freedom of movement.[19] Yet I am also well aware of the fact that my interest in the issues of everyday life in the prolonged crisis was triggered by a deeply personal puzzlement over the differences I have observed between my own "natural" responses to pressure and instability, and those I have en-countered among my university colleagues and friends in the United States. In this respect, my exploration into the forms of everyday life in Russia could be interpreted as an attempt at self-ethnography insomuch as this exploration was fueled by my appreciation of the affinities between my own modes of thought and action and those of my subjects.

My own position in this exploration, therefore, can be described as that of an insider/outsider, an individual sharing much of the cultural competence (as well as preoccupations) of her subjects, and at the same time, marked by the distance and self-estrangement conferred by academic training and a long ex-perience of living in another culture. While I take this peculiar position to be especially propitious for a self-reflexive investigation, it also presents significant dangers—those of over-identification on the one hand and of unwitting per-petuation of the dominant representations on the other. The dilemma of chart-ing a middle course between going native and remaining detached, between being a participant and remaining an observer, is something all ethnographers have to resolve. In my case, as is true for many other "native ethnographers,"[20] I was helped by knowing from the outset that I would not fit comfortably into either of the two identities. The tension between the two is much like the dynamic at play in the fundamental task of satisfying the Scylla of legitimation (by maximizing the credibility of the text) without, at the same time, falling prey to the Charybdis of power. But instead of dismissing these challenges as irresolvable, I maintain that they are profoundly and dialectically constructive. They prevent us from falling in too comfortably with either one of the poles they delineate. In this way, they continue to keep ethnographers productively uneasy in their skins, which means that they never stop asking questions.

Appendix 2. List of Respondents

Alena, 48, female, draftswoman. Lived with her two daughters and mother-in-law. Alena's husband, who was an engineer, died at a young age of a heart attack in 1996 and left her with children on a small salary and a pension. Toward the end of the fieldwork, Alena's older daughter graduated from university and got a well-paid job as a translator.

Alexei Ivanovich, 46, male, military engineer. Served in a military unit in the Moscow suburbs, and moonlighted every third night as a manager in a paging company. Lived with his wife (a school teacher) in military housing. Their son lived with his wife and her parents, and the daughter lived in a university dorm, but both children relied heavily on their parents' financial help. Throughout fieldwork Alexei Ivanovich's family was waiting to receive a permanent apartment through his job, and when it finally happened in 2000, he petitioned for early retirement in hopes of finding a better paying job as a security guard.

Alla Alekseevna, 53, female, office manager in a mid-sized Russian company. Previously occupied a high-ranking administrative position with a district Party committee, but was asked to leave at the beginning of the 1990s. Married to a criminal investigator, no children.

Andrei, 38, male, insurance manager. Lived with his wife, who worked as a nurse, his pensioner mother, and three children. In the course of fieldwork he left the insurance agency he was working for and began to work on commission.

Anna, 29, female, teacher of physics. Worked in a Moscow school and gave private lessons whenever she could. Lived with a grandmother and a husband who taught computers at the same school. At the time of fieldwork had no children.

Anton, 32, male, middle-ranking manager in a Western company, with a degree in international trade. Fluent in English, ambitious and upwardly mobile. Had a wife who worked as an accountant, and a baby son.

Dmitrii Kirillovich, 54, male, medical doctor. Worked long hours in a city hospital. Married to a journalist, had a daughter who lived separately.

Evgenii Alekseevich, 63, male, chemist. Married to Natalia Konstantinovna and lived with her, their daughter, and a baby grandson in a large apartment in a prestigious section of Moscow. Had an international reputation in his field, was often invited to participate in conferences, and published regularly. Despite his visibility, the lab he ran was strained financially, and the young scientists did not stay there long.

Gennadii, 43, male, engineer. Spent most of his career at a TV manufacturing factory. At the start of fieldwork he was unemployed; then he briefly had a job as a real estate agent and later found employment as an office equipment repairman. Married to an accountant and lived with her, her retired mother, and a son in a cramped two-room apartment in the center of Moscow. Throughout the duration of fieldwork, Gennadii's family was looking for opportunities to improve their living conditions, but they finally realized that their savings were insufficient for an apartment upgrade and bought a car instead.

Georgii, 43, male, car mechanic. Formerly worked as a zoologist and traveled widely across the country. Unmarried. In 1990, Georgii lost his mother, after which, as he himself confessed, he started having an alcohol problem. At the time of fieldwork was living alone in his apartment.

Igor, 31, male, car mechanic working independently. Lived with a student-girlfriend and a cat and spent a lot of time fishing or picnicking with a group of old friends who also served him as primary suppliers of clients.

Karina, 63, female, retired architectural designer. No children. Lived with her husband, an economist who, despite his poor health, continued to work in a private distance learning school. Shared grading assignments with him, and spent most of their income on expensive food supplements that were prescribed to her husband.

Klara, 45, female, clerk in a municipal health clinic. Klara was single and lived with her elderly mother, who was seriously ill and passed away in 1999. Klara herself received a disability pension because of an operation she had in 1992. Prior to the surgery she worked as a draftswoman in a construction bureau. Her job with the clinic was part-time and did not pay well, but Klara enjoyed it because it gave her an opportunity to socialize.

Konstantin, 53, male, engineer. Worked in an aviation research institute that had experienced problems in the mid-1990s. Had worked as a market salesman, sales manager, and construction worker, but returned to the institute after things there got better. Had a wife who was unemployed, and a school-aged daughter. Supplemented institute salary with a small income from occasional sub-contracted construction work and a room he rented out.

Kseniia Anatolievna, 43, female, cleaning lady, a former assembly line worker and saleswoman. Married to a construction worker. In the course of the fieldwork she left her cleaning job at an office to stay home and take care of their two school-aged sons. Lived with the family in a "communal apartment" which they shared with a single eighty-four-year-old woman.

Lena, 37, female, cleaning lady in a private market research company. Took all the contract jobs she could find, often staying after hours to help in the kitchen or to work on telephone surveys. Had a husband (a policeman) and two school-aged children, whose education, in the form of additional courses in preparation for the university, she considered the most important family investment.

Lina, 55, female, retired chemical engineer. Went on early retirement in the beginning of the 1990s in order to care for her grandchildren. Lived in a small two-bedroom apartment with her retired husband, who worked part time as a night watchman, their divorced daughter, and a small granddaughter. Had a son who lived separately but regularly left his son with her during the day. The family was struggling financially.

Liudmila Romanovna, 49, female, accounting manager in a drug rehabilitation clinic. Lived with her husband, a metal repairman, and had two grown daughters who lived separately. Liudmila Romanovna considered herself lucky because of the good fortune of her two daughters, both of whom were financially independent, and talked about them constantly. While her family seemed relatively comfortable financially, primarily because of her job, they remembered harder days when Liudmila Romanovna took typing jobs home in the evening and her husband worked several side jobs to make ends meet in the early 1990s.

Maria, 37, female, nurse in a municipal health clinic. Grew up and received nursing education in a small town four hours away from Moscow. Maria moved to Moscow after marrying a Muscovite and lived with her mother-in-law, her husband (who worked as a security guard), and their school-aged daughter.

Mikhail Aleksandrovich, 59, male, government employee. Married to Nelly Romanovna, and lived with her in a two-room apartment where they regularly took care of their teenage granddaughter, who often stayed with them after school. Long-time employee of the Ministry of Construction, was briefly fired in the course of the early 1990s, did odd jobs, but then was invited to return due to his administrative expertise.

Natalia Konstantinovna, 53, female, manager in a chemical research lab. Formerly worked as a chemist, but changed professions when her lab started to produce chemical substances for import.

Nelly Romanovna, 57, female, retired teacher. Gave private lessons at home, recruiting students through network connections. The couple supplemented its income by renting out a small apartment inherited by her husband Mikhail Aleksandrovich.

Nikolai, 31, male, freight operator with a major airline, who supplemented this income with occasional business transactions for a friend's company. Was married but divorced in the course of fieldwork because of what he referred to as "emotional incompatibility." No children.

Nina Alekseevna, 51, female, environmental engineer, in the course of fieldwork switched jobs within the same research institution and started to work as a clerk in a personnel office. Never married; she lived with her college-aged son and a much-loved cat. Had extensive experience of working several jobs at once, but did not want her son to find a job while in college, because she feared that it could compromise his studies.

Roman, 44, male, construction worker for a Yugoslav company, who also took independent contracts whenever possible. Formerly worked in a space equipment manufacturing plant and, afterward, in a metal casting workshop. Lived with his wife, school-aged daughter, and grown son in a three-room apartment. Cared for two elderly aunts and his mother-in-law who lived separately but depended on him for provisions. Toward the end of fieldwork, Roman's mother-in-law, who no longer could care for herself, moved in with them.

Sasha, 30, male, small entrepreneur. During the time of fieldwork was doing odd jobs that barely kept him afloat; continually looked for a big project to get involved with. Had a wife who was taking accounting courses, and a school-aged son.

Sergei Mikhailovich, 50, male, geologist. Juggled several jobs at once: did contract work at a research institute, teamed up with an old friend to work several nights a week as a security guard at a warehouse, and once or twice a year went as a supervisor on several months' long exploratory expeditions to Northern Siberia. Lived with a wife, who also worked two jobs, and their two grown daughters.

Tatiana, 68, female, retired postal worker. Worked as a groundskeeper. Lived with her unemployed daughter and a grandson who worked at a factory.

Valentina, 31, female, day care teacher. Lived and worked in a suburb of Moscow with her husband who worked at a nearby factory, and a school-aged daughter. Her family relied heavily on financial help from grandparents, and throughout the time of fieldwork Valentina was looking for a better paying job, albeit unsuccessfully.

Vera Vladimirovna, 43, female, cleaning lady. Formerly worked at a factory as an accountant's assistant. Married, with two children. Juggled two cleaning jobs, one in an elite furniture salon, and another in a courthouse. Was the sole breadwinner in the family. Her husband had left his factory job after an injury and was receiving a disability pension at the time of fieldwork.

Victor Vladimirovich, 56, male, former industrial engineer currently working as a lathe operator at a factory. Married to an accountant, lived in a small apartment with her and their college-aged son.

Vladimir, 40, male, actor. Struggling financially, single, lived in his friend's apartment. Took all side jobs he could find, including acting in promotions, company parties, etc. Had a permanent but poorly paid position in one of the Moscow theaters.

Zhenia, 34, female, accounting manager in an oil company. Avid camper. Lived with a boyfriend (computer specialist) and a school-aged daughter.

Appendix 3. List of Interviewed Experts

Aleksei Ageev, economist, Director of the Institute for Economic Strategies (interviewed in July 2001).

Daniil Dondurei, sociologist of culture, main editor of the *Iskusstvo Kino* [*Art of Cinema*] magazine (interviewed in June 2001).

Boris Dubin, the leading researcher of the Levada-Center (interviewed in June 2001).

Boris Kagarlitsky, left-wing activist and political journalist, Senior Research Fellow at the Institute for Comparative Political Studies and Director of the Institute of Globalization and Social Movements (interviewed in June 2001).

Aleksei Kara-Murza, historian and political scientist, member of the federal political council of the liberal SPS [Union of the Rightist Forces] Party, president of the Russian Liberal Heritage foundation (interviewed in July 2001).

Igor Kliamkin, political scientist, vice president of the Liberal Mission Foundation (interviewed in June 2001).

Andranik Migranian, vice president of the Reforma Foundation, long-term member of the Presidential Council (interviewed in June 2001).

Alexei Podberezkin, former deputy of the Russian Duma from the communist party faction, currently the leader of a national-patriotic movement, Dukhovnoe Nasledie [Spiritual Heritage] (interviewed in July 2001).

Georgii Satarov, political scientist, president of the Indem Foundation, one of the authors of Yeltsin's presidential program of 1996 (interviewed in June 2001).

Lev Timofeev, sociologist and former dissident, head of the Center of Informal Economy Research (interviewed in June 2001).

Valerii Tishkov, director of the Institute of Anthropology and Ethnography, consultant of the Carnegie Center (interviewed in June 2001).

Vladimir Vinnikov, journalist of the ultranationalist/communist newspaper *Zavtra* (interviewed in June 2001).

Oleg Yanitsky, environmental sociologist and the leading researcher of the Institute of Sociology (interviewed in May 2001).

Appendix 4. Discussion Topics

1. Tell me about the past 5–10 years in your life. What were the major events? What else?
2. What were the important periods, if any? How did your life change? Why?
3. How were these changes connected to the events in the larger society? Why?
4. When did the changes in the country begin? When did you personally realize it? How did you feel about the changes?
5. What was going on during the earlier stages of the transformation? What else? What happened later? Why did it take the course it did?
6. What did you expect when the changes started? What was your attitude back then? Why? Did it change later, and if yes, how? Why did it change?
7. How did the changes on the larger political scale affect your personal/family life? How else? Why?
8. How did you cope with these events in your life? How are you coping now? How did you decide how to cope?
9. What was the hardest thing for you to do/to deal with? Why? How did you deal with it? How are you dealing with it now?
10. How have the changes affected the members of your family? What about the society at large? How do most people deal with them? How successful are they?
11. What is a "good life," what does one need for it? How is it possible to achieve it in today's Russia?
12. If you had to make a guess, what do you think awaits Russia in the distant future, let's say in 50 years? Why? What would an optimistic person say? A pessimist? What about the next 5–10 years, how do you think events will develop?
13. What are your personal plans for the next 5 years? What will change in your/your family's life? Why do you think so? How do you feel about it?
14. How would you characterize the social groups that are the "winners" in the transformation? And who are the "losers"? Why? What is your attitude to this?
15. Speaking of you personally, how successful do you think you have been in dealing with the events of the last decade? Why? What about your family? Your friends? Your colleagues? Muscovites? Russians at large?

16. What qualities does one have to have in order to get by in our life? What does one have to do? Why? What is your attitude to this?
17. The events of the last decade were very diverse. What are you happy with when you look back at the past 5–10 years? What would you wish had not happened? Why? Would you like the things to have stayed as they were before 1985? Why?

Repeat Interviews

1. How are things, what news do you have (personal, professional, family)? What happened? What consequences did it bring for you and your family?
   (Questions 2–4 during the second wave only)
2. Describe the first weeks of the August financial crisis. Did you foresee it? How did you feel? What did you do? How did your friends/relatives feel/act? How did most Russian people feel?
3. What did the August default mean to you personally? What did it mean to most people? What did you decide to do? How did you make this decision?
4. What were the main effects of this event on your life? Your family? What about the rest of the nation, how did it affect it?
5. How often do you remember the days of the default? How has your life changed since it happened? How are you coping with it? Do you think another one would be possible right now?
6. Looking back, how has the August crisis made you reevaluate what is going on in the country? Looking back, did you act wisely during the days of the financial crisis?
7. Have there been changes for the better for you lately? For the worse? How has it been economically? How have you been coping? Have you or your family members managed to find any new sources of income? How did you find them?
8. Have you made any large purchases since we last talked? When did you make your last large purchase? Do you like to shop? What are the things you like buying most? How do you shop? Describe the last time you decided to buy something big. How did you choose the object, who did you discuss it with? Did you have to save for it? Are you usually satisfied with your purchases, and why? What is worth spending money on, and why? What do you do with your old things?
9. What about health, how do you feel about spending money on it? What types of healthcare do you use? How often have you been going to the doctor? Do you have a particular doctor you trust? Where does your doctor work? What is your attitude toward private medicine?
10. What is your regular day like right now? What about a regular weekend? Was the way you spend time different before? In what way, and why?

11. What have you been reading lately (books, newspapers, journals)? Did you read more/less before, and why? What are your favorite papers/TV programs, and why?
12. How closely have you been following politics lately? Why? What were the main events? What are your sources of information? What do you look for in a politician? Who do you support? Why? Would you like your child to be a politician?
13. How do the changes in larger politics affect everyday life? Why? Can the opposite happen: how can people affect politics? Have you ever tried to do it? Why? Did you always think this way? If not, when did you change your mind?
14. What is your take on voting? Do you vote? How do you decide who to vote for? Why do some people not vote?
15. What are your plans for the future, near and distant? What will you do for a vacation? Your family members? How do you think life in the country will be changing?
16. How will the past 10–15 years enter history? What about the history of your family? What have these years changed in your life? What was the hardest thing to cope with? How does this time compare with the other periods of your life? What do you remember with pleasure? With regret?

Notes

1. Introduction

1. *Khrushchevka* is a type of apartment building that was erected en masse during the 1960s, as a part of Nikita Khrushchev's efforts to deal with the housing crisis. Ubiquitous in Moscow as well as other Russian cities, *khrushchevka* buildings are also known pejoratively as *khrushchoby* (a merger of *khrushchevka* and *trushchoby,* the Russian word for slums) and are notorious for the small size of their apartments and the poor quality of construction. For more on khrushchoby and their social and cultural significance, see an entry in Sarnov (2002, 507–510) as well as Brumfield and Ruble (1993).

2. See Koselleck (2002).

3. Braudel writes: "If we reduce the length of time observed, we either have the event or the everyday happening. The event is, or is taken to be, unique; the everyday happening is repeated, and the more often it is repeated the more likely it is to become a generality or rather a structure" (1982, 29). See also Erikson (1976, 1994), Quarantelli and Dynes (1977), Bolin (1998), Quarantelli (1998).

4. See Lifton (1967), Jahoda, Lazarsfeld, and Zeisel (1971).

5. I am using the terminology of living, and not surviving, advisedly, because the significance of a permanent crisis is exactly that it normalizes whatever may otherwise be considered extreme.

6. This quality of everyday life became particularly interesting in the light of Foucault's conceptualization of the micro-workings of power. While for Garfinkel, individuals gloss over the shared foundations for interaction to avoid disruption of sociation, Foucault's subjects interiorize these (power-laden) foundations so deeply that they are inherently unable to question them.

7. Lefebvre (1984) and Lefebvre (1991). See also a special volume on everyday life published by *Yale French Studies* (1987), Vol. 73.

8. To a great extent these categories themselves are unsettled and inverted. Thus, de Certeau's (1984) treatise on the practice of everyday life starts with a dedication "To the ordinary man. To a common hero."

9. For criticisms of reification of everyday life, and of the conceptual ooziness of this category, see Elias (1998) and Kelly (2002).

10. My position as simultaneously an insider (a native Muscovite whose family continued to reside in Moscow) and an outsider (a person whose last few years had been spent mostly abroad) to the Russian setting gave me a certain leeway in violating assumptions of shared understanding: it was comprehensible to my subjects why certain practices could appear less intelligible to me than they would initially expect.

11. I would refer an interested reader to the works of Levada (1995), Rose and Carnaghan (1995), Rotkirch and Haavio-Mannila (1996), Buckley (1997), Burawoy and Verdery (1999), Dubin (1999), Kim (1999), Ashwin (1999, 2000), Burawoy et al. (2000), Markowitz (2000), Pilkington (2002), Ashwin and Lytkina (2004), and Kay (2000, 2006). For a seminal analysis tackling shared discursive and cultural frameworks during a somewhat earlier period, see Ries (1997).

12. See Ries (1997), Levada (2000). The strength of identification with "the people," as opposed to particular socioeconomic groups, could be explained at least partially by the fact that members of various economic, gender, and age groups were bound together in networks of mutual support and economic transfer that had become central to their ability to navigate the realities of postsocialism (Caldwell 2004).

13. See Jahoda, Lazarsfeld and Zeisel (1971).

14. Quotation in Russian: "Esli Rossii suzhdeno pogibnut', to . . . moskvichi umrut poslednimi!"

15. See Dubin (1997), Levada (2002).

16. My respondents (16 men and 17 women, 29 to 68 years of age) came from a variety of educational and occupational backgrounds and were recruited through a theoretically informed snowball sample which strove to diversify the set of respondents, ensuring, at the same time, that none of them had any professional knowledge of or involvement with the political and economic processes we were to discuss. I spoke with each three or four times. For more on sample selection, see appendix 1.

17. This argument is made in Crawford and Lijphart (1995), as well as in the collected works by Levada (2000).

18. The same argument is made by Fitzpatrick (1999) regarding the appropriateness of atomization terminology for the Stalinist period.

19. For an academic version of such an argument in the American context, see Putnam (2000).

20. The number of security guards in Russia is quite comparable to the United States, considering the differences in the population: 500,000 vis-à-vis just over 1 million (Sources: Gusev 2003, US Bureau of Labor Statistics, retrieved June 25, 2007, from http://www.bls.gov/oes/current/oes339032.htm). However, in the Russian case, they are concentrated predominantly in the large urban centers and have a far greater presence, because their responsibilities include, apart from merely maintaining order, checking the visitors' documents and essentially making public offices inaccessible to anyone who is not personally expected on a given day.

21. Thomas and Thomas drew attention to the significance of such definitions in what became known as the Thomas Theorem: "if men [sic] define situations as real they are real in their consequences" (1928, 572). This observation is pertinent to the role that notions of crisis played in the Russian public discourse in the late 1990s. However, I prefer the term "framework of interpretation" to W. I. Thomas's "definition of the situation," because "definition of the situation" implies more self-consciousness than is usually involved in everyday activity,

when cognitive assumptions about the nature of the environment are sub-merged rather than consciously articulated.

22. The term "practical competence" is inspired by Berger and Luckmann's notion of "pragmatic competence in routine performances" (1967, 42), which desig-nates the social stock of knowledge shared by individuals in a given society.

23. For a discussion of the two meanings of experience—*Erlebnis* and *Erfahrung,*—albeit in a different context, see Jay (1998).

2. How the Crisis of Socialism Became a Postsocialist Crisis

1. A detailed discussion of the perestroika era can be found in Hosking (1991), Sakwa (1991), Walker (1993), and Galeotti (1997).

2. Unlike Gorbachev, Yeltsin, who was at the vanguard of the democratic move-ment in the late 1980s, was consistently anti-Communist, pro-market, and in favor of the dissolution of the USSR.

3. The decree issued by then–prime minister of the USSR Valentin Pavlov an-nounced the abolition of 50- and 100-ruble banknotes, at the same time stipu-lating that the bank exchange of these notes would commence immediately and last only for three days.

4. By estimate of the Russian sociologist Tatiana Zaslavskaia (1997), the middle class, consisting primarily of professionals, managers, and entrepreneurs, com-prised about 20 percent of the Russian population prior to the 1998 economic breakdown. By the end of the decade, the estimate of *Expert* magazine was more conservative: no more than 20 percent of the population in Moscow and 6–10 percent in smaller cities. *Expert* considered the lower threshold of the middle class to be defined by a monthly income of $150 per capita (Gurova 2001).

5. See works by Lakoff and Johnson (1980), as well as Michaels and Ricks (1980).

6. Referring to the dismissal of Evgenii Primakov's cabinet in 1999.

7. Here and elsewhere, the respondent's pseudonym is followed by gender and age at the time of the first interview in 1998. For a brief biographical sketch on each respondent, see appendix 2.

8. A list of expert interviewees is available in appendix 3.

9. *Private Stock,* no. 6 (20), 2001, and *Pro et Contra* 4, spring 1999, respectively.

10. A testimony to the deficit of neutral names for the post-perestroika pe-riod were the hedges I frequently heard in everyday speech, such as "all these," or "so-called," as in: "When they began, all these changes . . . ," or "When it started, all this . . . I don't know how it's called . . . one can't call it perestroika . . ."

11. It is hard to give adequate estimates for trends prevailing in a broad array of sources. Some indication of the relative magnitude of the phenomenon, how-ever, is the relative frequency with which various terms for designating the 1990s were used in the Russian- and English-language press. For example, in July 1997, a relatively uneventful month in terms of political and economic developments, the term "crisis" was used more than three times as often as

the more neutral "changes" and more than twenty times as often as "transformation" in the Russian press, according to *Integrum*. A similar search done on *Lexis-Nexis* indicated an inverted proportion: "changes" were twice as popular as "crisis" in application to Russia, while "transformation" was used four times less often.

12. Voznesensky's title is a pun which makes use of the phonetic affinity between the sound of the words "Jesus Christ" and "Zhutkii Crisis" (Awful Crisis).

13. See Rancour-Laferriere (1995), Ries (1997).

14. As in Igor Kon, 1959. *Filosofskii idealizm i krizis burzhuaznoi istoricheskoi mysli* (*Philosophical Idealism and the Crisis of Bourgeois Historical Thought*). Moscow: ISEL; or Igor Kon, ed. 1966. *V tiskakh dukhovnogo krizisa* (*In the Grip of a Spiritual Crisis*). Leningrad: Lenizdat.

15. From Kon's February 24, 1960, letter to the Secretary of the Central Committee of CPSU, M. A. Suslov. In: Volkov, Pugacheva, and Iarmoliuk (2000, 465–466).

16. Voslenskii's book was first published in German in 1980 and circulated in USSR only in samizdat copies.

17. The publication date does not reflect the timing of the work's creation in 1978. As with many other publications mentioned in these pages, Timofeev's ideas were limited to samizdat circles before perestroika.

18. For more on socialist conceptions of history and their subsequent transformation, see Verdery (1996), especially chapter 2, and Verdery (1999) passim in pp.111–127.

19. For a critique of how privatization was conceived and managed, and of the American consultants' contribution to its pitfalls, see Wedel (1998).

20. Author interview, June 2001.

21. Consider, in this context, the following titles: *Myths of the Passing Era* (Osipov 1992) and *Landscape after the Battle* (Ivanova 1993a).

22. Author interview, June 2001.

23. Ibid.

24. See Bauman (1987, 8).

25. For the intellectual history of the concept of the Russian intelligentsia, as well as for the cultural history of the stratum itself, see Berlin (1979).

26. See Dubin (2001, 329–341).

27. For an overview, see Gessen (1997), though I do not share Gessen's optimistic belief that all rumors of the intelligentsia's demise have been grossly exaggerated.

28. Subscription rates for that champion of the perestroika years, the thick monthly *Novyi Mir,* dropped from 2,620,340 in 1990 to 241,340 in 1992 and continued to shrink (numbers reported for 2000 are 13,300). Much of the initial drop had to do with a radical rise in subscription prices in 1992 (Zasurskii 1999), as well as with an increased competition from other sources on the media and book market.

29. From the Greek *ou* (negative particle) and *topos* (place), i.e. no-place.

30. For a discussion of eschatological temporality as a distinctive mark of the postsocialist intelligentsia's sense of time, see Paperno (2002).

31. I am concentrating on humanities and social sciences as the two fields most centrally involved in shaping the terms of public discussion.

32. See Kuz'min et al. (2002).

33. According to Gudkov and Dubin (2003), in 1998, translations comprised 36.5 percent of all publications in philosophy, psychology, and sociology, 8.7 percent in history and 3 percent in comparative literature.

34. Author interview with Oleg Yanitsky (Leading Researcher, Institute of Sociology, Russian Academy of Sciences), May 2001.

35. *Zelenyi khrustiashchii ekvivalent*—a humorous reference to American dollars.

36. For some examples, see Rutkevich (1995, 1998); Kodin (2001).

37. See Mitrokhin (2003).

38. See Ianin (1999).

39. Compare, for example, the publications of Vladimir Shlapentokh (1996) to those of Mikhail Rutkevich, an orthodox Marxist functionary who in 1972 had led the suppression of the progressive Institute of Concrete Social Research where Vladimir Shlapentokh had worked.

40. Readers interested in the political underpinnings of privatization and the role of political and social capital in the forging of post-Soviet financial empires, as well as the role played in these struggles by the media, can consult Wedel (1998), Mickiewicz (1999), Zasurskii (1999), Freeland (2000), Belin (2002), Steiglitz (2003).

41. For a succinct synopsis of Gerbner's views, see Gerbner (1994).

42. Many voices from across the ideological spectrum brought up the issue of national identity and ideological vacuum prior to 1996. However, the question was raised "from above" only after Yeltsin's reelection as the president of Russia in 1996. At that point it produced an array of projects, from parliamentary hearings on the subject of "the Russian idea" to a research center founded by Igor Chubais and dedicated solely to resolving the Russian "ideational crisis." The debate added an interesting spin on the crisis rhetoric. Postulating the need for ensuring "ideological provisioning" (Dondurei 2001) for the transformation, its ideologues directed their efforts not at engaging the public in a discussion of state policies, but rather at creating a picture of reality that would console the disengaged masses by giving them a new illusion. Because this alternative to the crisis rhetoric smacked of the old Soviet-style approaches to ideology, it was not particularly appealing.

43. *Ot razrusheniia k sozidaniiu: Put' Rossii v XXI vek. Osnovnye polozheniia sotsial'no-ekonomicheskoi programmy G. A. Zyuganova, kandidata v prezidenty Rossii ot narodno-patrioticheskikh sil* (From Destruction to Creation: Russia's Way into the XXI Century: Main points of the socioeconomic program of G.A. Zyuganov, candidate for Russian Presidency on behalf of popular-patriotic forces). 1996. Moscow: Shcherbinskaia Tipografiia, p.13.

44. See Yeltsin's electoral brochure, *Prezident Yeltsin: 100 voprosov i otvetov* (President Yeltsin: 100 Questions and Answers). 1996.

45.　In the uninterrupted flow of paragraphs delineating the failure of Yeltsin's reforms, the following words and combinations were highlighted: decrease of GDP, production, economics, production base, agriculture, monetary circulation, finance, banks, property, system of foreign economic ties, social-economic structure of society, demographic processes, model of development, loss of national unity and of people's friendship.

46.　Crisis rhetoric continued to be used for negotiating economic privileges during the Putin era. For an example, see the report of the Khabarovsk regional governor, V. I. Ishaev, "On Social-Economic Development of the Far East and the Baikal Region," which was delivered by Ishaev during Vladimir Putin's visit to Vladivostok in August 2002. Retrieved October 8, 2007 from http://www.adm.khv.ru/Invest2.nsf/NewsRus/68c369e753d4c89aca256c22002c1cbb.

47.　Cf. a similar critique advanced by Michele Rivkin-Fish (2006) of the way the notion of demographic crisis circulated in the Russian public sphere.

3. A State of Emergency

1.　Russian for "complete disintegration."

2.　Ries' conceptualization of perestroika as consisting of three phases (separation—liminality—consummation) draws on Turner's (1967) discussion of the tripartite structure of passage rites, which in its turn develops the distinction made by Van Gennep (1960).

3.　See Cerf and Albee (1990).

4.　See also Buckley (1993), Urban (1994), Lewin (1995), Ries (1997), and Zasurskii (1999).

5.　*Khozrashchet* was a market mechanism dating back to the period of NEP in the early 1920s, which was promoted by Gorbachev as early as 1985. It was an integral part of what Geoffrey Hosking (1991) called *Perestroika Mark One*, i.e., the period from 1985 to mid-1986 when there was as yet no talk of a radical overhaul of a socialist system, and when the tightening of labor discipline and emphasis on modernization were thought sufficient to resolve the USSR's problems. In the system of *khozrashchet*, enterprises formerly supported through the state budget had to switch to financing themselves through contracts with the other enterprises. The workers in these enterprises received a certain percentage of the enterprise income, depending on their share of work.

6.　A set of Gorbachev-initiated policies aimed at raising the quality of the output and at analyzing the systemic roots of defects.

7.　The initiatives Gennadii is describing were actually launched in 1985–1986.

8.　*Perestroika* literally means rebuilding, or reorganization.

9.　*Subbotniki* were the effectively obligatory "volunteer" initiatives of the workers' collectives in which several Saturdays (*subboty*) in the course of the year were dedicated to joining efforts to achieve some labor-intensive task for one's institution, such as cleaning the area, repairing the building, and so on.

10.　About $150 in June 1998.

11. See, for instance, Eldar Riazanov's comedy *Garazh* (1979).

12. In 2003, the VTsIOM team was forced to quit working for the organization. They later founded a new organization under the name of VTsIOM-A, which was later changed again to the Levada Center. This happened when the "brand" of VTsIOM was overtaken, under a legalistic pretext, by a pro-Kremlin group of pollsters (for details, see Yablokova 2003). At the time of my fieldwork, VTsIOM was the most reputable independent polling organization in the country.

13. See VTsIOM's periodical, *Monitoring obshchestvennogo mneniia: Ekonomicheskie i sotsial'nye peremeny* for the corresponding years.

14. Iosif Kobzon is a well-known singer who first became popular in the 1960s, and who managed to convert his social prestige into political and business connections. On a number of occasions, materials appeared in the press that suggested that Kobzon was friendly with several known mafia figures.

15. The word *otdykh* used by Natalia Konstantinovna can be translated both as "*rest*" and as "*vacation*." Further on, she plays on this ambivalence, shifting from one meaning to the other.

16. While as a noun "the abroad" makes little sense in the English language, it was very meaningful in the context of an almost complete sense of isolation most citizens of the USSR felt in relation to the rest of the world.

17. Cf. the analysis in the previous chapter of similar reference shifts that were involved in Natalia Ivanova's discussion of the post-Soviet fates of Russian intelligentsia (1993b).

18. A joke I heard on several occasions spoke to this perception directly: A phone rings in the apartment, the host picks up the receiver:

    "Hello?"
    "Hi, how are you?"
    "Fine, thanks."
    "Sorry, I must have dialed the wrong number."

19. For a detailed discussion of media in Russia of 1990s, see Mickiewicz (1999).

20. *Field of Miracles* was the first of the many game shows on Russian TV adapted from a Western original. This particular show was based on *Wheel of Fortune,* and its title tellingly evoked the image of the "Field of Miracles in Fools' Land" ("Pole chudes v strane durakov") from the tale *Zolotoi Kliuchik* (*The Golden Key*), Alexei Tolstoi's Russian adaptation of *The Adventures of Pinocchio* by Carlo Collodi. In *Zolotoi Kliuchik,* of course, the field of miracles turned out to be a sham made up to fool and rob the gullible wooden doll Buratino, leaving one free to guess at the game show's conception of its audience.

21. Yet, ironically, the only functioning enterprises in the second town she described belonged to the state infrastructure.

22. The metaphor of the cultural tool-kit was developed in a seminal article by Ann Swidler (1986). While Swidler refers to Bourdieu in her discussion, her notion of the tool-kit does not address the deeper cognitive and generative dimensions of habitus, which I discuss below.

23. See Bourdieu (1977, 78).

24. This is almost certainly changing now, as the first truly postsocialist generation enters public life.

25. The shift was so dramatic that an entire genre of post-Soviet jokes emerged in which an engineer was juxtaposed to the stock figure of the transformation's "winner," the New Russian, as in the following joke. A New Russian and an engineer stand next to one another in church. "What are you praying for?" asks the New Russian. "I'm praying to finally get the salary I'm owed for the past five months," the engineer responds. The New Russian reaches for his pocket and takes out a pile of money: "C'mon, take it, and don't distract God with your petty requests." For more on the position of Russian technical intelligentsia, as well as some of the rhetorical approaches that its members adopted to deal with the situation, see Shevchenko (2002).

26. The comment refers to the non-Russian market traders from the former Soviet republics of Central Asia and the Caucasus: Azerbaijan, Armenia, Uzbekistan, and so on. In lumping all of them into the same category, Azerbaijani, Konstantin demonstrated a prejudice common to Muscovites who, as Humphrey (1999, 49) points out, usually "neither know nor care about the traders' [actual] ethnic identity."

27. Arguably, this resentment was compounded by the general ambivalence of the postsocialist Russians toward money. Many of the traumatic changes that occurred during the 1990s, from the liberation of the prices in the early 1990s to the currency devaluation of 1998, were closely associated with monetary instability, which gave to the realm of money overtones of danger, injustice, and lack of control. Even apart from people's personal experiences, the objectifying and impersonal qualities of money, its deep implication in the project of capitalist modernity made it a good target for voicing criticism of the entire postsocialist transformation and of the shift in relationships that it engendered.

28. For an insightful discussion of the assumption of immutability shared by the citizens in regard to the late socialist system in all its incarnations, see Yurchak 2006.

4. The Routinization of Crisis

1. I am grateful to Oksana Sarkisova for sharing this quotation with me.

2. The Russian notion of normality stands in contrast here with the meaning this term acquired in other postsocialist countries, such as Hungary or Estonia. While for Russians the ideal of "normal life" belonged to the realm of pure normative imaginary, of what *should be,* for their East European counterparts, the notion of "normal life" was linked to their idea of what their standard of living *would have been* without the "unnatural" and imposed period of Soviet rule (see Fehérváry [2002] on Hungary and Rausing [2002] for Estonia). This difference further highlights the discrepancy between the Russian case and that of its East European neighbors.

3. Yeltsin's resignation took place on December 31, 1999.

4. The same spirit permeated many academic discussions. See, for example, Lisichkin's essay "Has Time Stopped in Russia?" published in *Russia and the Contemporary World* (2002).

5. Giddens' work on ontological security rethinks sociologically the concept that originally appeared in the writings of the existentialist psychiatrist R. D. Laing (1969).

6. See Smith (2002) for a detailed discussion of the post-Soviet commemorative calendar. In 2002, the day was renamed *Russia Day* (*Den' Rossii*), but for the few following years the initiative passed largely unnoticed and the two designations coexisted comfortably in newspapers, radio announcements, and street displays.

7. For a discussion of Russia's historical politics in the 1990s, see Smith (2002), as well as Zorin (2003).

8. While to an extent all postsocialist countries had to deal with the issue of temporality, the Russian case was complicated by its imperial and messianic legacies, which make the construction of an alternative linear timeline after the fall of socialist utopia more problematic.

9. These and other changes in political rhetoric after August 1998 are discussed in Shevchenko (2001).

10. Cf. Nancy Ries' suggestion that tales of suffering and absurdity, when recited and exchanged in a group, "help . . . to fabricate a sense of shared experience and destiny" and "provide a mode of cultural connection among vastly different people" (1997, 46, 51). I have benefited a great deal from Ries' insightful analysis. However, here I want to emphasize not the unintended effects of the crisis discourse, but the ways in which it was consciously used as a lubricant in social settings.

11. About forty dollars at the time.

12. This is in line with observations of Susan Gal (1991) regarding the differences in male and female speech styles.

13. This explains, among other things, the pleasure low-income Muscovites took in reciting a chain of prices, both current and socialist-era, as a way of indicating their discontent with the rapidity of inflation. Monotonously recounting the amounts charged for products ("Carrots now are twenty-five rubles. Eggs—seventeen, three times what they were! Cold cuts—thirty-five a kilo. Sugar is expensive, eleven in the least, and twelve on the market"), individuals who could not master these prices in reality controlled them at least in the narrative, attaining a fragile sense of competence that likely dissipated again as soon as they reached the market.

14. Italics in the original. This "double superlative," Wacquant suggests, "speaks volumes about the finely differentiated micro-hierarchies elaborated at the very bottom of society" (1994).

15. RAO ES is a nationwide energy monopoly, while Rem Viakhirev was (until June 2001) the head of Gazprom, a natural gas giant.

16. I am borrowing the term "damage control" from Herzfeld's (1992) discussion of fatalism. While Herzfeld applies it to self-serving justifications of failure after the fact, the concept seems equally applicable to the discussion of the future.

17. This is also how Ries (1997) interpreted the persistent imagery of suffering she

observed in perestroika-era public discourse. The concentration on suffering, rather than crisis, is a telling disciplinary choice by an anthropologist whose interests pertain more to the problematics of emotions and subjectivity than of social organization and self-presentations.

18. Cf. Stephen Kotkin's suggestion that studies of Soviet history could benefit from a shift of emphasis, from "what the party and its proponents *prevented* to what they *made possible*, intentionally or unintentionally" (1995:22, italics in the original).

19. This suggestion follows in spirit the comment made by my Czech colleague Marcel Tomášek in a different context: "For thirteen years, everyone talks about the legacies of socialism. But where are the legacies of *post*socialism?" (personal communication)

20. This strategy of exaggerated emotional distance from postsocialist turbulences was especially frequently displayed by men, perhaps due to the cultural taboo on admitting one's vulnerability.

21. Literally: "In my soul I wasn't disposed to this deceit" (*U menia dusha ne lezhala k etomu obmanu*).

22. See Shlapentokh (1995), Levada (2000).

23. For a rich ethnographic account of the way doctors misrecognize their participation in the deplored "system," see Rivkin-Fish (2005), especially chapters 4 and 5.

24. An article in the popular monthly *Itogi* followed this logic closely. Criticizing the inefficiencies of the suburban rail system and simultaneously dispensing advice on the art of traveling without paying for the ticket, it suddenly ended up siding with the railroad employees (the ticket collectors and ticket office personnel), through the device of portraying them as wronged by the system themselves. After a detailed explication of the scheme for riding trains for free, the article unexpectedly concluded, "and if you start feeling guilty—remind the ticket collector what your money would have gone to should you have paid it. It certainly wouldn't have been the pay for her overtime" (Zhukov 2000).

25. Meaning the financial breakdown of August 1998.

26. While the literal translation of this expression is not too illuminating, the Russian meaning expresses the notion of nonstop motion in the search for any opportunities, however small and trivial, of enhancing one's economic status.

27. Lifton (1967) in his work on Hiroshima made a similar observation when he suggested that the interpretation of fatalism as passivity has to be reconsidered. Referring to what is usually thought of as "Asian fatalism," he emphasized the active element of the "principle of resignation" that is usually overlooked: "No matter what happens, I carry on" (Lifton 1967, 186).

5. Permanent Crisis, Durable Goods

1. This chapter describes some of these ethnographic puzzles; for example, the ease with which some of my worst-off informants parted with their hard-earned savings in order to purchase expensive and seemingly unnecessary pieces of domestic equipment.

2. Consumer polls had documented vibrant consumer spending in the sphere of domestic durables at levels striking for a country that was conventionally seen as undergoing economic decline. According to COMCON-International market research data for 1999, 80 percent of Russian households purchased at least one TV set during the previous ten years, 62 percent obtained a new refrigerator, 37 percent a new VCR, with figures somewhat higher in large cities, such as Moscow and St. Petersburg. The data is based on a R-TGI (Russian Target Group Index) survey carried under the license of BMRB International—a detailed monitoring of lifestyles and consumption patterns of the Russian population, which has been conducted since 1995. In 1999, the data was collected from 14,000 households in forty-two Russian cities across the country and explored consumption of more than 400 categories of goods and services and over 3,900 brands. I thank Elena Koneva, Petr Zalesskii and the TGI team of COMCON-International for sharing this data with me.

3. By "family" I mean not only nuclear family, but the entire multiplicity of kinship ties in which an individual is embedded, including the most distant ones.

4. In fact, the divorce rate remained relatively stable throughout the late 1980s and 1990s (Vishnevskii 1999).

5. About $150 in June 1998.

6. The attraction of some of the low-income jobs in Russia was exactly that they could supplement earnings of other family members with access to other resources, such as status, privileges, or diverse connections (the profession of teacher here seems to be among the best positioned, due to the possibility of exchanging favors with the students' parents; see Lonkila [1998]). Similarly, the contributions of pensioners, although small, had unique advantages: they were regular and monetary, which was of great value in a situation of payment arrears; pensioners often became the only contributors of actual money to the household, with other household members being paid in kind (if at all). For that reason, according to Clarke (1999), it was almost as important for urban households to include a pensioner as it was to have a wage earner.

7. For an approach to employment strategies as products of purely individual choices, see Kupriianova (1997) and Biziukov (1999). While Burawoy et al. (2000) make it their central claim that households, not individuals or enterprises, should be treated as units of analysis of strategies of production and redistribution in the postsocialist context, their treatment of the subject firmly positions the female household head as the sole engine of survival, and thus overlooks the collective nature of the household economic project.

8. I am borrowing the notion of the "diversified portfolio of household activities" from an article by Richard Rose (1994).

9. About two dollars.

10. Yuri Luzhkov, longtime Moscow mayor.

11. Because the dollar rate escalated in August 1998 three-fold, it was a common complaint that the prices had become "three times as high" and people "three times as poor." While it is hard to deny the very real nature of the dilemmas many of my informants had to face daily in providing for the household, these turns of phrase seem to reflect the shock of the sudden increase more than

its realistic proportion: by December 1998, most consumer prices were about 1.5–2 times what they had been a year before, and average adjusted income was 78.3 percent of what it was December 1997 (Goskomstat 1999). In addition, due to this misbalance, individual savings, which were predominantly preserved in dollars, retained their value and even gained in purchase capacity.

12. "This is an unusual finding," write Braithwaite et al., "and the fact that one of the highest poverty rates recorded was for a single-male adult family type is even more surprising. One would expect that a single male adult would have no dependents and presumably would have a reasonable earning potential. Age only partly explains this finding, since two-thirds of these single male adults are *younger* than 65" (2000, 51–52; italics in the original).

13. While materials of my interviews concentrate on the recent period, historical evidence suggests that changes in the ideologies and practical circumstances of consumption have accompanied political turns throughout Soviet history (Stites 1989, Buchli 1999).

14. Consumer cards, introduced in Moscow in the fall of 1990, were issued to all Muscovites in an effort to limit shortages in the city by excluding out-of-town shoppers from obtaining products in the better-provided stores of the capital. For an excellent discussion and analysis of this and other rationing practices, as well as their social-psychological effects, see Nikolaev (2000).

15. According to time-budget research, working female Muscovites spent an average of 24 hours a week on shopping and housework in 1990–1991, while the corresponding figure for working males is 13 hours (Patrushev, Karakhanova, and Kushnareva 1992).

16. Literally "Go stand" (*Idite stoite*).

17. Detskii Mir—the largest children's department store in Moscow, located in a monumental building on Lubyanka Square.

18. "To hack a window through to Europe" (*prorubat' okno v Evropu*) is an expression originating from a line in Alexander Pushkin's 1833 narrative poem *The Bronze Horseman*, which refers to the founding of St. Petersburg by Peter the Great. Now the phrase is commonly used satirically to reference any Westernization project.

19. For an excellent discussion of the market's fundamental embeddedness in moral categories, see Zelizer (1979). Several fascinating case studies on the subject are in Mandel and Humphrey (2002).

20. Vera implies that the Moscow mayor, in exchange for a substantial sum of money, gave to ethnic Azerbaijani diaspora the exclusive monopoly on running the produce markets in city—a rumor I did not hear from anyone else, but which goes well with the general logic of total corruption and deceit.

21. I heard similar comments from people of all class and educational backgrounds.

22. There were finer sub-categorizations in this hierarchy, too. Thus, an appliance assembled in Malaysia ranked higher among the Russian consumers than an identical item assembled in China. These positions were not fixed and could undergo transformations: thus, according to a Russian market researcher, the

image of Korea as manufacturer and assembler of equipment made an evolution under the influence of aggressive LG and Samsung advertising, from a "secondary one, worse than Malaysia /Indonesia" to one of the "market leaders" (Sergei Sarkisov, personal communication).

23. In 2001, an entire issue of *Spros* was dedicated solely to the art of avoiding fraud on the market. More commonly, however, articles on the subject were dispersed throughout magazines, intermingling with coverage of consumer tests, interviews with lawyers, discussions of readers' letters, and so on. For an example of fraud coverage in the very first issue of *Spros*, see "Anti-ad: fake jeans, cognac, perfume," *Spros* 1 (1), 1992, a selection of articles beginning, characteristically, with "*In our insane market,* new fruits of competition have appeared" (4; italics added). Articles published later addressed issues ranging from investment fraud ("What is a deceived investor to do?" *Spros* 1 [19], 1996) to manufacturing fraud ("It only burns with a white flame if it's natural," *Spros* 5, 2000). The latter article suggested a rather unorthodox way of outsmarting the "tricksters from the textile industry" who blend cotton with synthetic ingredients in sheets. The suggestion was to burn a thread from the suspicious sheet and to inspect the color of the flame. The article stopped short of discussing the effects such vigilant consumer behavior might have on retail workers.

24. In prices of spring 2001, a high-quality German refrigerator cost about 21,000 rubles (roughly $740) in a store, while the same model could be purchased at the Gorbushka (an open-air market with a reputation for good prices and a wide selection of household goods) for about 16,800 rubles ($590), some 20% cheaper.

25. Personal communication.

26. VDNKh is the Russian acronym for the Exhibition of Achievements of the People's Economy. After 1991 the exhibition's monumental pavilions, formerly dedicated to different branches of industry and agriculture, were leased to various trading firms and stores, which sold everything from diapers to foreign cars. While not in the way originally intended, the vibrancy of consumer life one could observe in front of shop displays there could still serve as a testimony to the achievements of the people's economy.

27. According to COMCON-International data for 1999, every sixth Russian family owned more than one fridge, and an even larger proportion had multiple TV sets.

28. This claim was all the more powerful when it referred to household equipment—a category of goods which, from the time of the American National Exhibition in 1959, has been widely used as a symbol of the competition between the superpowers (Crowley and Reid 2000). For a similar point in discussion of the equally vibrant Hungarian home improvement practices, see Fehérváry (2002).

29. See Kon (1993), Lapin (1993), Evgenieva (1999), Kara-Murza (1999).

30. See the cover page feature in *Spros,* the Moscow-based consumer monthly (*Spros* 5, 2000).

31. In VTsIOM's 1998 survey *Power and Society*, 56 percent of those surveyed confessed having little to no interest in politics, as opposed to 9 percent expressing great or substantial interest (VTsIOM 1998).

32. See Ledeneva (1998).

33. In his analysis of the uses of furniture in the context of postsocialist Romania, Drazin (2001, 2002) comes to similar conclusions regarding the importance of domestic objects for managing uncertainty. However, while I concur with him in his argument, I also suggest that these objects carried a performative and not merely an adaptive function. In other words, they were used not only to protect one from the dangers of the crisis, but also to affirm the existence and gravity of the crisis itself.

6. Building Autonomy in Everyday Life

1. The imagery of a retreating state should not be taken uncritically. Even during the 1990s drift to neoliberalism, the Russian state was far from absent in the large-scale projects of resource distribution and economic and political management of the country. However, the increasing inadequacy of the welfare system, as well as mounting financial problems in the so-called budget sphere (health care, education, law enforcement, fundamental research), were much more noticeable and consequential to the individual Russians than the ways in which the state remained an organizing force in their lives.

2. It is telling in this respect that metal doors were more popular than the alarm service offered by the municipal police itself. With the latter, an alarm signaling the unauthorized opening of the entrance door is transmitted through telephone lines directly into the police station. The service was cheaper than the installation of the second door in the late 1990s and available to anyone with a telephone line (Smirnova 2002).

3. The data is for 1999, and is taken from Gudkov (2000b).

4. Resolution 723 of the Moscow city government "On the work of the district administration regarding the regulation of the construction of non-stationary objects and the creation of conditions for the preservation of personal auto transport belonging to the district's inhabitants," August 10, 1999. Published in *Oktiabr'skoe Pole*, September 20, 1999.

5. Ibid.

6. For quantitative data on the stable dynamic of distrust toward social institutions, see Naumova (1995) and Gudkov (2000b).

7. Mikhail Aleksandrovich is confusing the order of events here, since the "Gaidar crisis" of price liberalization came in 1992, a year after the "Pavlov crisis," which was prompted by the currency reform.

8. This bridging was, of course, primarily rhetorical. As I will discuss below, means for ensuring one's autonomy from the systemic crisis were distributed among these groups highly unequally.

9. See Zdravomyslov (1993), Crawford and Lijphart (1995), Toshchenko (1995), and Levada (2000).

10. While the city government supported the idea of supplying every residential building with coded access locks and took it upon itself to provide such locks after the explosions, most Muscovites found that their quality was low. More importantly, by the time they became an option most buildings already had fortified coded lock doors installed on the initiative and at the expense of the building residents themselves.

11. See Brown and Rusinova (1997) for some examples from the early 1990s.

12. While there must be cases when healthy individuals draw on the body of alternative medical knowledge in order to enhance well-being (through such practices as yoga, holistic nutrition, etc.), I did not encounter such uses in my sample. Overwhelmingly alternative medicine was employed in order to protect an individual from various negative influences rather than to enhance physical fitness for its own sake. Speaking in economic terms, people were less interested in maximizing their assets than in minimizing their losses.

13. A brand of over-the-counter painkiller analogous to Excedrin.

14. The country-level data suggests that use of medical institutions actually rose during the 1990s (Vishnevskii 1999).

15. See also Lindquist (2002). In order to describe the coexistence of multiple medical frameworks used by the patients simultaneously, Lindquist uses the notion of *pentimento* (first introduced to medical anthropology by Arney and Bergen [1984]), an art historical term that designates elements in old paintings that have been painted over, but so thinly that the underlying images remain visible.

16. See Rivkin-Fish (2005).

17. This form was particularly familiar to me personally, since during the last three years of graduate school I functioned as a shuttle trader, delivering dozens of bottles of herbal food supplements to my mother and her many acquaintances.

18. See Fehérváry (2002) for an enlightening discussion of the functions such sites of imaginary Westernness (which the author, following Foucault, labels *heterotopias*) carried for Hungarian consumers in the mid-1990s.

19. Note that Zhenia's professed optimism existed hand-in-hand with the assumption of total crisis.

20. For classic works on holidays and celebrations, see Huizinga (1955), Eliade (1959), Caillois (1959). For more recent sociological analyses, see Zerubavel (1982, 2003), Connerton (1989).

21. See Karakhanova (2001).

22. See Smith (2002).

23. Maria is referring to the mineral springs located in a park within walking distance of her house.

24. New Year's Eve was one of the most popular holidays during late socialism. It absorbed many aspects of traditional Christmas (a New Year's tree in place of a Christmas tree, Father Frost in place of Santa Claus) and was associated with nightly TV entertainment programs and with abundant cooking and champagne. The popularity of the holiday was such that Jewish emigrants from

Russia often continued celebrating it in America, taking advantage of the fact that Christmas trees and decorations are available after December 25 at practically no cost.

25. An important detail in this respect is that the significance of family holidays (such as relatives' birthdays or wedding anniversaries) suffered comparatively less, while the "state" holidays were increasingly interpreted as occasions to do something private (and often family-minded), like cultivating one's dacha orchard or visiting relatives (Dubin 2003).

26. Leonid Sladkov, one of the leading figures in the puzzle industry in Russia and the main editor of over a dozen puzzle weeklies and monthlies under the "777" logo, switched to this position after working for the *Pole Chudes* (*Field of Miracles*) quiz show in the mid-1990s.

27. See Dubin (2001).

28. This weekly publication, which was selling 1,171,927 copies a week in 2003, received from the National Circulation Service that year the Record Circulation of the Year prize in the Entertainment Periodicals category. The only publication with greater coverage that year was a weekly tabloid, *Komsomolskaia Pravda-Tolstushka*, whose circulation (2,601,478) received a prize in the Weekly Newspaper category. All "serious" dailies and weeklies, as well as entertainment magazines, lagged far behind.

29. According to the Gallup National Readership Survey for 2002, about 58 percent of the puzzle readership were women. All ages and income groups actively partook in solving puzzles, with a somewhat greater proportion enjoying "average income," possessing a high school education, and falling between 35 and 44 years of age. I thank Leonid Sladkov for making this Gallup data available to me.

30. *Scanvord* in the singular, which stands for "Scandinavian crossword."

31. Instructive in this context is the appropriation of the word "crossword" to refer to the less challenging scanwords.

32. Letter from V. N. Zhuravlev, published in *Tri Semerki* 19, 1999.

33. Letter from the Storzhuk family in Nizhnii Novgorod, published in *Pole Chudes* 9, 1998.

34. Letter from T. Selezneva in Irkutsk, published in *Russkii Krossvord* 7, 2000.

35. Despite the prevalence of such criticisms, I observed no instances of protesting, or even acknowledging, what I found to be rather tacky popular culture elements in the puzzle publications themselves, for example, borderline-decent jokes and abundant provocative photos of half-naked women.

36. Letter from F. Tregupova and two families, the Evlashins and the Ionovs, in Saransk, published in *Tri Semerki* 31, 1999.

37. Author interview with Leonid Sladkov, March 2003.

38. Editorial comment in *Zolotaia Rybka* 2, 2001.

39. Editorial comment in *Russkii Krossvord* 1, 1998.

40. Letter published in *Tri Semerki* 22, 1999.

41. Letter published in *Teshchin Iazyk* 2, 2000.

42. Many letters were written in a "we" format, and even such effects as the cross-words' presumed role in "extending lives" were phrased in plural terms, as in "*we* eagerly anticipate every issue of your paper. Thank you for extending *our* lives by your creative activity" (in a letter from the Golovanov family from Moscow, published in *Tri Semerki* 32, 1999; italics added)

43. Published in *Teshchin Iazyk* 5, 2000.

44. Letter from I. Kolodina in Urai, published in *Tri Semerki* 29, 1999.

45. Letter from L. Khaustova, published in *Tri Semerki* 21, 1999.

46. Letter published in *Russkii Krossvord* 4, 2000.

47. This attitude would also explain the frequency with which readers' letters closed with ritualized wishes of "good health and well-being," which are usually used in personal correspondence to close friends and kin.

48. Letter from E. Serebrennikova in Dzhizak, Uzbekistan, published in *Russkii Krossvord* 8, 2000.

49. I am assuming that the information about significant dates for particular readers was collected from the correspondence, although the papers never made this apparent.

50. "Vse drug drugu pomogaiut, / Govoriat o tom, chto znaiut" (my translation). *Ogo!-Scanvord* 3, 2001.

7. What Changes When Life Stands Still

1. Karina seems to be conflating two instances of civil unrest in Moscow: the coup of August 1991, when people came out into the streets to defend Yeltsin and the White House from the communist hardliners, and the conflict in October 1993, in which the White House was occupied by Yeltsin's opponents, including then-speaker of the Russian Supreme Soviet (and Yeltsin's former ally) Ruslan Khazbulatov.

2. While Karina's firm belief in the exceptionally antipolitical attitude of the Russian electorate was shared by others, her choice of indicators for this sensibility could be questioned. In fact, voter turnout in the parliamentary and presidential elections at the turn of the millennium was higher in Russia than in the United States: 60.5 percent (parliamentary, 1999) and 68.6 percent (presidential, 2000) in Russia, versus the corresponding 48.5 percent and 51.2 percent in the United States, according to the International Institute for Democracy and Electoral Assistance (http://www.idea.int/). It was the motivation of the voters to come to the polling stations that differed distinctly, as will be shown below.

3. See Keenan (1986), Pipes (1993).

4. This explains the retrospective tendency, noted by Harley Balzer (2005), for today's Russians to underestimate and underreport the extent of popular participation in protest activity in Russia during the 1991 putsch. While Balzer holds the Russian political elites to be primarily responsible for this puzzling silence, the reluctance of the former protesters themselves to remember and take pride in their participation appears to be a far more central factor in its perpetuation.

5. The article, titled "Goodness, how naïve we have been," was dedicated to the ten-year anniversary of the 1991 putsch. Some of the responses the journalist received to her inquiry as to whether it was worthwhile to resist the communist hardliners include "Who are we to defend? No one. They have broken and destroyed our lives," "One needs to live and make ends meet, and all the rest is vanity of vanities," "The Kremlin is now nothing but a thieves' den: they don't need defending" (Liuboshits 2001).

6. See also Yurchak 2006.

7. See Guseinov (1996). This explains the wide currency of debates about the contents of the new "positive mythology" for Russia (for an example, see Dondurei [2001]), and, for that matter, the belief that such a unified and artificially created mythology should exist in the first place.

8. The critical potential and the leverage of such programs diminished noticeably with the gradual takeover of the most outspoken television channel, NTV, by the pro-Kremlin shareholders associated with Gazprom in the course of 2000–2001 (for details on this takeover, see Belin [2002]).

9. *Novaia Gazeta* 6, February 15–21, 1999 (circulation 535,000), and *Moskovskii Komsomolets* 37, February 26, 1999 (circulation 1,877,000), respectively.

10. This explains the higher ratings of NTV at the height of its popularity, when its analytical programs and political satire consistently claimed a higher audience share in Moscow than programs aired on other channels (Gallup Media data, reported in *Obshchaia Gazeta* 7 [341], February 17–23, 2000). The balance in the regions was different, largely because NTV programs could be received only by 58 percent of the Russian population, while the coverage of the state channels—ORT and RTR—was close to 95 percent (Zadorin and Siutkina 2000, 85).

11. See Noelle-Neumann (1974), McChesney (1999).

12. This appears to have been a relevant factor in the popularity of Vladimir Putin and Evgenii Primakov, both of whom served as prime minister during the time of my fieldwork. The two were widely seen as competitors in their presidential ambitions in 1999–2000 (Primakov eventually dropped out of the race), and shared much in common above and beyond their KGB past: they did not seek to rally support, they were appointed to their positions, they appeared preoccupied with administrative questions, and they participated in the election campaign almost reluctantly (Putin, in particular, did not even take part in presidential debates, declaring that he was too busy with his duties as acting president to be wasting time on political self-promotion).

13. Organization for Security and Cooperation in Europe.

14. The leader of the liberal-democratic Yabloko party.

15. Cf. the section on the imagery of games and luck in chapter 3.

16. See Zasurskii (1999) on the role of electoral consultants in the presidential campaign of 1996.

17. See Zasurskii (1999), Mukhin (2000).

18. FSB is the abbreviation for the Federal Security Service, successor of the KGB.

19. Alexei Ivanovich is referring to the televised and widely discussed instances of Putin's performance as an acting president before the elections.

20. See chapter 4.

21. Time of Troubles (*smutnoe vremia*) refers to the period of social and political unrest and struggles over the Russian throne in the early seventeenth century, up until 1613 when Mikhail Romanov was elected to the throne.

22. All other subsections in the History section of the store were arranged chronologically and thematically ("The Middle Ages," "Recent Russian History," etc.), so the decision to set aside a separate "Fomenko" subsection, although probably motivated by high consumer demand and the versatile nature of his writings, had the unintended effect of giving this body of writing the status of a historical period.

23. Fomenko and Nosovskii lay out their theory in detail in numerous volumes, including *Imperiia: Rus', Turtsiia, Kitai, Evropa, Egipet: Novaya Matematicheskaia Khronologiia Derevnosti* (Empire: Rus', Turkey, China, Europe, Egypt: A New Mathematical Chronology of Antiquity) (1996); *Rus' i Rim* (Rus' and Rome), 2 vol. (1997); *Bibleiskaia Rus': Russko-ordynskaia Imperiya i Bibliya: Novaya Matematicheskaia Khronologiia Drevnosti* (Biblical Rus': The Russian-Horde Empire and the Bible: A New Mathematical Chronology) 2 vol. (1998); *Vvedenie v Novuiu Khronologiiu: Kakoi Seichas Vek?* (Introduction to the New Chronology: What Century Is This?) (1999); *Novaia Khronologiia Rusi, Anglii i Rima* (A New Chronology of Rus', England, and Rome) (1999).

24. See Chashchikhin (2001).

25. See Stakhov (1997), Begunov (2001).

26. *The Tale of Bygone Years* is a medieval chronicle of Russian history covering the period from the ninth to the eleventh century.

27. Nelly Romanovna is referring to Leonid Brezhnev's largely ghost-written memoir about the battle at Malaia Zemlia, near Novorossisk, in which he participated in 1943. This relatively insignificant episode of World War II was transformed in the memoir into a major battle, and the book was used widely to augment his personality cult.

28. Author of popular historical novels and literary biographies.

29. See Epstein (1995).

30. For an application of Luhmann's work on trust to postsocialist Russia, see Lindquist (2000).

31. Financial pyramid schemes are investment scams in which returns depend exclusively on the exponentially widening circle of new investors. These fast-money scams find recruits around the world. The website of the Federal Trade Commission has a prepared statement on pyramid schemes at http://www.ftc.gov/speeches/other/dvimf16.htm.

32. For an account of a pyramid scheme run by the Russian pyramid magnate Sergei Mavrodi and his associate Oksana Pavliuchenko out of the Dominican Republic and for an international clientele, see RFE/RL Security Watch, 4 September 2000, 1 (7). For a firsthand account of Romanian pyramid schemes in which the anthropologist herself participated, see Verdery (1995).

33.   For a discussion of the ways in which Moscow luxury housing complexes lay claims on the public space, see Makarova (2006).

8. Conclusion

1.   See the special issue of the magazine *Neprikosnovennyi Zapas* dedicated to the ten-year anniversary of the 1991 coup (6 [20], 2001), as well as Orlowski 2001, Starodubrovskaia and Mau 2001.

2.   Buckley refers to the putsch of August 1991, justly warning against treating it as a "neat historical divide for demarcating a new phase of change."

3.   See also Swidler 2001.

4.   For a discussion of how Soviet cultural legacies, especially the late Soviet cult of privacy, impacted the formation of post-Soviet urban space, see Makarova (2006).

5.   I am borrowing the term from Lief and Fox's discussion of medical students' training (Lief and Fox 1963).

6.   On the "inordinately, unbelievably high" level of reported satisfaction with family relationships at the time, see Dubin (1999, 23).

7.   For a recent and particularly hostile reiteration of this critique, see Pipes (2006).

Appendix 1. Methodology

1.   It would be hard to argue, however, that simply by splitting the sample between the city and a rural area one could claim a better representation of the Russian society, since the differences found between regions were as significant as the differences found between rural and urban areas (see, for example, Clem and Craumer [1995]).

2.   For more on the distinctiveness of Moscow, see Dubin (1997).

3.   For instance, Kolosov and Vendina write, "Moscow itself is far from homogenous, and a careful analysis uncovers contradictions characteristic for Russia as a whole. The intensity and diversity of the political and socioeconomic life of the capital . . . reflect the general Russian situation, and comprehension of the processes unfolding here allows for a better understanding of our current reality" (1996, 168).

4.   The inevitably small size of a longitudinal qualitative sample precluded a systematic exploration of the differences in perspectives of Muscovites of different class, gender, and educational backgrounds. While I could, and did, address the variation in the forms of crisis discourse, a systematic cross-sectional comparison would have required a much larger sample.

5.   Age was a particularly salient criterion for diversification, since older Russians tend to be especially susceptible to postsocialist problems characteristic for inhabitants of non-metropolitan areas (for example, poor health and hopelessness) (Levada [1995]; Dubin [1999]; Kim [1999]).

6.   See Lamont (1992) for an example.

7. During my fieldwork, telephone and address listings were available in Moscow markets on compact disks. Their publication, however, was not sanctioned by the telephone company, and the very fact of their existence was understandably perceived by most Muscovites as illegal.

8. Moreover, it appears questionable that selection bias in the case of a random sample would have been any smaller. Recalling the difficulty of obtaining a legitimate source of Muscovites' addresses and telephones for such a sample, one could speculate that individuals who would agree to reveal details of their everyday lives to a stranger who obtained their phone number from an obscure source would constitute a very peculiar sample.

9. The list of the respondents is given in appendix 2, together with a brief biographical blurb on each person. As I have agreed with them in the course of the interviews, respondents' names are replaced by pseudonyms in order to ensure anonymity.

10. This, of course, does not mean that either of them should be prioritized over the other or granted the status of the final truth. Rather, they are to be juxtaposed and viewed in the light of one another to reveal the regularities and criteria according to which events are translated into narratives, and vice versa.

11. For similar concerns, see Bosk (2001).

12. Since not all of the respondents had the dedication, time, and desire to record all of their month's expenditures, I decided not to quantify the budget data I received, but instead to use it as an additional source of insight into the circumstance of those respondents who did.

13. See Van Maanen (1988); Steier (1991); Denzin and Lincoln (1998).

14. The term "validity" itself has been critically questioned on the grounds that the fundamental presumption behind the concept of validity remains that the explored phenomena can have only one correct interpretation. A number of ethnographers have proposed to speak of "credibility" of ethnographic research, or of "verisimilitude" of its findings (Lincoln and Guba 1985; Janesick 1994; Marshall and Rossman 1995).

15. In my particular case, the fact that I was receiving education abroad could not help but contribute to this dynamic.

16. An additional sign of the somewhat patronizing attitude that many respondents developed over the course of the fieldwork was that, no matter how much I protested, I could rarely manage to escape from the later waves of the interviews without some token of sympathy (a bag of candy, a piece of cake, or a sandwich) that my respondents literally forced upon me in order to make my way home more pleasurable.

17. I did try hard, however, to keep such instances of self-disclosure neutral in emotional tone and sufficiently boring in order not to make them central to the discussion.

18. This, of course, does not make an author the last link in the chain of power, since authorial interpretations are themselves subject to the interpretation and disciplining of the academic community the author addresses.

19. I was a graduate student at the time of the fieldwork, so the "financial stability"

I was enjoying was questionable by American standards. But it is certainly an accurate description of how my respondents construed me, as well as of my own self-perception at the time.

20. For useful critiques of this notion, see Narayan (1993), Chawla (2006).

Works Cited

Adler, Patricia A., and Peter Adler. 1998. "Observational Techniques." In *Collecting and Interpreting Qualitative Materials,* ed. Norman K. Denzin and Yvonna S. Lincoln. Thousand Oaks, Calif.: Sage.

Afanas'ev, Iurii N., ed. 1988. *Inogo ne dano* [There Is No Other Way]. Moscow: Progress.

Arney, William Ray, and Bernard J. Bergen. 1984. *Medicine and the Management of Living: Taming the Last Beast.* Chicago: University of Chicago Press.

Ashwin, Sarah. 1999. *Russian Workers: The Anatomy of Patience.* Manchester, UK: Manchester University Press.

———, ed. 2000. *Gender, State, and Society in Soviet and Post-Soviet Russia.* New York: Routledge.

Ashwin, Sarah, and Tatyana Lytkina. 2004. "Men in Crisis in Russia: The Role of Domestic Marginalization." *Gender and Society* 18 (2): 189–206.

Balzer, Harley. 2005. "Ordinary Russians? Rethinking August 1991." *Demokratizatsiya* 13 (2), 193–218.

Baudrillard, Jean. 1996. *The System of Objects.* Trans. James Benedict. New York: Verso.

Bauman, Zygmunt. 1987. *Legislators and Interpreters: On Modernity, Post-modernity, and Intellectuals.* Ithaca, N.Y.: Cornell University Press.

Begunov, Iurii K., ed. 2001. *Russkaia istoriia protiv "novoi khronologii": Antifomenko.* [Russian History Against the "New Chronology": Anti-Fomenko]. Moscow: Russkaia Panorama.

Belin, Laura. 2002. "The Rise and Fall of Russia's NTV." *Stanford Journal of International Law* 38 (Winter): 19–42.

Bellah, Robert N., Richard Madsen, William M. Sullivan, Ann Swidler, and Steven M. Tipton. 1996. *Habits of the Heart: Individualism and Commitment in American Life.* Berkeley: University of California Press.

Berger, Peter L., and Thomas Luckmann. 1967. *The Social Construction of Reality: A Treatise in the Sociology of Knowledge.* New York: Doubleday.

Berlin, Isaiah. 1979. *Russian Thinkers.* New York: Penguin.

Biziukov, Petr V. 1999. *Otsenka faktorov, vliiaiushchikh na stabil'nost' zaniatosti* [Assessment of the Factors Influencing the Stability of Employment]. In *Zaniatost' i povedenie domokhoziaistv. Adaptatsiia k usloviiam perekhoda k rynochnoi ekonomike v Rossii* [Employment and Household Behavior: Adaptation to the Conditions of Market Transition in Russia], ed. Veronika Kabalina and Simon Clarke. Moscow: ROSSPAN.

Bolin, Robert. 1998. *The Northridge Earthquake: Vulnerability and Disaster.* In collaboration with Lois Stanford. London: Routledge.

Bosk, Charles L. 2001. "Irony, Ethnography, and Informed Consent." In *Bioethics in Social Context,* ed. Barry Hoffmaster. Philadelphia: Temple University Press.

Bourdieu, Pierre. 1977. *Outline of a Theory of Practice.* Trans. Richard Nice. Cambridge, UK: Cambridge University Press.

———. 1984. *Distinction: A Social Critique of the Judgment of Taste.* Trans. Richard Nice. Cambridge, Mass.: Harvard University Press.

———. 1998. *On Television.* New York: New Press.

Bourdieu, Pierre, and Loïc J. D. Wacquant. 1992. *An Invitation to Reflexive Sociology.* Chicago: University of Chicago Press.

Boym, Svetlana. 1994. *Common Places: Mythologies of Everyday Life in Russia.* Cambridge, Mass.: Harvard University Press.

Braithwaite, Jeanine, Christiaan Grootaert, and Branko Milanovic. 2000. *Poverty and Social Assistance in Transition Countries.* New York: St. Martin's Press.

Braudel, Fernand. 1982. *Civilization and Capitalism, 15th–18th Century, Vol. 1: The Structures of Everyday Life: The Limits of the Possible.* New York: Harper and Row.

Brown, Julie V., and Nina L. Rusinova. 1997. "Russian Medical Care in the 1990s: A User's Perspective." *Social Science & Medicine* 45 (8): 1265–1276.

Brumfield, William C., and Blair A. Ruble, eds. 1993. *Russian Housing in the Modern Age: Design and Social History.* New York: Cambridge University Press.

Buchli, Victor. 1999. *An Archaeology of Socialism.* Oxford, UK: Berg.

Buckley, Mary. 1993. *Redefining Russian Society and Polity.* Boulder, Colo.: Westview Press.

———, ed. 1997. *Post-Soviet Women: From the Baltic to Central Asia.* Cambridge, UK: Cambridge University Press.

Burawoy, Michael. 1998. "The Extended Case Method." *Sociological Theory* 16 (1): 4–33

Burawoy, Michael, and Katherine Verdery, eds. 1999. *Uncertain Transition: Ethnographies of Change in the Postsocialist World.* New York: Rowman and Littlefield.

Burawoy, Michael, Pavel Krotov, and Tatyana Lytkina. 2000. "Involution and Destitution in Capitalist Russia." *Ethnography* 1 (July): 43–65.

Caillois, Roger. 1959. *Man and the Sacred.* Glencoe, Ill.: Free Press of Glencoe.

Caldwell, Melissa L. 2004. *Not by Bread Alone: Social Support in the New Russia.* Berkeley: University of California Press.

Cerf, Christopher, and Marina Albee. 1990. *Small Fires: Letters from the Soviet People to Ogonyok Magazine, 1987–1990.* New York: Summit Books.

Certeau, Michel de. 1984. *The Practice of Everyday Life.* Trans. Steven Rendall. Berkeley: University of California Press.

Chashchikhin, U. V. 2001. Estestvennonauchnye vozrazheniia protiv "novoi khronologii" [Natural-Scientific Objections to the "New Chronology"]. In *Russkaia istoriia protiv "novoi khronologii": Antifomenko* [Russian History Against the "New Chronology": Anti-Fomenko], ed. Iurii Begunov. Moscow: Russkaia Panorama.

Chawla, Devika. 2006. "Subjectivity and the 'Native' Ethnographer: Researcher Eligibility in an Ethnographic Study of Urban Indian Women in Arranged Marriages." *International Journal of Qualitative Methods* 5 (4). http://www.ualberta .ca/~iiqm/backissues/5_4/html/chawla.htm (accessed June 20, 2007).

Clarke, Simon. 1999. *New Forms of Employment and Household Survival Strategies in Russia.* Coventry, UK: Centre for Comparative Labour Studies, University of Warwick.

Clem, Ralph S., and Peter R. Craumer. 1995. "A rayon-level analysis of the Russian election and constitutional plebiscite of December 1993." *Post-Soviet Geography* 36 (8): 459–475.

Connerton, Paul. 1989. *How Societies Remember.* Cambridge, UK: Cambridge University Press.

Crawford, Beverly, and Arend Lijphart. 1995. "Explaining Political and Economic Change in Post-Communist Eastern Europe: Old Legacies, New Institutions, Hegemonic Norms, and International Pressures." *Comparative Political Studies* 28 (2): 171–199.

Crowley, David, and Susan E. Reid. 2000. "Style and Socialism: Modernity and Material Culture in Post-War Eastern Europe." In *Style and Socialism: Modernity and Material Culture in Post-War Eastern Europe,* ed. Susan E. Reid and David Crowley. Oxford, UK: Berg.

D'Agostino, Anthony. 1998. *Gorbachev's Revolution.* New York: New York University Press.

Denzin, Norman K., and Yvonna S. Lincoln, eds. 1998. *The Landscape of Qualitative Research.* Thousand Oaks, Calif.: Sage.

Derluguian, Georgi. 2003. Introduction to *A Small Corner of Hell: Dispatches from Chechnya,* by Anna Politkovskaia. Chicago: University of Chicago Press.

DiMaggio, Paul. 1991. "Social Structure, Institutions, and Cultural Goods: The Case of the United States." In *Social Theory for a Changing Society,* ed. Pierre Bourdieu and James S. Coleman. New York: Russell Sage Foundation.

Dondurei, Daniil. 2001. "Poprobuem podkupit' intelligentsiiu" [Let's Try Bribing the Intelligentsia]. *Ekspert,* March 26.

Drazin, Adam. 2001. "A Man *Will* Get Furnished: Wood and Domesticity in Urban Romania." In *Home Possessions: Material Culture Behind Closed Doors,* ed. Daniel Miller. Oxford, UK: Berg.

———. 2002. "Chasing Moths: Cleanliness, Intimacy, and Progress in Romania." In *Markets and Moralities: Ethnographies of Postsocialism,* ed. Ruth Mandel and Caroline Humphrey. Oxford, UK: Berg.

Dubin, Boris V. 1997. "Rossiiane i moskvichi" [Russians and Muscovites]. *Monitoring obshchestvennogo mneniia: Ekonomicheskie i sotsial'nye peremeny* 32: 14–19.

———.1999. "Zhizn' po privychke: byt' pozhilym v Rossii 1990kh godov" [Life By Inertia: Being Elderly in Russia in the 1990s]. *Monitoring obshchestvennogo mneniia: Ekonomicheskie i sotsial'nye peremeny* 44 (6): 18–26.

———. 2001. *Slovo—Pis'mo—Literatura: Ocherki po sotsiologii sovremennoi kul'tury* [Word—Writing—Literature: Essays in Sociology of Contemporary Culture]. Moscow: NLO.

———. 2003. "Budni i prazdniki" [Everyday Life and Holidays]. *Vestnik Obshchestvennogo Mneniia: Dannye. Analiz. Diskussii* 68 (2): 52–62.

———. 2005. "Postoronnie: Vlast', massa i massmedia v segodniashnei Rossii" [Bystanders: Power, Masses and Mass Media in Today's Russia]. *Otechestvennye Zapiski* 6. http://www.strana-oz.ru/?numid=27&article=1167 (accessed June 27, 2007).

Dunlop, John B. 1993. *The Rise of Russia and the Fall of the Soviet Empire.* Princeton, N.J.: Princeton University Press.

Eliade, Mircea. 1959. *Cosmos and History: The Myth of the Eternal Return.* Trans. Willard R. Trask. New York: Harper.

Elias, Norbert. 1998. "On the Concept of Everyday Life." In *The Norbert Elias Reader: A Biographical Selection,* ed. Johan Goudsblom and Stephen Mennell. Oxford, UK: Blackwell.

Eliasoph, Nina. 1998. *Avoiding Politics: How Americans Produce Apathy in Everyday Life.* Cambridge, UK: Cambridge University Press.

Epstein, Mikhail N. 1995. *After the Future: The Paradoxes of Postmodernism and Contemporary Russian Culture.* Trans. Anesa Miller-Pogacar. Amherst: University of Massachusetts Press.

Erikson, Kai T. 1976. *Everything in Its Path: Destruction of Community in the Buffalo Creek Flood.* New York: Simon and Schuster.

———. 1994. *A New Species of Trouble: Explorations in Disaster, Trauma, and Community.* New York: W. W. Norton.

Evgenieva, T. V. 1999. "Arkhaicheskaia mifologiia v sovremennoi politicheskoi kul'ture" [Archaic Mythology in Contemporary Political Culture]. *Politia* 11 (1): 33–47.

Fadin, Andrei. 1991. "Tretii Rim v tret'em mire. Razmyshleniia na ruinakh imperii" [Third Rome in the Third World: Reflections on the Ruins of an Empire]. *Vek XX i Mir* 9: 20–28.

Faraday, George. 2000. *Revolt of the Filmmakers: The Struggle for Artistic Autonomy and the Fall of the Soviet Film Industry.* University Park: Pennsylvania State University Press.

Fehérváry, Krisztina. 2002. "American Kitchens, Luxury Bathrooms, and the Search for a 'Normal' Life in Postsocialist Hungary." *Ethnos* 67 (3): 369–400.

Fitzpatrick, Sheila. 1999. *Everyday Stalinism. Ordinary Life in Extraordinary Times: Soviet Russia in the 1930s.* New York: Oxford University Press.

Fraser, Nancy. 1992. "Rethinking the Public Sphere: A Contribution to the Critique of Actually Existing Democracy." In *Habermas and the Public Sphere,* ed. Craig Calhoun. Cambridge, Mass.: MIT Press.

Freeland, Chrystia. 2000. *Sale of the Century: Russia's Wild Ride from Communism to Capitalism.* New York: Crown Business.

Gal, Susan. 1991. "Between Speech and Silence: The Problematics of Research on Language and Gender." In *Gender at the Crossroads of Knowledge: Feminist Anthropology in the Postmodern Era,* ed. Micaela di Leonardo. Berkeley: University of California Press.

Galeotti, Mark. 1997. *Gorbachev and His Revolution.* New York: St. Martin's Press.

Garfinkel, Harold. 1967. *Studies in Ethnomethodology.* Englewood Cliffs, N.J.: Prentice-Hall.

Geertz, Clifford. 1973. *The Interpretation of Cultures: Selected Essays.* New York: Basic Books.

Gerbner, George. 1994. "Reclaiming Our Cultural Mythology." In *Context* 38 (Spring): 40–42.

Gergen, Kenneth J., and Mary M. Gergen. 1991. "Toward Reflexive Methodologies." In *Research and Reflexivity,* ed. Frederick Steier. Newbury Park, Calif.: Sage.

Gessen, Masha. 1997. *Dead Again: The Russian Intelligentsia After Communism.* London: Verso.

Gibson, James L. 2001. "Social Networks, Civil Society, and the Prospects for Consolidating Russia's Democratic Transition." *American Journal of Political Science* 45 (1): 51–68.

Giddens, Anthony. 1990. *The Consequences of Modernity.* Stanford, Calif.: Stanford University Press.

Gordon, Leonid A., and Eduard V. Klopov. 2000. "Dinamika uslovii i urovnia zhizni naseleniia" [Dynamics of Conditions and Standard of Living of the Population]. *Monitoring obshchestvennogo mneniia: Ekonomicheskie i sotsial'nye peremeny* 49 (5): 25–34.

———. 2001. *Poteri i obreteniia Rossii devianostykh: Istoriko-sotsiologicheskie ocherki ekonomicheskogo polozheniia narodnogo bol'shinstva* [Losses and Gains of Russia's 1990s: Historical-Sociological Sketches of the Economic Condition of Society]. Moscow: Editorial URSS.

Goskomstat. 1999. *Sotsial'no-Ekonomicheskoe Polozhenie Rossiiskoi Federatsii, 1999 god* [Social-Economic Condition of the Russian Federation, 1999]. Moscow: Goskomstat.

Granovetter, Mark S. 1973. "The Strength of Weak Ties." *American Journal of Sociology* 78 (6): 1360–1380.

Grindstaff, Laura. 2002. *The Money Shot: Trash, Class, and the Making of TV Talk Shows.* Chicago: University of Chicago Press.

Gross, David. 1985. "Temporality and the Modern State." *Theory and Society* 14 (1): 53–82.

Gudkov, Lev D. 2000a. "K probleme negativnoi identifikatsii" [Regarding the Problem of Negative Identification]. *Monitoring obshchestvennogo mneniia: Ekonomicheskie i sotsial'nye peremeny* 49: 30–39.

———. 2000b. "Otnoshenie k pravovym institutam v Rossii" [Attitudes toward Legal Institutions in Russia]. *Monitoring obshchestvennogo mneniia: Ekonomicheskie i sotsial'nye peremeny* 47: 34–39.

———. 2004. *Negativnaia identichnost': stat'i 1997–2002 godov* [Negative Identity: Articles 1997–2002]. Moscow: NLO, VTsIOM-A.

Gudkov, Lev D., and Boris V. Dubin. 2001. "Obshchestvo telezritelei: Massy i massovye kommunikatsii v Rossii kontsa 1990kh godov" [TV-Viewer Society: Masses and Mass Communications in Russia During the Late 1990s]. *Monitoring obshchestvennogo mneniia: Ekonomicheskie i sotsial'nye peremeny* 52: 31–46.

———. 2003. "Izdatel'skoe delo, literaturnaia kul'tura i pechatnye kommunikatsii v segodniashnei Rossii" [Publishing, Literary Culture, and Print Communications in Today's Russia]. In *Liberal'nye Reformy i Kul'tura* [Liberal Reforms and Culture], ed. Denis Dragunskii, 13–89. Moscow: OGI.

Gurova, Tat'iana. 2001. "Deti porazheniia" [Children of defeat]. *Ekspert* 23: 58–69. http://www.expert.ru/printissues/expert/2001/23/23ex-middle/ (accessed June 27, 2007).

Guseinov, Gasan. 1996. "IAzyk politiki i publitsistiki v pervyi posovetskii god Rossii" [Language of Politics and Press During the First Russian Po-Soviet Year]. In *Portfel': Literaturnyi Al'manakh* [Briefcase: A Literary Anthology], ed. Aleksandr Sumerkin. Dana Point, Calif.: Ardis.

Gusev, Anatolii. 2003. "Okhranniki pugovits" [Guardians of Buttons]. *Izvestiia,* March 19.

Habermas, Jürgen. 1989. *The Structural Transformation of the Public Sphere: An Inquiry into a Category of Bourgeois Society,* trans. Thomas Burger and Frederick Lawrence. Cambridge, Mass.: MIT Press.

Herzfeld, Michael. 1992. *The Social Production of Indifference: Exploring the Symbolic Roots of Western Bureaucracy.* New York: Berg.

Hilgartner, Stephen, and Charles L. Bosk. 1988. "The Rise and Fall of Social Problems: A Public Arenas Model." *American Journal of Sociology* 94 (1): 53–78.

Hosking, Geoffrey A. 1991. *The Awakening of the Soviet Union.* Cambridge, Mass.: Harvard University Press.

Huizinga, Johan. 1955. *Homo Ludens: A Study of the Play-Element in Culture.* Boston: Beacon Press.

Humphrey, Caroline. 1995. "Creating a Culture of Disillusionment: Consumption in Moscow, A Chronicle of Changing Times." In *Worlds Apart: Modernity through the Prism of the Local,* ed. Daniel Miller. London: Routledge.

———. 1999. "Traders, 'Disorder,' and Citizenship Regimes in Provincial Russia." In *Uncertain Transition: Ethnographies of Change in the Postsocialist World,* ed. Michael Burawoy and Katherine Verdery. New York: Rowman and Littlefield.

———. 2002. *The Unmaking of Soviet Life.* Ithaca, N.Y.: Cornell University Press.

Ianin, Igor T. 1999. *Kul'tura Protiv Krizisa, ili iskusstvo zhit' v Rossii* [Culture vs. Crisis, or the Art of Living in Russia]. Moscow: RAU-Universitet.

Ivanova, Natalia. 1993a. "Peizazh posle bitvy" [Landscape after the Battle]. *Znamia* 9: 189–198.

———. 1993b. "Dvoinoe samoubiistvo (intelligentsiia i ideologiia)" [A Double Suicide: Intelligentsia and Ideology]. *Znamia* 11: 170–183.

Jahoda, Marie, Paul F. Lazarsfeld, and Hans Zeisel. 1971. *Marienthal: The Sociography of an Unemployed Community.* Chicago: Aldine.

Janesick, Valerie J. 1994. "The Dance of Qualitative Research Design: Metaphor, Methodolatry, and Meaning." In *Handbook of Qualitative Research,* ed. Norman K. Denzin and Yvonna S. Lincoln. Thousand Oaks, Calif.: Sage.

Jay, Martin. 1998. *Cultural Semantics: Keywords of Our Time.* Amherst: University of Massachusetts Press.

Jorgenson, Jane. 1991. "Co-constructing the Interviewer/Co-constructing 'Family.'" In *Research and Reflexivity,* ed. Frederick Steier. Newbury Park, Calif.: Sage.

Karakhanova, T. M., ed. 2001. *Biudzhet vremeni i peremeny v zhiznedeiatel'nosti gorodskikh zhitelei v 1965–1998 godakh* [Time Budgeting and the Lifestyle Changes of Urban Dwellers, 1965–1998]. Moscow: ISRAN.

Kara-Murza, Aleksei A. 1999. *Kak vozmozhna Rossiia?* [*How Is Russia Possible?*]. Moscow: Sovetskii Sport.

Karpov, Viacheslav. 1990. "Starye dogmy na novyi lad" [Old Dogmas in New Form]. *Oktiabr'* 3: 142–158.

Kay, Rebecca. 2000. *Russian Women and Their Organizations: Gender, Discrimination, and Grassroots Women's Organizations, 1991–96.* New York: St. Martin's Press.

———. 2006. *Men in Contemporary Russia: The Fallen Heroes of Post-Soviet Change?* Aldershot, UK: Ashgate.

Keenan, Edward L. 1986. "Muscovite Political Folkways." *Russian Review* 45 (2): 115–181.

Kelly, Catriona. 2002. "Ordinary Life in Extraordinary Times: Chronicles of the Quotidian in Russia and the Soviet Union." *Kritika* 3 (4): 631–651.

Kim, N. 1999. "Nadezhda, ustalost', starost'" [Hope, Weariness, Old Age]. *Monitoring obshchestvennogo mneniia: Ekonomicheskie i sotsial'nye peremeny* 39: 56–58.

Kodin, Mikhail I. 2001. *Rossiia v "sumerkakh" transformatsii: Evoliutsiia, revoliutsiia ili kontrrevoliutsiia?* [Russia in the Twilight of Transformation: Evolution, Revolution, or Counterrevolution?]. Moscow: Molodaia Gvardiia.

Kolosov, Vladimir A., and Ol'ga I. Vendina. 1996. "Sotsial'naia poliarizatsiia i politicheskoe povedenie moskvichei" [Social Polarization and the Political Behavior of Muscovites]. *Sotsiologicheskii Zhurnal* 3–4.

Kon, Igor'. 1993. "Identity Crisis and Post-Communist Psychology." *Symbolic Interaction* 16 (4), 395–410.

Koselleck, Reinhart. 2002. "Some Questions Regarding the Conceptual History of 'Crisis.'" In *The Practice of Conceptual History: Timing History, Spacing Concepts,* trans. Todd Samuel. Stanford, Calif.: Stanford University Press.

Kostikov, Viacheslav. 1991. *Blesk i nishcheta nomenklatury* [The Splendor and Misery of the Nomenklatura]. *Ogonek* 1.

Kotkin, Stephen. 1995. *Magnetic Mountain: Stalinism as a Civilization.* Berkeley: University of California Press.

Koval', Boris I., ed. 1993. *Rossiia segodnia. Politicheskii portret v dokumentakh, 1985–1991*

[Russia Today: A Political Portrait in Documents 1985–1991]. Vol. 2. Moscow: Mezhdunarodnye Otnosheniia.

Kupriianova, Zoia. 1997. "Real'naia i potentsial'naia professional'naia mobil'nost' v Rossiiskoi Federatsii" [Real and Potential Professional Mobility in the Russian Federation] *Monitoring obshchestvennogo mneniia: Ekonomicheskie i sotsial'nye peremeny* 30 (4): 26–30.

Kuz'min, Evgenii I., B. K. Nikolaeva, I. A. Vaganova, L. A. Dubrovina, V. V. Il'ina, and A. D. Makeeva. 2002. *Biblioteki Rossii na poroge XXI veka: Tsifry i fakty: Sbornik statisticheskikh i analiticheskikh materialov o sostoianii bibliotechnoi sfery* [Russian Libraries at the Threshold of the 20th Century: Facts and Figures: A Collection of Statistical and Analytical Materials on the State of Libraries]. Moscow: Libereia.

Laing, Ronald David. 1969. *The Divided Self: An Existential Study in Sanity and Madness.* London: Tavistock Publications.

Lakoff, George, and Mark Johnson. 1980. *Metaphors We Live By.* Chicago: University of Chicago Press.

Lamont, Michèle. 1992. *Money, Morals and Manners: The Culture of the French and the American Upper-Middle Class.* Chicago: University of Chicago Press.

Lapin, Nikolai I. 1993. "Sotsial'nye tsennosti i reformy v krizisnoi Rossii" [Social Values and Reforms in Crisis-Era Russia]. *Sotsiologicheskie Issledovaniia* 20 (9): 17–28.

Ledeneva, Alena V. 1998. *Russia's Economy of Favors: Blat, Networking, and Informal Exchange.* Cambridge, UK: Cambridge University Press.

Lefebvre, Henri. 1991. *Critique of Everyday Life.* London, New York: Verso.

———. 1984. *Everyday Life in the Modern World.* New Brunswick, N.J.: Transaction.

Lemon, Alaina. 2000. *Between Two Fires: Gypsy Performance and Romani Memory from Pushkin to Postsocialism.* Durham, N.C.: Duke University Press.

Levada, Iurii A. 1995. "Tri pokoleniia perestroiki" [Three Generations of Perestroika]. *Monitoring obshchestvennogo mneniia: Ekonomicheskie i sotsial'nye peremeny* 17: 7–10.

———. 2000. *Ot mnenii k ponimaniiu: Sotsiologicheskie ocherki, 1993–2000* [From Opinions to Understanding: Sociological Essays, 1993–2000]. Moscow: Shkola Politicheskikh Issledovanii.

———. 2002. "2002: Pod znakom katastrof i ispytanii" [2002: Under the Sign of Catastrophe and Trial]. *Moskovskie Novosti* 51.

Lewin, Moshe. 1988. *The Gorbachev Phenomenon: A Historical Interpretation.* Berkeley: University of California Press.

Lief, Harold I., and Renée C. Fox. 1963. "Training for 'Detached Concern' in Medical Students." In *The Psychological Basis of Medical Practice,* ed. Harold I. Lief, Victor F. Lief, and Nina R. Lief. New York: Harper and Row.

Lifton, Robert J. 1967. *Death in Life: Survivors of Hiroshima.* New York: Random House.

Lincoln, Yvonna S., and Egon G. Guba. 1985. *Naturalistic Inquiry.* Beverly Hills: Sage.

Lincoln, Yvonna S., and Norman K. Denzin. 1998. "The Fifth Moment." In *The Landscape of Qualitative Research,* ed. Norman K. Denzin, Yvonna S. Lincoln. Thousand Oaks, Calif.: Sage.

Lindquist, Galina. 2000. "In Search of the Magical Flow: Magic and Market in Contemporary Russia." *Urban Anthropology and Studies of Cultural Systems and World Economic Development* 29 (4): 315–357.

———. 2001. "Wizards, Gurus, and Energy-Information Fields: Wielding Legitimacy in

Contemporary Russian Healing." *The Anthropology of Eastern Europe Review* 19 (1): 16–28.

———. 2002. "Healing Efficacy and the Construction of Charisma: A Family's Journey Through the Multiple Medical Field in Russia." *Anthropology and Medicine* 9 (3): 337–358.

Linz, Juan J., and Alfred Stepan. 1996. *Problems of Democratic Transition and Consolidation: Southern Europe, South America, and Post-Communist Europe.* Baltimore, Md.: Johns Hopkins University Press.

Lisichkin, Gennadii S. 2002. "V Rossii vremia ostanovilos'?" [Has Time Stopped in Russia?]. *Rossiia i Sovremennyi Mir* 34 (1): 144–147.

Liuboshits, Svetlana. 2001. "Bozhe, kakimi my byli naivnymi!" [Goodness, How Naïve We Have Been!]. *Moskovskii Komsomolets,* August 22.

Lonkila, Markku. 1998. "The Social Meaning of Work: Aspects of the Teaching Profession in Post-Soviet Russia." *Europe-Asia Studies* 50 (4): 699–712.

Luhmann, Niklas. 1979. *Trust and Power: Two Works,* ed. Tom Burns and Gianfranco Poggi, trans. Howard Davis, John Raffan, and Kathryn Rooney. New York: Wiley.

Makarova, Ekaterina. 2006. "The New Urbanism in Moscow: The Redefinition of Public and Private Space." Paper presented at the Annual Soyuz Symposium, March 3–5, in Smithfield, R.I.

Mandel, Ruth, and Caroline Humphrey, eds. 2002. *Markets and Moralities: Ethnographies of Postsocialism.* Oxford, UK: Berg.

Markowitz, Fran. 2000. *Coming of Age in Post-Soviet Russia.* Urbana: University of Illinois Press.

Marshall, Catherine, and Gretchen B. Rossman. 1995. *Designing Qualitative Research,* 2nd ed. Thousand Oaks, Calif.: Sage.

Mauss, Marcel. 1967. *The Gift: Forms and Functions of Exchange in Archaic Societies,* trans. Ian Cunnison. New York: W. W. Norton.

Mbembe, Achille, and Janet Roitman. 1995. "Figures of the Subject in Times of Crisis." *Public Culture* 7: 323–352.

McChesney, Robert W. 1999. *Rich Media, Poor Democracy: Communication Politics in Dubious Times.* Urbana: University of Illinois Press.

Meyer, Gordon W. 1994. "Social Information Processing and Social Networks: A Test of Social Influence Mechanisms." *Human Relations* 47 (9): 1013–1048.

Michaels, Leonard, and Christopher Ricks, eds. 1980. *The State of the Language.* Berkeley: University of California Press.

Mickiewicz, Ellen, P. 1999. *Changing Channels: Television and the Struggle for Power in Russia.* Durham, N.C.: Duke University Press.

Miller, Daniel. 1998. *A Theory of Shopping.* Ithaca, N.Y.: Cornell University Press.

Mironov, Arsenii S. 2001. *Razduvai i vlastvui: Tekhnologii sovremennoi "miagkoi" propagandy* [Exaggerate and Rule: Technologies of Contemporary "Soft" Propaganda]. Moscow: Dobrosvet.

Mitrokhin, Nikolai. 2003. *"Russkaia partiia": Dvizhenie russkikh natsionalistov v SSSR, 1953–1985 gody* ["Russian Party": The Russian Nationalist Movement in the USSR, 1953–1985]. Moscow: NLO.

Morawska, Ewa. 1996. *Insecure Prosperity: Small-town Jews in Industrial America, 1890–1940.* Princeton, N.J.: Princeton University Press.

Mukhin, Aleksei. 2000. *Informatsionnaia voina v Rossii: Uchastniki, tseli, tekhnologii* [Information War in Russia: Participants, Objectives, Technologies]. Moscow: Tsentr Politicheskoi Informatsii.

Narayan, Kirin. 1993. "How Native Is a 'Native' Anthropologist?" *American Anthropologist* 95 (3): 671–686.

Naumova, Nina F. 1995. "Zhiznennaia strategiia cheloveka v perekhodnom obshchestve" [Life Strategy of an Individual in a Transitional Society]. *Sotsiologicheskii Zhurnal* 2: 5–22.

Nikolaev, Vladimir G. 2000. *Sovetskaia ochered' kak sreda obitaniia: Sotsiologicheskii analiz* [The Soviet Queue as a Living Environment: A Sociological Study]. Moscow: INION RAN.

Noelle-Neumann, Elisabeth. 1974. "The Spiral of Silence: A Theory of Public Opinion." *Journal of Communication* 24 (2): 43–51.

Nosovskii, Gleb V., and Anatolii T. Fomenko. 1997. *Novaia khronologiia Rusi* [New Chronology of Rus']. Moscow: Faktorial.

Orlowski, Lucjan T., ed. 2001. *Transition and Growth in Post-Communist Countries: The Ten-Year Experience*. Northampton, UK: Edward Elgar.

Orwell, George. 1968. *The Collected Essays, Journalism, and Letters of George Orwell*, Vol. 4, ed. Sonia Orwell and Ian Angus. London: Secker and Warburg.

Osipov, Gennadii. 1992. "Mify ukhodiashchego vremeni" [Myths of the Passing Era]. *Sotsiologicheskie Issledovaniia* 19 (6): 3–14.

Oushakine, Serguei A. 2000a. "In the State of Post-Soviet Aphasia: Symbolic Development in Contemporary Russia." *Europe-Asia Studies* 52 (Sept. 2000): 991–1016.

———. 2000b. "The Quantity of Style: Imaginary Consumption in the New Russia." *Theory, Culture & Society* 17 (5): 97–120.

Palosuo, Hannele, Irina Zhuravleva, Anti Uutela, Nina Lakomova, and Liudmila Shilova. 1998. *Vospriiatie zdorov'ia i sviazannykh s nim privychek i ustanovok: Sravnitel'noe issledovanie vzroslogo naseleniia v Khel'sinki i Moskve* [Perceptions of Health and of the Corresponding Habits and Dispositions: A Comparative Study of the Adult Population in Helsinki and Moscow], trans. R. S. Drozdova, T. N. Sorokina. Moscow: ISRAN.

Paperno, Irina. 2002. "Personal Accounts of the Soviet Experience." *Kritika* 3 (4): 577–610.

Patrushev, V. D., T. M. Karakhanova, and O. N. Kushnareva. 1992. "Vremia zhitelei Moskvy i Moskovskoi oblasti" [Time of Muscovites and Moscow Region Residents]. *Sotsiologicheskie Issledovaniia* 6: 98–101.

Pilkington, Hilary, ed. 2002. *Looking West? Cultural Globalization and Russian Youth Cultures*. University Park, PA: Pennsylvania State University Press.

Pipes, Richard. 1993. *Russia under the Bolshevik Regime*. New York: A. A. Knopf.

———. 2006. "Why the Bear Growls." *Wall Street Journal*, March 1, A14, Eastern edition.

Poster, Mark. 1997. "Cyberdemocracy: The Internet and the Public Sphere." In *Virtual Politics: Identity and Community in Cyberspace*, ed. David Holmes. London: Sage.

Promptova, Ol'ga. 2000. "Rastet spros na travy i chesnok" [Demand for Herbs and Garlic is Growing]. *Vedomosti*, October 11, B5.

Putin, Vladimir V. 2000. *First Person: An Astonishingly Frank Self-portrait by Russia's President Vladimir Putin*, with Natalia Gevorkian, Natalia Timakova, and Andrei V. Kolesnikov, trans. Catherine A. Fitzpatrick. New York: Public Affairs.

Putnam, Robert D. 1993. *Making Democracy Work: Civic Traditions in Modern Italy*, in collaboration with Robert Leonardi and Raffaella Y. Nanetti. Princeton, N.J.: Princeton University Press.

———. 2000. *Bowling Alone: The Collapse and Revival of American Community*. New York: Simon and Schuster.

Quarantelli, Enrico L., ed. 1998. *What Is a Disaster? Perspectives on the Question.* London, New York: Routledge.

Quarantelli, Enrico L., and Russell R. Dynes. 1977. "Response to Social Crisis and Disaster." *Annual Review of Sociology* 3: 23–49.

Rancour-Laferriere, Daniel. 1995. *The Slave Soul of Russia: Moral Masochism and the Cult of Suffering.* New York: New York University Press.

Rausing, Sigrid. 2002. "Re-constructing the 'Normal': Identity and the Consumption of Western Goods in Estonia." In *Markets and Moralities: Ethnographies of Postsocialism,* ed. Ruth Mandel and Caroline Humphrey. Oxford, UK: Berg.

Ricœur, Paul. 1971. "The Model of the Text: Meaningful Action Considered as a Text." *Social Research* 38 (3): 529–562.

Ries, Nancy. 1997. *Russian Talk: Culture and Conversation during Perestroika.* Ithaca, N.Y.: Cornell University Press.

Rivkin-Fish, Michele R. 2005. *Women's Health in Post-Soviet Russia: The Politics of Intervention.* Bloomington: Indiana University Press.

———. 2006. "From 'Demographic Crisis' to 'Dying Nation'—The Politics of Language and Reproduction in Russia." In *Gender and National Identity in Twentieth-Century Russian Culture,* ed. Helena Goscilo and Andrea Lanoux. DeKalb: University of Northern Illinois Press.

Rose, Richard. 1994. "Getting By Without Government: Everyday Life in Russia." *Daedalus* 123 (3): 41–62.

Rose, Richard, and Ellen Carnaghan. 1995. "Generational Effects on Attitudes to Communist Regimes: A Comparative Analysis." *Post-Soviet Affairs* 11 (1): 28–56.

Rose, Richard, William Mishler, and Christian Haerpfer. 1997. "Social Capital in Civic and Stressful Societies." *Studies in Comparative International Development* 32 (3): 85–111.

Rotkirch, Anna, and Elina Haavio-Mannila, eds. 1996. *Women's Voices in Russia Today.* Aldershot, UK: Dartmouth.

Rubtsov, Aleksandr. 1992. "Brain demobilization?" [Mozgovaia demobilizatsiia?] *Moskovskie Novosti,* March 15.

Rutkevich, Mikhail N. 1995. "O roli sub'ektivnogo faktora v sovremennoi situatsii" [About the Role of the Subjective Factor in Contemporary Situation]. *Sotsiologicheskie Issledovaniia* 22 (10): 31–38.

———. 1998. "Protsessy sotsial'noi degradatsii v Rossiiskom obshchestve" [Processes of Social Degradation in Russian Society]. *Sotsiologicheskie Issledovaniia* 25 (6): 3–12.

Sakwa, Richard. 1991. *Gorbachev and His Reforms, 1985–1990.* New York: Prentice-Hall.

Sarnov, Benedikt M. 2002. *Nash Sovetskii Novoiaz [Our Soviet Newspeak].* Moscow: Materik.

Scott, James C. 1985. *Weapons of the Weak: Everyday Forms of Peasant Resistance.* New Haven, Conn.: Yale University Press.

Sewell, William H., Jr. 1980. *Work and Revolution in France: The Language of Labor from the Old Regime to 1848.* Cambridge, UK: Cambridge University Press.

———. 1992. "A Theory of Structure: Duality, Agency, and Transformation." *The American Journal of Sociology* 98 (1): 1–29.

———. 2005. *Logics of History: Social Theory and Social Transformation.* Chicago: University of Chicago Press.

Shafarevich, Igor P. 1989. *Rusofobiia* [Russophobia]. *Nash Sovremennik* 6.

Shevchenko, Olga. 2001. "Bread and Circuses: Shifting Frames and Changing References in Ordinary Muscovites' Political Talk." *Communist and Post-Communist Studies* 34 (1): 77–90.

———. 2002. "'Esli ty takoi umnyi, to pochemu takoi bednyi?' Utverzhdaia muzhestvennost' tekhnicheskoi intelligentsii" ["If You're So Smart, How Come You're So Poor?" Rhetorical Strategies of Affirming Masculinity Among the Members of the Technical Intelligentsia]. In *O Muzhe(n)stvennosti* [On Masculinity], ed. Serguei Oushakine, 288–302. Moscow: NLO.

Shlapentokh, Vladimir. 1995. "Russian Patience: A Reasonable Behavior and a Social Strategy." *Archives Européennes de Sociologie* 36 (2): 247–280.

———. 1996. "Russia: Privatization and Illegalization of Social and Political Life in Russia." *The Washington Quarterly* 19 (1): 65–85.

Simakov, A. G. 1995. "Esli Rossii suzhdeno pogibnut', to . . . moskvichi umrut poslednimi!" [If Russia is Doomed to Perish . . . Muscovites Will Be the Last Ones to Die!] In *Gorod. Reformy. Zhizn'. Moskva v Tsifrakh: 1992–1995* [City. Reforms. Life. Moscow in Numbers: 1992–1995], ed. L. B. Arshon, G. S. Barabanshchikov, and G. N. L'vov. Moscow: Intergraf Service.

Simpura, Jussi, and Galina Eremitcheva. 1997. "Dirt: Symbolic and Practical Dimensions of Social Problems in St. Petersburg." *International Journal of Urban and Regional Research* 21 (3): 467–479.

Slater, Don. 1997. "Consumer Culture and the Politics of Need." In *Buy This Book: Studies in Advertising and Consumption,* ed. Mica Nava, Andrew Blake, Iain MacRury, and Barry Richards. London: Routledge.

Smirnova, Tatiana. 2002. "Domushniki 'rabotaiut' bez vykhodnykh" [Home Thieves "Work" Without Vacations]. *Petrovka 38,* January 22. http://archives.maillist .ru/85589/407896.html (accessed May 27, 2007).

Smith, Kathleen E. 2002. *Mythmaking in the New Russia: Politics and Memory During the Yeltsin Era.* Ithaca, N.Y.: Cornell University Press.

Solzhenitsyn, Aleksandr I. 1990. *Kak nam obustroit' Rossiiu: Posil'nye soobrazheniia* [Rebuilding Russia: Reflections and Tentative Proposals]. Leningrad: Sovetskii Pisatel'.

Spradley, James P. 1980. *Participant Observation.* New York: Holt, Rinehart and Winston.

Stakhov, Dmitri. 1997. "Novaia khronologiia" [New Chronology]. *Russkii Zhurnal,* August 18. http://old.russ.ru/journal/chtenie/97-08-18/stahov.htm (accessed July 2, 2007).

Starodubrovskaia, Irina V., and Vladimir A. Mau. 2001. *Velikie revoliutsii: ot Kromvelia do Putina* [Great Revolutions: From Cromwell to Putin]. Moscow: Vagrius.

Steier, Frederick, ed. 1991. *Research and Reflexivity.* Newbury Park, Calif.: Sage.

Stiglitz, Joseph E. 2003. *Globalization and Its Discontents.* New York: W. W. Norton.

Stites, Richard. 1989. *Revolutionary Dreams: Utopian Vision and Experimental Life in the Russian Revolution.* New York: Oxford University Press.

Swidler, Ann. 1986. "Culture in Action: Symbols and Strategies." *American Sociological Review* 51 (2): 273–286.

———. 2001. *Talk of Love: How Culture Matters.* Chicago: University of Chicago Press.

———. 2002. "Cultural Repertoires and Cultural Logics: Can They Be Reconciled?" *Newsletter of the Sociology of Culture Section of the American Sociological Association* 16 (2): 6–8.

Sztompka, Piotr. 1991. "The Intangibles and Imponderables of the Transition to Democracy." *Studies in Comparative Communism* 24 (3): 295–311.

———. 1993. "Civilizational Incompetence: The Trap of Post-Communist Societies." *Zeitschrift für Soziologie* 22 (2).

Thomas, William I., and Dorothy S. Thomas. 1928. *The Child in America: Behavior Problems and Programs.* New York: Knopf.

Timofeev, L. 1990. *Tekhnologiia chernogo rynka, ili krest'yanskoe iskusstvo golodat'* [Technology of the Black Market, or The Peasant Art of Starvation]. In *Ya—osobo opasnyi prestupnik* [I am a Highly Dangerous Criminal]. Moscow: SP Vsia Moskva.

Tocqueville, Alexis de. 1945. *Democracy in America,* 2 vols., rev. ed., trans. Henry Reeve. New York: Knopf.

Toshchenko, Zh. T. 1995. "O paradoksakh obshchestvennogo soznaniia" [On Paradoxes of Mass Consciousness]. *Sotsiologicheskie Issledovaniia* 22 (11): 3–11.

Turner, Victor. 1967. *The Forest of Symbols: Aspects of Ndembu Ritual.* Ithaca, N.Y.: Cornell University Press.

Ugrešić, Dubravka. 1999. *The Museum of Unconditional Surrender,* trans. Celia Hawkesworth. New York: New Directions.

Urban, Michael E. 1994. "Politics of Identity in Russia's Postcommunist Transition: The Nation against Itself." *Slavic Review* 53 (3): 733–765.

———. 1997. *The Rebirth of Politics in Russia.* In collaboration with Viacheslav Igrunov and Sergei Mitrokhin. Cambridge, UK: Cambridge University Press.

Van Gennep, Arnold. 1960. *The Rites of Passage.* Chicago: University of Chicago Press.

Van Maanen, John. 1988. *Tales of the Field: On Writing Ethnography.* Chicago: University of Chicago Press.

Verdery, Katherine. 1993. "Ethnic Relations, Economies of Shortage, and the Transition in Eastern Europe." In *Socialism: Ideals, Ideologies, and Local Practice,* ed. C. M. Hann. London: Routledge.

———. 1995. "Faith, Hope, and Caritas in the Land of the Pyramids: Romania, 1990 to 1994." *Comparative Studies in Society and History* 37 (4): 625–669.

———. 1996. *What Was Socialism, and What Comes Next?* Princeton, N.J.: Princeton University Press.

———. 1999. *The Political Lives of Dead Bodies: Reburial and Postsocialist Change.* New York: Columbia University Press.

Vishnevskii, Anatolii G., ed. 1999. *Naselenie Rossii: 1998. Shestoi ezhegodnyi demograficheskii doklad* [The Population of Russia: 1998. Sixth Annual Report]. Moscow: Universitet.

Volkov, Aleksandr I., Marina G. Pugacheva, and S. F. Iarmoliuk, eds. 2000. *Pressa v Obshchestve, 1959–2000: Otsenki zhurnalistov i sotsiologov, dokumenty* [*Press in Society, 1959–2000: Assessments of Journalists and Sociologists, Documents*]. Moscow: Moskovskaia shkola politicheskikh issledovanii.

Voslenskii, Mikhail S. 1991. *Nomenklatura.* Moskva: Sovetskaia Rossiia.

Voznesensky, Andrei. 1999. *Zhutkii Crisis Super Star* [Awful Crisis Super Star]. Moscow: Terra.

VTsIOM. 1997. *Monitoring obshchestvennogo mneniia: Ekonomicheskie i sotsial'nye peremeny* 30.

VTsIOM. 1998. *Monitoring obshchestvennogo mneniia: Ekonomicheskie i sotsial'nye peremeny* 36.

VTsIOM. 2001. *Monitoring obshchestvennogo mneniia: Ekonomicheskie i sotsial'nye peremeny* 54.

Wacquant, Loïc J. D. 1994. "Inside the 'Zone': The Social Art of the Hustler in the Dark

Ghetto." Russell Sage Foundation, Working Papers. Quoted in Bellah et al. 1996, xxxvii.

Walker, Rachel. 1993. *Six Years That Shook the World: Perestroika—The Impossible Project*. New York: St. Martin's Press.

Wedel, Janine R. 1998. *Collision and Collusion: The Strange Case of Western Aid to Eastern Europe, 1989–1998*. New York: St. Martin's Press.

White, Hayden. 1978. *Tropics of Discourse: Essays in Cultural Criticism*. Baltimore, Md.: Johns Hopkins University Press.

White, Stephen. 2000. *Russia's New Politics: The Management of a Postcommunist Society*. Cambridge, UK: Cambridge University Press.

Yablokova, Oksana. 2003. "Levada Leaves VTsIOM for VTsIOM-A." *The Moscow Times*, September 10. http://www.eng.yabloko.ru/Publ/2003/PAPERS/9/030910_2_mt .html (accessed July 2, 2007).

Yurchak, Alexei. 1997. "The Cynical Reason of Late Socialism: Power, Pretense, and the *Anekdot*." *Public Culture* 9: 161–188.

———. 2006. *Everything Was Forever, Until It Was No More: The Last Soviet Generation*. Princeton, N.J.: Princeton University Press.

Zadorin, I. V., and A. P. Siutkina. 2000. "Osobennosti potrebleniia politicheskoi informatsii i ee vliianie na electoral'nye predpochteniia" [Consumption of Political Information and Its Influence Upon Electoral Preferences]. In *SMI i politika v Rossii: Sotsiologicheskii analiz roli SMI v izbiratel'nykh kampaniiakh* [Mass Media and Politics in Russia: A Sociological Analysis of the Role of Mass Media in Electoral Campaigns], ed. I. V. Zadorin. Moscow: Socio-Logos.

Zaslavskaia, T., and L. Arutiunian, eds. 1994. *Kuda idet Rossiia?: Al'ternativy obshchestvennogo razvitiia: Mezhdunarodnyi simpozium 17–19 dekabria 1993 g.* [Whither Russia?: Alternatives of Societal Development: International Symposium, December 17–19, 1993]. Moscow: Interpraks.

Zaslavskaia, Tatiana. 1997. "Sotsial'naia struktura sovremennogo rossiiskogo obshchestva" [Social Structure of Contemporary Russian Society]. *Obshchestvennye Nauki i Sovremennost'* 2: 5–23.

Zasurskii, Ivan. 1999. *Mass Media Vtoroi Respubliki* [*Mass Media of the Second Republic*]. Moscow: MGU.

Zdravomyslov, Andrei G. 1993. "Fundamental'nye problemy sotsiologii konflikta i dinamika massovogo soznaniia" [The Fundamental Problems of the Sociology of Conflict and the Dynamics of Mass Consciousness]. *Sotsiologicheskie Issledovaniia* 20 (8): 12–21.

Zelizer, Viviana A. R. 1979. *Morals and Markets: The Development of Life Insurance in the United States*. New York: Columbia University.

Zerubavel, Eviatar. 1982. "Easter and Passover: On Calendars and Group Identity." *American Journal of Sociology* 47 (2): 284–289.

———. 1996. "Lumping and Splitting: Notes on Social Classification." *Sociological Forum* 11 (3): 421–433.

———. 2003. *Time Maps: Collective Memory and the Social Shape of the Past*. Chicago: University of Chicago Press.

Zhukov, Boris. 2000. "Ministerstvo perekrytiia putei soobshcheniia" [The Ministry of Rail Travel Impediments]. *Itogi*, August 1: 9.

Zhuravlev, Valerii V., ed. 1990. *Na poroge krizisa: Narastanie zastoinykh iavlenii v partii i obshchestve* [On the Brink of a Crisis: The Intensification of Stagnation in the Party and in Society]. Moscow: Politizdat.

Zorin, Andrei L. 2003. "Guliaem?" [Are We Having Fun Yet?]. In *Gde sidit fazan: Ocherki poslednikh let* [Where the Pheasant Hides: Recent Essays]. Moscow: NLO.

Zorkaia, Natal'ia. 1997. "Kommunikativnaia aktivnost' moskvichei: Chtenie knig, gazet, zhurnalov" [Muscovites' Mass-Communicative Activity: Readership of Books, Newspapers, Magazines]. *Monitoring obshchestvennogo mneniia: Ekonomicheskie i sotsial'nye peremeny* 30: 18–22.

Index

corruption, 28, 29, 78; and capitalism, 41,
90; and communication, 74; as external,
84; inconsistent complaints about, 44, 48;
and media, 151; and medicine, 84, 118; as
normal, 65; of police, 85; and politics, 153,
155–156, 161, 164; and power, 167; and
trust, 123
coup of 1991, 16, 22, 44, 148
crime, 23, 40–41, 73, 113–114
crisis, 69–87; acceptance of, 146, 170; acknowledgement of, 21; as a historical condition,
11; and aphasia, 37; and autonomy, 81, 144,
170; changing meaning of, 18, 19–25, 33,
145, 148; civilizational, 32; common understanding of, 2, 3; and competence, 11–12,
13, 174; and consumption, 13, 106, 110; and
control, 11, 76, 80, 81, 82; and discourse vs.
practices, 10; and domestic routine, 133;
eternally recurring, 13, 68; and everyday life,
2, 3, 8, 34–37, 77, 88; as failure of reforms,
32; and family, 174; geography of, 139–143;
and golden age, 70–71; and healthcare/
medicine, 119, 121, 122, 123; and identity,
3, 12, 174, 175; as inevitable, 33; inflation
of concept of, 14; institutionalization of
responses to, 11, 175; as insurmountable,
22; of intelligentsia, 25–27, 33; and interest
struggle, 32–34; and interpretation, 11, 12,
27, 58, 116–117; judgment of, 70–71; on
macro- and micro-social levels, 35; and
Marxism, 21; and media, 29–31, 35, 76,
150; as new habitus, 69; as omnipresent
and familiar, 34; as outside family, 176;
permanence of, 9, 13, 17, 33, 62, 63–68, 69;
in personal vs. national life, 71, 72–73; and
politics, 173; and postsocialism, 43–49, 61,
176; practical knowledge in, 4; of reforms,
22–25, 33; repetitiveness of, 63, 69–70;
rhetoric as normalizing, 145; as routine condition, 2, 3, 13, 62; as second nature, 11; and
self-conception, 12; and self-presentation,
12; and skepticism, 144; and stability, 8, 173;
as surmountable obstacle, 37; as symbolic
resource, 9–10, 11, 144; temporal dimension
of, 13, 23, 86; traumatic symptoms related
to, 2–3
crisis, total, 62; adaptation to, 173; and community, 174; and competence, 78, 80; and
consumption, 90–96; continuity of, 173;
and crime, 73; defined, 2; and economy, 70,
71–73; evidence of, 73; flexibility of, 69–70;
and fraud, 175; and hysteresis of habitus, 69,
77–81, 80; and identity, 78; instrumental application of, 75–77; as interpretative system,

69, 72–73; and media, 76; navigation of, 6,
8, 9, 11, 12, 33, 78, 88; and politics, 73–74,
160, 173; and puzzles, 135, 136, 137; and
self-presentation, 80, 81; as shared framework, 74; and temporality, 78; uses of, 69–77;
and work, 75
crisis rhetoric: in academia, 28; as analytic tool,
33–34; and autonomy, 116–118; changing
meaning of, 12–13; and collective action,
153; and collective identities, 144; and
competence, 62; as contradictory, 47–48;
cross-class use of, 118; as deflating future
expectations, 145; development of, 19–20;
and economics, 33; finality and timelessness
in, 11; and ideology, 20–21; as inconsistent,
44–49; and inflation, 34; and intelligentsia,
27; as normalizing crisis, 145; as pacifier,
73; and perestroika, 35; and political actors,
31–32; and politics, 154, 156; as pretext for
non-Marxist approaches, 20; in print media,
23; selective use of evidence in, 45–49; and
solidarity, 62; strategic use of, 62; success as
atypical in, 46; and universalism, 32–33
cultural capital, 9, 51, 56, 134, 135, 136, 146,
175
cultural categories, 10
cultural tool-kit, 50–52, 78, 170
currency: and consumer goods, 109, 110; devaluation of, 7, 22, 29; fluctuations of, 109,
110; 1998 devaluation of, 16, 71, 86, 116; and
Pavlov's reforms, 15; and perestroika, 39;
and political interests, 107. See also monetary reform

de Certeau, Michel, 4, 5
delo, 153, 154, 155
democracy, 4, 29, 36, 98, 155, 168
deterioration: as common theme, 13; continuity of, 65; and economic breakdown of
1998, 63; of housing, 40; and media, 17;
permanence of, 69, 74, 78; and postsocialist
decade, 17; and puzzles, 136; as relevant idea,
35–36; and stability, 69; terminology of, 17;
and wellness greetings, 17
dirty technologies, 158, 159
domesticity, 9, 13, 131–133. See also family;
household
doors, fortified, 9, 10, 113–114, 115, 116, 118,
139–140, 141
doxa, 74

Eastern bloc, 58
Eastern Europe, 15, 23–24
economy, 15–16, 23, 29; and consumption,

revolution, 73
Russian All-People's Union, 31
Russian Democratic Reform Movement, 31
Russian nationalism, 28–29, 32

safety, 5, 88
Satarov, Georgii, 24
savings, 111, 114, 115, 127. *See also* banks;
  income
scientific communism, 28
security guards, 10, 139–140
self-image, 138
self-presentation, 9, 12, 78, 80, 81, 88, 145
self-protection, 9, 109, 111, 113–118, 123, 137
Shafarevich, Igor, *Russophobia,* 21
Situationist movement, 4
skepticism: about media, 150–152; and autonomy, 9; of collective action, 168; in
  consumption, 166; and crisis, 144; development of, 165–166; and history, 162; and
  postsocialist decline, 39; toward politics,
  148; toward the system, 84–85. *See also*
  trust/distrust
sociability. *See* personal relations
social change, 11, 40–41, 50, 173
social mobility, 43, 50
social networks, 118, 168
social security, 67
socialism: and consensus, 32; and consumption, 96, 97–98, 100; crisis of, 21, 22; and
  economy, 21, 111; fall of, 28; guaranteed
  employment in, 67; human relationships
  under, 42–43; humane, 37; lost collectivity
  of, 41–42; and mass media, 29; open discussion of problems of, 29; reform of, 25; and
  universalism, 32; welfare networks of, 67
solidarity, 3, 10, 62
Solzhenitsyn, Aleksandr I., *Rebuilding Russia,* 22
Soviet Russia, 36–37, 56, 164
Soviet Union, 22, 29, 65
stability: before and after perestroika, 40; and
  autonomy, 117; changing sense of, 68; and
  crisis, 8, 173; and deterioration, 69; lack of,
  17, 18, 44–46; preservation of, 9; and public
  sphere, 90; and wellness greetings, 17
Starodubrovskaia, Irina, *Great Revolutions,*
  19, 20
state: autonomy from, 14, 166, 169–170, 174;
  breakdown of, 100; and crisis, 69; failure of,
  6, 166; and fraud, 175; funding from, 33;
  games with, 59, 81; and healthcare, 118, 126;
  and informal parallel structures, 14, 170;
  as integrating framework, 58; intrusion of,

82, 108; minimized interaction with, 118;
  and *narod,* 108; and postsocialist decline,
  44; recognition of role of, 144; responsibilities of, 82; retreat of protective, 39, 81, 113,
  115–116; Soviet, 39; withdrawal from, 14,
  127, 128. *See also* politics
statistical sameness, 64–65
Stepashin, Sergei, 71–72
system, the, 127–130; concept of, 84–85

taxes, 78
temporality/time: and crisis, 13, 23, 25, 78,
  86; and domesticity, 133; and living day by
  day, 86; and perceptions of permanence and
  eternal return, 62; postsocialist conceptions
  of, 66–68; sameness in, 65–68. *See also* eternal return; history
Ten Years That Shook Us (television program), 19
Timofeev, Lev, 22
trade, 100
transportation, 141
travel, 45, 51
trust/distrust: and banks, 166; and crisis, 3,
  10, 88; and government and political elites,
  72; and healthcare/medicine, 121, 123, 125,
  126; and history, 161–165; and identity, 165;
  and media, 152; particularized, 169; and
  perestroika, 40; and politics, 152–156, 165,
  168; and solidarity, 169; and state, 14. *See
  also* skepticism

ultrasound stations, 123, *124,* 140
United States, 20, 26, 63
universalism, 32, 66
us-them opposition, 107–109

VITATRESS advertisement, 82–84, *83*
Voslenskii, Mikhail, 22
voting. *See* elections
Voznesensky, Andrei, *Zhutkii Crisis Super
  Star,* 20
Vzgliad (television program), 29

wages, 54, 94. *See also* income
welfare, 67
West, 20, 27–29, 114
women, 6, 93, 94, 96
work/employment, 51–59; and academia, 29;
  before and after perestroika, 39, 42, 43; and
  autonomy, 127; and family, 91, 92, 111; guaranteed, 67; instability in, 44–46, 61, 90; and
  politics, 154; and postsocialism, 44, 50; restructuring of, 67; and sense of temporality,

68; time off from, 130–133; and total crisis framework, 75. *See also* income; job market

World War II, 73

Yasin, Evgenii, 19

Yeltsin, Boris, 98, 150; and academics, 28, 29; and Communist Party, 15; criticism of, 151; era of, 172; and ideology, 24; inner circle of, 150, 151, 167; and Kirienko, 71; and media, 29; and parliament, 7, 29, 44, 73; reforms of, 31

Zhirinovsky, Vladimir, 16, 24, 32

Zhizni, Lavka, 122

Zhuravlev, Valerii V., *On the Brink of a Crisis,* 22

Zyuganov, Gennadii, 32, 33

OLGA SHEVCHENKO is Assistant Professor of Sociology at Williams College.

Milton Keynes UK
Ingram Content Group UK Ltd.
UKHW022003211124
451438UK00005B/159